Understanding the Tacit

This book outlines a new account of the tacit, meaning tacit knowledge, presuppositions, practices, traditions, and so forth. It includes essays on topics such as underdetermination and mutual understanding, and critical discussions of the major alternative approaches to the tacit, including Bourdieu's *habitus* and various practice theories, Oakeshott's account of tradition, Quentin Skinner's theory of historical meaning, Harry Collins's idea of collective tacit knowledge, as well as discussions of relevant cognitive science concepts, such as non-conceptual content, connectionism, and mirror neurons. The new account of tacit knowledge focuses on the fact that in making the tacit explicit, a person is not, as many past accounts have supposed, reading off the content of some sort of shared and fixed tacit scheme of presuppositions, but rather responding to the needs of the Other for understanding.

Stephen P. Turner is Distinguished University Professor of Philosophy at the University of South Florida.

Routledge Studies in Social and Political Thought

For a full list of titles in this series, please visit www.routledge.com.

47 The Politics and Philosophy of Michael Oakeshott
Stuart Isaacs

48 Pareto and Political Theory
Joseph Femia

49 German Political Philosophy
The Metaphysics of Law
Chris Thornhill

50 The Sociology of Elites
Michael Hartmann

51 Deconstructing Habermas
Lasse Thomassen

52 Young Citizens and New Media
Learning for Democratic Participation
Edited by Peter Dahlgren

53 Gambling, Freedom and Democracy
Peter J. Adams

54 The Quest for Jewish Assimilation in Modern Social Science
Amos Morris-Reich

55 Frankfurt School Perspectives on Globalization, Democracy, and the Law
William E. Scheuerman

56 Hegemony
Studies in Consensus and Coercion
Edited by Richard Howson and Kylie Smith

57 Governmentality, Biopower, and Everyday Life
Majia Holmer Nadesan

58 Sustainability and Security within Liberal Societies
Learning to Live with the Future
Edited by Stephen Gough and Andrew Stables

59 The Mythological State and its Empire
David Grant

60 Globalizing Dissent
Essays on Arundhati Roy
Edited by Ranjan Ghosh & Antonia Navarro-Tejero

61 The Political Philosophy of Michel Foucault
Mark G.E. Kelly

62 Democratic Legitimacy
Fabienne Peter

63 Edward Said and the Literary, Social, and Political World
Edited by Ranjan Ghosh

64 Perspectives on Gramsci
Politics, Culture and Social Theory
Edited by Joseph Francese

65 Enlightenment Political Thought and Non-Western Societies
Sultans and Savages
Frederick G. Whelan

66 Liberalism, Neoliberalism, Social Democracy
Thin Communitarian Perspectives on Political Philosophy and Education
Mark Olssen

67 Oppositional Discourses and Democracies
Edited by Michael Huspek

68 The Contemporary Goffman
Edited by Michael Hviid Jacobsen

69 Hemingway on Politics and Rebellion
Edited by Lauretta Conklin Frederking

70 Social Theory in Contemporary Asia
Ann Brooks

71 Governmentality
Current Issues and Future Challenges
Edited by Ulrich Bröckling, Susanne Krasmann and Thomas Lemke

72 Gender, Emotions and Labour Markets - Asian and Western Perspectives
Ann Brooks and Theresa Devasahayam

73 Alienation and the Carnivalization of Society
Edited by Jerome Braun and Lauren Langman

74 The Post-Colonial State in the Era of Capitalist Globalization
Historical, Political and Theoretical Approaches to State Formation
Tariq Amin-Khan

75 The Psychology and Politics of the Collective
Groups, Crowds and Mass Identifications
Edited by Ruth Parkin-Gounelas

76 Environmental Solidarity
How Religions Can Sustain Sustainability
Pablo Martínez de Anguita

77 Comedy and the Public Sphere
The Rebirth of Theatre as Comedy and the Genealogy of the Modern Public Arena
Arpad Szakolczai

78 Culture, Class, and Critical Theory
Between Bourdieu and the Frankfurt School
David Gartman

79 Environmental Apocalypse in Science and Art
Designing Nightmares
Sergio Fava

80 Conspicuous and Inconspicuous Discriminations in Everyday Life
Victor N. Shaw

81 Understanding the Tacit
Stephen P. Turner

Understanding the Tacit

Stephen P. Turner

NEW YORK LONDON

First published 2014
by Routledge
711 Third Avenue, New York, NY 10017

Simultaneously published in the UK
by Routledge
2 Park Square, Milton Park, Abingdon, Oxfordshire OX14 4RN

First issued in paperback 2015

Routledge is an imprint of the Taylor & Francis Group, an informa business

Library of Congress Cataloging-in-Publication Data

Turner, Stephen P., 1951–
Understanding the tacit / by Stephen P. Turner.
pages cm. — (Routledge studies in social and political thought ; 81)
Includes bibliographical references and index.
1. Tacit knowledge. 2. Knowledge, Theory of. I. Title.
BF317.5.T87 2014
153.4—dc23
2013022302

ISBN13: 978-1-138-92964-7 (pbk)
ISBN13: 978-0-415-70944-6 (hbk)

Typeset in Sabon
by IBT Global.

To my sons, Evan and Douglas, in admiration, and with gratitude for our life together

Contents

PART III
The Alternative: Tacitness, Empathy, and the Other

Acknowledgments

Chapter 1, "Tacit Knowledge and the Problem of Computer Modeling Cognitive Processes in Science," was published in *The Cognitive Turn: Sociological and Psychological Perspectives on Science*, edited by Steve Fuller, Marc de Mey, Terry Shinn, and Steve Woolgar. Dordrecht: Reidel, 1989, pp. 83–94. Reprinted by permission of the publisher.

Chapter 2, "Davidson's Normativity," was published in *Dialogues with Davidson: On the Contemporary Significance of His Thought*, edited by Jeff Malpas. Cambridge, MA: MIT Press, 2011, pp. 343–70. Reprinted by permission of the publisher.

Chapter 3, "Starting with Tacit Knowledge, Ending with Durkheim?" was published in *Studies in History and Philosophy of Science* 42: 472–76, 2011. Reprinted by permission of Elsevier.

Chapter 4, "Practice Then and Now," was published in *Human Affairs* 17(2): 110–25, 2007. Reprinted by permission of the publisher.

Chapter 5, "Practice Relativism," was published in *Crítica, Revista Hispanoamericana de Filosofía* 39(115): 3–27, 2007. Reprinted by permission of the publisher.

Chapter 6, "Mirror Neurons and Practices: A Response to Lizardo," was published in the *Journal for the Theory of Social Behavior* 37(3): 351–71, 2007. Reprinted by permission of the publisher.

Chapter 7, "Tradition and Cognitive Science: Oakeshott's Undoing of the Kantian Mind," was published in *Philosophy of the Social Sciences* 33(1): 53–76, 2003. Reprinted by permission of the publisher.

Chapter 8, "Meaning without Theory," was published in the *Journal for the Philosophy of History* 5: 352–69, 2011. Reprinted by permission of the publisher.

Chapter 9, "Making the Tacit Explicit," was published in the *Journal for the Theory of Social Behavior* 42(4): 386–402, 2012. Reprinted by permission of the publisher.

Chapter 10, "The Strength of Weak Empathy," was published in *Science in Context* 25(3): 383–99, 2012. Reprinted by permission of the publisher.

Chapter 11, "Collective or Social? Tacit Knowledge and Its Kin," was published in a variant form in *Philosophia Scientiæ* 17(3), 2013. Reprinted by permission of the publisher.

Introduction
Tacit Knowledge: Between Habit and Presupposition

The tacit, as I will treat it here, encompasses a poorly bounded domain that appears repeatedly in the history of philosophy and social and political thought, under different names with different emphases and different associations. Aristotle says that moral virtue is a *hexis* (Aristotle [350 B.C.E.] 1915: 1103a). In more recent writers it is second nature (McDowell 1994: 84), the background (Searle 1995), habit or custom (Hume [1748] 1995: 88–89), *habitus*—with different meanings in Bourdieu, where it is a collective fact (1977: 17), and Weber, where it is ascribed to individuals ([1922] 1988: 391, 532). Michael Polanyi called it tacit knowledge (1966a). Gilbert Ryle distinguished knowing how from knowing that (1949: 27–32). In its historical sense, it can refer to the climate of opinion or *Zeitgeist* of the time, and especially to the "assumptions" that are evident to later interpreters but obscured to the historical persons who think in terms of them—the historical a priori, as Dilthey put it ([1959] 1988: 51). In its sociological sense, it refers to the taken-for-granted and the distinctive but unacknowledged habits of mind or meaning-structures that make something taken for granted.

What all of these locutions refer to is the unspoken and often inarticulable conditions of thought and articulation, normally conditions that are acquired or learned other than through the kind of explicit claims normally associated with the term "knowledge." Michael Polanyi's slogans capture this thought: "All knowledge either is or is rooted in tacit knowledge"; "we know more than we can say." Wittgenstein went from saying, in the *Tractatus*, that "the tacit conventions on which the understanding of everyday language depends are enormously complicated" ([1921] 1961: 37, para. 4.002) to his later view that justification dead-ended in facts about what we do. Regress arguments of this kind are important motivations for appealing to the tacit: Chains of justification do indeed end in something like unspoken mutual understandings. The problem is to make sense of what these understandings are, or what they themselves rest on, and what produces them.

If the problem is to make sense of what these understandings are, or what they themselves rest on, there are some obvious constraints on the solution. These are social facts. They vary from society to society and setting to setting. They underlie the differences between political orders and the possibilities of constructing political orders. In this theoretical context, "understandings" is an awkward analogy: There is nothing like a contract or agreement. Nor does the term "understandings" capture the whole of the relevant domain. Understanding shades into skills, skills of interacting with others. If the end point is the way something is done in a group or setting, it shades into more ordinary kinds of skills: riding a bicycle, manipulating a laboratory instrument, and the like. These skills are "conditions" of certain kinds of communication and interaction as well. One cannot function in a laboratory without them or ride competently in a closely packed group of bicycle racers without possessing skills at a high level. Interactional skills and bodily skills are intertwined. So is skill and most of evaluative language, a point Wittgenstein made in his "Lecture on Aesthetics" ([1938] 1967: 1–40): Using the language requires a bit, at least, of knowing how, and using the evaluative language in a sophisticated way may require a high level of competence in performing the tasks being evaluated.

WHAT AN ACCOUNT OF THE TACIT NEEDS TO DO

Making sense of the realm of the tacit is not easy, but it is possible to specify a few desiderata for an adequate approach. The short list would include the following:

1. Explain what is going one when the tacit gets articulated or turned into something explicit.
2. Understand the fact that we stumble over the tacit, that it is usually obvious only to outsiders needs to be part of any account of the tacit. However it is described—tacit knowledge, presuppositions, techniques of the body—it must be understood in terms of the conditions under which these descriptions of the tacit are themselves made possible. Moreover, there is something comparison-relative about our constructions of the tacit. This leads to an additional problem that can be phrased as a question: What if not only the recognition of the tacit in others but the content we ascribe to the tacit in others is relative to our own tacit background and would differ for persons with different tacit backgrounds?
3. Acknowledge that much of what is discussed as tacit is embodied: Perhaps all of it should be understood in this way. But there needs to be some sort of fit between claims about the tacit and the actual physical world from which it produces its effects: with the brain and with ordinary senses, cognitive processes, and the like.
4. Square with the usual things that claims about the tacit are taken to explain: communication, mutual understanding, skills, moments of discovery in which unarticulated understanding is articulated, and

the kinds of political and social facts that accounts of the tacit, notably accounts of practice, have explained.

5. Avoid nonexplanatory shortcuts. Many of the most repeated terms in discussions of the tacit are concepts with a one-directional explanatory structure—that is to say that they are invoked as explanations, but are themselves not explainable. Notions of practice often have this character: They are treated as explainers, but are descriptions that need to be given some sort of additional explanatory background or force to actually explain. Sometimes it is assumed that they have this force, or that just by describing something as having a force one has explained it. This is an issue that cannot be addressed in detail here, although I will discuss some dimensions of it in this Introduction in connection with the next issue.
6. Explain how the tacit stuff gets there or is produced. One can call this the joint problems of transmission and sameness. If one has a picture of communication in which each party to the communication must decode the utterances of the other and can do so because they each have, so to speak, a secret decoder ring that decodes and encodes in the same way as the other party decodes and encodes, one must ask how they got that ring. If one chooses to jettison this picture and claim that the tacit is deeply private and distinctive to each person, one must account in some way for how the tacit in this sense is acquired, but also how it enables people to do what they can in fact do, such as understand one another in spite of having different tacit backgrounds.
7. Recognize metaphors as metaphors, and analogies as analogies. Metaphorical usages, such as "frameworks," abound in this literature, usually without any sense that they need to be able to be cashed in. Similarly, terms that make sense in the context of explicit formulation, such as "rule" and "knowledge," are applied analogically to the tacit without reminding us that these are analogies only. An adequate account needs to be careful with these distinctions and not assume that the analogies are licit.
8. Be careful with the distinction between explanation and description. It is one thing to describe a practice, but quite another to treat the practice as itself something that explains anything.

OBSTACLES, DILEMMAS, AND EXPLANATORY LACUNAE

In what follows, I will briefly outline the main obstacles and conflicts that lie in the path of any account of the tacit. Most of these have the form of explanatory dilemmas, in which there are two explanatory problems that overlap and two solutions, each of which works for one part of the problem, but leads to implausibilities when it is applied to other parts.

Habits and Presuppositions

One can see the roots of the most central of these dilemmas in the history of a particular philosophical dispute, the fundamental conflict between Hume and Kant. Kant responded to Hume's idea that casual inferences could not be grounded by a principle, but only by custom or habit, that is to say inferential habits. Kantianism and neo-Kantianism responded by arguing that there were logical conditions for judgments about causality. These conditions were of course normally tacit as well: But they could be articulated. Hegel and the neo-Kantians extended this insight in a radical direction. Hegel argued that habits were already conceptual. The neo-Kantians argued that not just physics but any organized domain of thought presupposed conceptual content, which could be revealed by transcendental arguments.

These two lines of reasoning were not directly or simply opposed to one another, and developed, indeed flourished, independently, in part because they largely took different domains of thought and action as paradigmatic. Yet neither of them could quite shake the fundamental problem they faced: The transcendental side needed to connect to the real world of causality; the habit side needed to account for the fact that the things it explained seemed to be the sorts of things that could be restated as "assumptions" or premises to arguments.

The "habit" side made arguments summarized by Friedrich Hayek in his discussion of tradition, a key term in this discourse:

> [Constructivist rationalism] produced a renewed propensity to ascribe the origin of all institutions of culture to invention or design. Morals, religion and law, language and writing, money and the market, were thought of as having been deliberately constructed by somebody, or at least as owing whatever perfection they possessed to such design. . . .
>
> Yet . . . [m]any of the institutions of society which are indispensable conditions for the successful pursuit of our conscious aims are in fact the result of customs, habits or practices which have been neither invented nor are observed with any such purpose in view. . . .
>
> Man . . . is successful not because he knows why he ought to observe the rules which he does observe, or is even capable of stating all these rules in words, but because his thinking and acting are governed by rules which have by a process of selection been evolved in the society in which he lives, and which are thus the product of the experience of generations. (Hayek 1973: 10–11)

With claims like these, the muddle becomes apparent. The "rules" which are observed but not stated or even perhaps capable of being stated are a peculiar object. They are not rules at all, except in an analogical sense, analogous to explicit or non-tacit rules. But sometimes, it seems, they can be stated. Genealogically they arise through means that are not conscious. They are not invented, although things that were invented, such as explicit doctrines or norms, can become habitualized, and thus tacit.[1] But the crucial point is this: When we attempt to explain or articulate them we do *so as though* they were invented or as though there was an explicit rule or presupposition hidden somewhere which we were revealing by stating it explicitly. So these "customs, habits, or practices" behave like the kinds of things that evolve through a "process of selection" involving experience, but are otherwise like rules invented by people.

The "transcendental" side has its own problems that are the mirror image of this one: the problem of relating to the causal world (Beiser 2009). But it has a powerful "method." By asking for justifications of something that is done or claimed but which is normally not justified, one can create a novel question for which an answer can be supplied in the form of an explicit premise, rule, or concept. But this method is too powerful, because it manufactures too many presuppositions and rules, and too many that conflict with one another. Attributing "presuppositions" is done very casually in the philosophical literature. Several examples are given in Chapters 3, 4, 5, 6, 7, and 8. This complicates the problem of connecting to the natural world: If we are to understand these presuppositions as representing something that actually happens in the minds of people, we have no grounds within these regress arguments themselves for thinking that we have the right presupposition. And this raises questions about what sorts of things these presuppositions are supposed to be.

Presuppositions or Enthymemes?

In the technical literature on the transcendental method, mere regress arguments, which may result in varying and conflicting attributions of presuppositions, are distinguished from transcendental arguments that not only end the regress but exclude all alternatives (Paulson [1934] 1992). It is questionable whether there are such arguments. The neo-Kantians never arrived at them. For reasons familiar from Quine, we know that for whatever set of premises we derive a set of sentences from, a conflicting set of premises can be constructed from which the original set of premises may also be derived. And this is more or less what happened with neo-Kantianism: Philosophers invented system upon system to conceptually order and explain such domains as the law. The systems conflicted and thus undermined their own claim for themselves, which was that the premises were "necessary."

This result should be a warning for appeals to "presuppositions" generally. The issue is connected with the problem of whether the content of the tacit we ascribe to others will vary according to our own tacit background. Here it is useful to distinguish two distinct things: presuppositions and enthymemes, or inferences with "suppressed premises." In the case of enthymemes, we are encountering an inference that someone is making that we would not make or would not make unless we knew something else, something that would enable us to accept the inference. If we are attempting to understand someone who is reasoning in a way we find unfamiliar or wrong, we are able, routinely, to makes sense of the other person by supplying this something in the form of a premise that would make the inference valid or enable us to explain it as an intelligible error, an error of the kind we already would be able to understand.

These somethings have a different character than what we usually have in mind when speaking of presuppositions: They are supplied or constructed for a specific purpose, and they are relative to the starting point of the person who is using them to understand someone else. Moreover, there are going to be many inferential bridges that will work to make the inference valid, so there is underdetermination. Moreover, what is an enthymeme for me is not necessarily one for you. Indeed, in the normal situation, one is ascribing a missing premise in order to understand a person who is already making the inference for which the "missing" premise is being supplied.

In the case of tacit knowledge, we would like to think that there is something fixed or stable to which the term refers. Presuppositions, understood in a more or less Kantian way, have this stability. But it is questionable whether there are such things, that they are in fact stable, or that they exist at all. And these questions are linked to the problem of their accessibility, at least in the "necessary" sense. If they are inaccessible to us, as analysts, in this fixed form, how could they be accessible to those who are supposed to share them? How could they be transmitted tacitly if they could not be accessed explicitly? What grounds could we have for saying some fixed thing of this kind is shared?

Explanatory Lacunae

These questions point to a set of muddles over explanation. They become especially apparent in the writings of Charles Taylor. As he is normally interpreted, he is an advocate of tacit knowledge, and part of a long tradition:

> Following Heidegger, Merleau-Ponty, Gadamer, Michael Polanyi, and Wittgenstein, Taylor argues that it is mistaken to presuppose that our understanding of the world is primarily mediated by representations. It is only against an unarticulated background that representations can make sense to us. On occasion we do follow rules by explicitly representing them to ourselves, but Taylor reminds us that rules do not contain the principles of their own application: application requires that we draw on an unarticulated understanding or "sense of things"—the background. (*Wikipedia* n.d.)

And he is understood as interpreting Wittgenstein in accordance with this picture:

> Taylor argues that Wittgenstein's solution is that all interpretation of rules draws upon a tacit background. This background is not more rules or premises, but what Wittgenstein calls "forms of life." More specifically, Wittgenstein says in the *Philosophical Investigations* that "Obeying a rule is a practice." Taylor situates the interpretation of rules within the practices that are incorporated into our bodies in the form of habits, dispositions, and tendencies. (*Wikipedia* n.d.)

But when it comes to the problem of what is going on when we articulate rules, Taylor falls into the same problem as Hayek, although in a slightly different way.

Taylor explains himself in terms of "frameworks." This is a metaphor, and a cliché. But Taylor treats frameworks as genuine explanations, which explain what happens when we make the tacit explicit:

> Frameworks provide the background, explicit or implicit, for our moral judgments, intuitions, or reactions. . . . To articulate a framework is to explicate what makes sense of our moral responses. That is, when we try to spell out what it is that we presuppose when we judge that a certain form of life is truly worthwhile, or place our dignity in a certain achievement or status, or define our moral obligations in a certain manner, we find ourselves articulating inter alia what I have been calling here "frameworks." (Taylor 1989: 26)

This is a straightforward appeal to presuppositions and a claim that when we explain ourselves to others, we are articulating a framework that is already there, providing the background to our moral responses. The picture is clear: When articulating tacit presuppositions we are reading off something that actually is present in the tacit realm, ready to be read off. "Presuppose" is not used analogically, or in an "as if" form, but to state some sort of fact.

One might ask what evidence Taylor has for the existence of frameworks of this sort, and indeed, he raises the question himself by his criticisms of the denial of frameworks by unnamed "naturalists." His answer to the naturalists seems to be that they are an explanatory necessity. Frameworks need to be there for things to have meaning for us: The "framework-definitions are answers, providing the horizon within which we know where we stand, and what meanings things have for us" (Taylor 1989: 29).

Taylor acknowledges that some frameworks cannot be articulated. But he treats this as a property of the frameworks themselves.

> Plato's ethic requires what we might call today a theory, a reasoned account of what human life is about, and why one way is higher than the others. This flows inescapably from the new moral status of reason. But the framework within which we act and judge doesn't need to be

> articulated theoretically. It isn't, usually, by those who live by the warrior ethic. They share certain discriminations: what is honorable and dishonoring, what is admirable, what is done and not done. It has often been remarked that to be a gentleman is to know how to behave without ever being told the rules. (And the "gentlemen" here are the heirs of the former warrior nobility.) (Taylor 1989: 20–21)

He notes, "In the case of some frameworks it may be optional whether one formulates them or not. But in other cases, the nature of the framework demands it, as with Plato, or seems to forbid it, as with the warrior-citizen ethic he attacked: this does seem to be refractory to theoretical formulation." He goes on to suggest that we can sometimes articulate, and sometimes need to articulate, frameworks, for example to show how an inarticulate "sense" of right and wrong established in one narrow setting applies in new situations.

But what does the fact that we can sometimes articulate something in the way of premises or explanations tell us about "frameworks"? Are we, as Taylor insists, articulating a real thing which is tacit? Or are we doing something like this: When we are explaining ourselves to someone who doesn't understand us, we can and do imagine what they would need to know in order to understand us and articulate it. In short, we fill in our own enthymemes, if we think others are taking them as enthymemes. There is no reason to think that by doing so we are articulating a "framework" or that doing so requires a "framework." The fact that we articulate things is not evidence that there is a complex unified object like a framework that we presuppose. It is evidence of our ability to respond to the needs of others and to put ourselves into their position.

Similarly, the fact that there are such things as explicit frameworks—ideologies, in the traditional sense of the word, that is to say something explicitly constructed and imposed—does not tell us that there are analogous tacit things in people's heads, tacitly constructed or imposed. To reason, emote, or feel *as if* one is doing it according to an ideology is not the same as doing it according to a tacit ideology. To ignore this is to erase the distinction between the tacit and the explicit by assuming it away.

IS TACIT KNOWLEDGE "KNOWLEDGE"?

If knowledge is, in the famous formula, justified true belief, the definition excludes what is known as tacit knowledge, the unarticulated or inarticulable knowledge that enables the scientist to perform experiments, make discoveries, and also to understand the reasoning in an area of science. What is tacit is by definition not "justified" and cannot be justified until it is no longer tacit, nor is the tacit "belief," in the usual sense.

What is tacit is not reasoned about in the same way as an explicit claim, justified according to more or less explicit conventions of evidence, such as the conventions of reporting results in scientific journals. We can recognize that there is a tacit component to knowledge and accept Polanyi's famous claim that all knowledge is either tacit or rooted in tacit knowledge. But this does not tell us what tacit knowledge is or how it works. There is no formula, analogous to "justified true belief," that we can treat even as a first approximation to an account of the "knowledge" part of the phrase "tacit knowledge."

Much of what is called tacit knowledge is "knowing how" rather than "knowing that" in Gilbert Ryle's terms (cf. Ryle 1949). But even this concept is clouded in controversy. "Knowing that" is a relation between a thinker and a true proposition. Arguably, knowing how to ride a bicycle, to take the standard example, involves some sort of "knowing that," such as knowing that *x* is the right way to ride a bicycle, with "way" meaning a way to engage in an action (Stanley and Williamson 2001). This is useful, because it enables us to distinguish knowledge-relevant abilities from such abilities as the ability to digest starch, although we could make the relevant distinctions in other ways, such as in terms of the manner by which an ability is acquired.

But in the end formulations of this kind do not help very much: We don't know what a "way" is, despite being able to put the term in a "knowledge that" proposition like "Hazel knows that there is a way to ride a bike." Indeed, the status of such a "way" is what is at issue in most discussions of tacit knowledge. If one asks how a "way" explains, there is no good answer. Where is it located? How does it causally interact with the world, with intentions, and how are ways produced and transmitted? There is no answer to these questions: The "way" is simply there, filling a place in an explanation schema. The question of whether tacit knowledge is really knowledge is a definitional quibble, but it points to a more fundamental problem which involves all of the analogical uses of concepts. Put "tacit" in front of terms like "rules," "norms," "premises," and so forth and one gets a problematic analogy. The analogy is justified because something in the way of a rule, norm, premise, and the like can be made explicit—although what this means and what exactly it is that is being made explicit is an open question. What is less of an open question is this: What is the difference between the acquisition of something tacit and the acquisition of something explicit?

Tacit knowledge, if we count it as knowledge, avoids some issues associated with propositional knowledge, not least Gettier problems. One can easily believe false propositions: We often accept something as true that we are told by others, for example. Learning something tacitly requires at least some sort of feedback. One could not mislearn the language you were raised in. To be sure, acquiring a habitual response or making a habitual inference as a result of feedback may produce errors, that is to say bad habits that prove to be bad in new contexts. And of course one can be induced to form bad habits by being given a diet of feedback that produces them.

The fact that tacit learning requires feedback makes it radically unlike explicit learning. But in actual cases the two are mixed together: One learns a language of appraisal together with learning how to do things, for example. Each kind of learning has its own tacit component, because it has feedback that is not explicitly constructed, as an experiment or test of a hypothesis would be.

INDIVIDUAL OR COLLECTIVE?

A major issue with tacit knowledge is whether it is collective or individual. Start with the idea of a "way." Is it something that can be shared? And if so, what does it mean to be shared? That it is externally similar and produces more or less the same result? Or something stronger. Does it *have* to be shared, or shareable, as a proposition would be, in order to be knowledge? Does it function to enable mutual understanding if it is shared? And if the sharing is not merely about externals and results, or emulation, how exactly can tacit things be shared? There is no standard story here, but there is a commonplace one, derived from Kuhn's use of the concept as part of the concept of paradigm. It reappears in Foucault's accounts of power/knowledge and epistemes, not to mention such notions as Bourdieu's account of *habitus* and Harry Collins' account of collective tacit knowledge. These accounts run into their own problems: There is no plausible mechanism by which the tacit stuff can be reproduced in different minds, or "shared" (Turner 1994).

Habits, however, are individual: They are personally acquired, as a result of personal experiences and the particular processes of feedback that stabilize them, on the basis of a personal past, in accordance with other habits which are themselves personal and based on a personal past. And this seems to be not enough to make sense of our common life: of communication and mutual understanding. The temptation is to say that these things must be based on something that is shared.

The most influential recent version of this argument is Bourdieu's. His notion of *habitus* is wildly expansive. Bourdieu explains the effectiveness of customary law by *habitus*, noting that

> the rules of customary law have some practical efficacy only to the extent that, skillfully manipulated by the holders of authority within the clan . . . they "awaken," so to speak, the schemes of perception and appreciation deposited, in their incorporated state, in every member of the group, i.e., the dispositions of the *habitus*. (1977: 17)

These dispositions account for

> the practical mastery of the symbolism of social interaction—tact, dexterity, or savoir-faire—presupposed by the most everyday games of sociability and accompanied by the application of a spontaneous semiology, i.e., a mass of precepts, formulae, and codified cues. (1977: 10)

To make any sense in terms of his larger explanatory model, which involves the role of the inculcation of *habitus* in the reproduction of an oppressive social order, it needs to be a fixed and shared thing, "incorporated into every member of the group," as he says, with so to speak a mind of its own and a teleological directionality that overrides and directs individual motivation. Most important, of course, is that it is a collective object, not just a set of individual habits and dispositions. It directs individuals to collective ends.

The concept illustrates a crucial problem with "sharing." The more that one loads into the concept, the less plausible it becomes, because the more power to direct the mind and the more content that is ascribed to it the more difficult it becomes to explain how this thing actually comes to be shared. Not only "a mass of precepts, formulae, and codified cues" but "schemes of perception and appreciation," dispositions, and so forth need to be "incorporated" in "everymember of the group." The more that needs to be incorporated the more difficult it becomes to explain how it all can be incorporated in every member of the group. And there is a related problem: Ascribing too much power of direction to the *habitus* risks turning people into what Harold Garfinkel called cultural dopes—automata enacting routines (1967). People are not like this. The solution to the problem for Bourdieu is to say that people share it, but improvise. But this is a tricky gambit: If you allow too much improvisation, you lose the sense that *habitus* determines anything, that it meets some sort of explanatory need, and lose the sense that there is any hard-core collectively shared fact about *habitus*.

"Ways" opens up a much larger question about buried or hidden forms of knowledge. What about the knowledge contained in instruments? The users of tools, no less than the users of expert systems, are relying on knowledge that they typically do not possess but which has been, so to speak, built into the object. Similarly with routines: One may follow them mindlessly, as long as they succeed, vary them and so forth, but without knowing or caring about their invention, design, or the knowledge behind them.

But this raises a question about underdetermination. The same result can be produced using different routines. So producing a routine tells us nothing about the actual processes involved. Moreover, the solutions are solutions to artificially limited problems selected or defined by the researcher. This is a point that applies very widely, for example to the claims of ethnomethodologists to reveal underlying rules of social interaction. In each of these cases, we are faced both with underdetermination, or the existence of a vast number of alternative ways of modeling the supposed process, and artificiality resulting from the selection of a particular characterization of the process as the correct representation of the thing to be modeled. If routines can be produced in a variety of ways, there is no reason not to think that this applies to persons as well—that the tacit conditions of their performances are different from the tacit conditions of others performing the same thing.

This has direct implications for the idea that there can be anything collective and tacit. What we learn, acquire, and assimilate tacitly we can only do through the surfaces of things: We can emulate another person's actions, or performances, perform actions for which we get feedback, and otherwise respond to data from the world. This feedback may be extensive enough to produce behavioral uniformity. And uniformity may be produced by explicit means—by drill or instruction. But there is no alternative pipeline into the tacit that assures that the tacit contents are the same or shared by the rest of the collectivity. There is nothing analogous to a central computer server providing constant updates to computer programs that reproduces identical programs in multiple computers.

A FINAL NOTE ON WITTGENSTEIN

One of the reviewers of this manuscript suggested that I add a chapter on Wittgenstein and the relation of this argument to Wittgenstein. There are of course Wittgensteinian roots to this discussion, which can be best explained in terms of my earlier *Sociological Explanation as Translation* (1980), which was heavily Wittgensteinian, and a more Quinean approach to the same problems, "Translating Ritual Beliefs" (1979). Both of these texts, and especially the first, were concerned with what I later called the Mauss problem (1994: 19–24), which results from the fact that stating and recognizing a practice as "social," as distinct, for example, from natural or rational, required an alternative social starting point, that is to say familiarity with another practice that differed from the practice one was characterizing, or at least a starting point in which the practice did not exist. Moreover, recognizing one's own practices as practices required this.

This implied that calling a practice "social" in the first place, or indeed calling it a practice at all, was relative to a starting point in another practice, but also, and importantly, that what appeared as "the practice" would also be relative to a starting point. I expressed this in *Sociological Explanation as Translation* by the phrase "same-practices hypothesis," by which I meant that when the sociologist enters a new social situation she must continue to take for granted what she was already taking for granted. The "must" here is a de facto must: The analyst cannot avoid doing this. The same-practices hypothesis is an "as if" construction, however: This is not something researchers consciously do or can consciously do. What they consciously do is to construct accounts of the practices of others for an audience which has practices of its own, which are similar in some respects and different in others—similar enough for them to be made sense of, different enough that the sense needs to be explicated. The similarity between this claim and Davidson's notion of interpretive charity is evident, although Davidson was concerned with beliefs rather than practices, that is to say the explicit rather than the tacit. But if the explicit is dependent on the tacit, interpretive charity needs to be extended to practices as well.

This issue appears in various forms in Wittgenstein, notably in his discussion of natural signs of an intention, his discussions of "agreement," and his characterization of the problem of understanding Martians. "Agreement" is an analogical term, but Wittgenstein's meaning is captured in this passage:

> Suppose someone heard syncopated music of Brahms played and asked: "What is the queer rhythm which makes me wobble?" "It is the 3 against 4." One could play certain phrases and he would say: "Yes. It's this peculiar rhythm I meant." On the other hand, if he didn't agree, this wouldn't be an explanation. ([1938] 1967: 20–21)

This corresponds with what I will discuss in Chapter 10 as *Evidenz*. In discussing the problem of interpreting in anthropological contexts, he contrasts what we would do with what we would do if we faced Martians instead:

> If you came to a foreign tribe, whose language you didn't know at all and you wished to know what words corresponded to 'good', 'fine', etc., what would you look for? You would look for smiles, gestures, food, toys. ([Reply to objection:] If you went to Mars and men were spheres with sticks coming out, you wouldn't know what to look for. ([1938] 1967: 2)

With Martians, we lack natural signs of intention, among other things. This marks the distinction between the universal and the realm of practices or agreement. But Wittgenstein does not concern himself with the question of how we distinguish natural signs from signs that are signs by agreement when we encounter a situation where we are struggling to understand another person. Our knowledge of both kinds of signs is tacit.

It is a commonplace anthropological observation that we can be misled by taking signs or facial expressions as natural when they are in fact conventional and have a different meaning in the target culture. In these cases we stumble into the difference and need to construct for ourselves an analogue to a translation manual. This translation manual is going to be relative to the needs we have and therefore to what we already understand tacitly as the significance of the signs: If we learn that a frown means anxiety rather than disapproval, we calibrate accordingly, and at the same time recognize the sign as conventional or cultural. If we came from a society that frowned when anxious, we would not need a manual.

This is simple enough. But complications arise when we get into the subtleties of characterizing a different culture or follow Wittgenstein when he says about aesthetic taste that

> The words we call expressions of aesthetic judgment play a very complicated role, but a very definite role, in what we call a culture of period. To describe their use or to describe what you mean by cultured taste, you have to describe a culture. ([1938] 1967: 8)

To "describe" a culture one must deploy many comparisons to one's own culture, or in the idiom that one is explaining. The object cannot be characterized in any other way than in one's native idiom. So the object one describes is constructed as a practice in a way that is relative to that idiom, and not in some universal idiom. Facts about practices are thus not universal or culture-free, but are relative to the idiom in which they are explicated. This is not in Wittgenstein, although it is implied. And there is more that is consistent with Wittgenstein that bears on these formulations.

The tacit knowledge required for a particular performance or act—throwing a curve ball, for example—is individual in a complex way: It is embodied, and people with different physical characteristics need to adapt in different ways to get the result; some people do naturally what others need to be coached to do, and the tacit knowledge possessed by one person learning to perform the act is different from the knowledge possessed by others; moreover, in the end, the performances are not "the same" in a microscopic sense, but different in ways that reflect the combination of first-nature embodiment, second-nature embodiment of tacit knowledge, and explicit knowledge that produce the performance. What holds here holds for the tacit generally: What we make explicit when we help someone to understand, or perform, is relative to the need for understanding that they have in a particular situation in which they already possess tacit knowledge. But what each person possesses varies, and thus so does the need and the explicit formulation that responds to it.

Wittgenstein does not go this far. Nor does he need to, given the therapeutic purposes of his later writings, in which, for example, an analogical use of the notion of rule to apply to tacit rules can serve a purpose without committing him to some sort of ontology of rules.[2] In a sense, the recognition of the situated character of the tacit parallels the shift from the model of a set of "enormously complicated" presupposed tacit conventions in the *Tractatus* ([1921] 1961) to the therapeutic model of the *Investigations* ([1953] 2009) and also reflects the recognition that the solution of philosophical problems is always situated in specific linguistic contexts, and is possible only from within. The lesson of Wittgenstein is that there is no external "transcendental" presuppositional order to which one can go to solve philosophical problems—a lesson too often forgotten today. The problem of the a priori, in short, is a part, but not the whole, of the problem of the tacit.

Part I

Two Key Philosophical Issues

Underdetermination and Understanding Others

The two chapters in this section deal with the two key philosophical elements of the argument that is developed in the rest of the book: the problem of underdetermination and the problem of understanding. The first chapter is also chronologically the first of the previously published papers in the volume, and its content reflects this. It was written during the period of the greatest influence of computationalist approaches to the mind, when the project of modeling tacit mental processes seemed reasonable, and ideas like knowledge engineering and replacing experts with computational expert systems were novel. Yet this somewhat antique topic is still revealing. Tacit knowledge can be modeled by computers, but the models give us no reason to believe that the contents of the model correspond to anything going on in the mind or brain, simply because there are multiple models that can emulate any given skill or tacit process.

The second is the denial of the idea of "frames" that is ubiquitous in many literatures that relate to tacit knowledge, and especially the idea that shared tacit frames are conditions of communication and understanding. The key document in this denial is Donald Davidson's "On the Very Idea of a Conceptual Scheme" ([1973] 1984). But this famous text needs to be properly understood, especially in relation to Davidson's later views. The product of this understanding is an account of intelligibility that does not rest on frames. Davidson's account provides an answer to the question of how we can understand each other that does not require the assumption that there is something tacit, like a frame, which the two parties to understanding already have in common. This provides one of the key desiderata listed in the Introduction: an answer to the question of how something normally explained by reference to the tacit can be explained without reference to tacit collective facts. In the next section, "meanings" are treated in a parallel manner.

1 Underdetermination

Tacit Knowledge and the Problem of Computer Modeling Cognitive Processes in Science

In what follows I propose to bring out certain methodological properties of projects of modeling the tacit realm that bear on the kinds of modeling done by those concerned with scientific cognition by computer as well as by ethnomethodological sociologists, both of whom must make some claims about the tacit in the course of their efforts to model cognition. The same issues, I will suggest, bear on the project of a cognitive psychology of science as well.

Tacitness has had a small but persistent role in the writings of critics of computer modeling of cognition, a role smaller than that of intuition, a concept with which it is often confused. In what follows the terms will be distinguished: "tacitness" will refer strictly to the reproducible expectations, assumptions, presuppositions, cognitive skills, and what not that I have elsewhere called "sub-beliefs." By "reproducible" I mean simply socially transmitted, as the training of a clinician is, as distinct from wholly private, which intuition might be thought to be. The role of the concept of tacitness in the critical literature on computer modeling or human reasoning has been to identify a residual category of things allegedly "essential" to "real thinking" or "real discovery" that are unmodeled and perhaps unmodelable by computer programs. Joseph Weizenbaum, for example, uses Polanyi (Weizenbaum 1976: 71, 124–25), Chomsky (1976: 137), and Chief Justice Holmes (1976: 226) as sources for examples of tacitness and, in addition to his remarks on intuition, stresses the idea that machines cannot be socialized in the same way as humans, if only because certain primal experiences cannot be shared with machines as they are with other humans.

The argument in this paper in no way depends on this thesis about ultimate or essential unmodelability, and indeed because it is in large part about methodological troubles with the concept of tacitness that extend all the way from the statisticians' concept of "belief structures" to the intellectual historians' concept of "structures of consciousness" in the historical past, it potentially undermines uses such as Weizenbaum's, especially when these involve potentially troubled assertions about the tacit realm, such as claims about their essential character.

The relevance of problems of tacitness to discussions of scientific discovery is evident from discussions of the more familiar "search procedures" of statistics, such as the kinds of curve-fitting done using least squares. The difficulties are dramatized in the following suggestion made by the statistician David Freeman:

> Suppose a few of us were transported back in time to the year 1600, and were invited by the Emperor Rudolph II to set up an Imperial Department of Statistics in the court at Prague. Despairing of those circular orbits, Kepler enrolls in our department. We teach him the general linear model, least squares, dummy variables, everything. He goes back to work, fits the best circular orbit for Mars by least squares, puts in a dummy variable for the exceptional observation—and publishes. And that's the end, right there in Prague at the beginning of the 17th century. (Freeman 1985: 359)

If this sounds a bit fantastic, there is another case closer to home. In the dispute between biometers and Mendelians at the beginning of this century, the inventors of these same regression methods did in fact settle for a correlational view of heredity, at least for a time. It is said that Pearson, who lived long after the dispute, never accepted the Mendelian hypothesis. He thus fulfilled precisely the fears which earlier critics of statistics, such as Mill and Comte, had expressed, the fear that the investigations would settle for statistical results that were a conceptual dead end. Clark Glymour has responded to Freeman's suggestion by arguing that Kepler would have been saved from a dead end in much the same way as the experimental tradition saved genetics: The separate problem-tradition of Newtonian physics, and especially Newton's derivation of elliptical orbits from his law of gravitation (Glymour 1983: 129–30), would have forced these scientists to push on.

Glymour's use of the term "problem-tradition" should suffice to make a small point: The search procedures themselves do not suffice to explain why these curve-fitting efforts were not dead ends. One need not be a believer in any sort of mystical doctrine of tacitness to claim that to model discoveries of this kind, it is not enough to describe a search procedure based on the explicit assumptions initially held by the researchers. Some account needs to be taken of the ways in which these assumptions were or could be revised. And because they are typically revised by importations from other traditions rather than from mechanical revisions of the explicit assumptions of the search procedures, the imported assumptions and assumptions that make importation possible need also to be modeled. Such assumptions are "tacit" at least in the sense that they are not a part of the modeled search procedure itself. To call the assumptions tacit does not imply that they are irretrievably tacit, or unmodelable, but simply that they have not yet been made explicit or not yet been made part of the model; this limited sense of "tacit" will suffice for the discussion here. What I will have to say concerns the problem of the identification of such assumptions or traditions, and the peculiarities of their logical status. The problem of irretrievability does not, of course, vanish because we cannot assume that the assumptions are modelable.

THE *MENO* ACCORDING TO POLANYI AND SIMON

Perhaps the clearest confrontation on the topic of tacitness in the AI literature is found in the discussion of Herbert Simon of Polanyi's use of the *Meno* in *The Tacit Dimension* (Polanyi 1966a). The *Meno* is a dialogue about whether virtue can be taught, and the point Socrates makes at the end of the dialogue is essentially that, if it could be, either the Sophists could teach it, or virtuous men could. His audience agrees with Gorgias that the Sophists only make men clever at speaking, and Socrates disposes of the idea that virtuous men might teach virtue by showing that various virtuous men had assured that their sons were well instructed in those things which are a matter of knowledge or skill, but failed to make them "virtuous"; virtue, he concludes, is divinely given. The slave boy in the dialogue is brought in to make a related point, which is well described by Polanyi's phrase "we know more than we can tell," but is nevertheless oddly incongruent with Polanyi's larger thesis, and oddly congruent with Simon's.

Socrates establishes a) that the boy cannot correctly answer the question ("cannot tell," in Polanyi's language), of how much larger the sides of a square with double the area of another square will be, and b) that the boy thinks he knows that if a square has twice the area the sides will also be doubled (Plato *Meno*: 99). He then leads the boy through a series of inferences, each of which the boy could "tell," at least could assent in response to Socrates' "questions," formulating those influential steps, and that he could correctly multiply and add when asked. After these queries led him to the correct solution, Socrates turns to Menon, asks whether any of the opinions the boy gave in response to the queries were not his own, and then asks whether the correct opinions were not in the boy all along. Menon assents (Plato *Meno*: 81–82).

Polanyi thinks the *Meno* shows conclusively that if all knowledge is explicit, i.e., capable of being clearly stated, then we cannot know a problem or look for its solution. And the *Meno* also shows, therefore, that if problems nevertheless exist and discoveries can be made by solving them, we can know things, and important things, that we cannot tell (Polanyi 1966a: 22).

How exactly the *Meno* does this is not made clear by Polanyi. Presumably he has in mind that the boy had a kind of precognition of the solution that he could employ when coaxed but could not formulate in response to Socrates' direct query. He claims that "the kind of tacit knowledge that solves the paradox of the *Meno* consists in the intimation of something hidden, which we may yet discover," and suggests that there are parallels in the history of science. The Copernicans "must have meant to affirm" a "kind of foreknowledge" when they "passionately maintained during the hundred and forty years before Newton proved the point, that the heliocentric theory was not merely a convenient way of computing the paths of the planets, but was really true" (Polanyi 1966a: 23). The scientist's "valid knowledge of a problem," sense of "approaching its solution," and "valid anticipation of the yet indeterminate implications of the discovery" (meaning the sense that the discovery will lead to additional but "as yet undisclosed, perhaps as yet unthinkable, consequences") are thus accounted for by tacit knowing (Polanyi 1966a: 24).

Michael Bradie presented a counterexample directed not at this broader set of claims, but at Polanyi's formulation of the paradox—that "to search for the solution of a problem is an absurdity; for either you know what you are looking for, and then there is no problem; or you do not know what you are looking for, and then you cannot expect to find anything" (Polanyi 1966a: 22). One horn of this dilemma, that if you know what you are looking for, there is no problem, is false, Bradie suggests. He gives the example of a mathematician who is trying to refute Goldbach's conjecture: He knows what he is looking for, namely an even number which is not the sum of two primes, but he still has the problem of finding one (Bradie 1974: 203). One suspects that Polanyi would not accept this formulation, and indeed it seems like a pun on "problem." But it is a serious pun, as Simon's appropriation of the example makes evident, for, to the extent that "problems" are those cases where "you know what you are looking for," it may be possible to represent the problem solving process formally.[1]

Simon's expansion of this point runs as follows. It is possible to have an effective procedure for testing and an effective procedure for generating candidates; we will have a "problem," i.e., an unsolved problem, where we nevertheless "know what we are looking for" without actually having it. In the case of Goldbach's conjecture, we can set up the following procedures: Generate even numbers, generate numbers named by their prime factors, and make judgments of equality. The problem then can be defined as follows: "Find a number *k* generated by the first procedure that does not belong to the numbers generated by the second procedure" (Simon 1971a: 340). Thus the example fits the "general scheme for defining problem solutions prior to finding them" (Simon 1971a: 340) as elaborated in such papers as "The Logic of Heuristic Decision-Making," in which Simon also discusses the *Meno* paradox. In this essay he defines "solution," following John McCarthy, as "the object that satisfies the following test" (1971b: 161).

WHAT DID THE SLAVE BOY KNOW?

Did the slave boy possess a procedure for testing? Presumably he did not, or he would have been able to see that his first answer to Socrates was wrong. Socrates shows him that he was wrong by making him go through certain inferential steps which lead to an inconsistency with his original answer, and he recognizes the inconsistency. We might describe this in computational terms by saying that the knowledge the boy possessed consisted of the subroutines that generated each inferential step, plus subroutines that matched the outcomes and recorded a failure to match. On the basis of this description of the first part of the dialogue with the slave boy, one might question whether Socrates has in fact merely "queried" the slave boy: The slave boy apparently could not have performed the routine producing the result on his own; Socrates, by putting the pre-existing subroutines together into a routine measuring the area of squares in fact taught him something, namely the higher-level routine.

It is perhaps less clear that the boy possessed a procedure for matching answers in order to test candidate solutions: After all, he didn't recognize his original answer was wrong until Socrates showed that using the boy's matching and calculating subroutines, one comes to a different numerical result. It is the inconsistency that the boy recognizes as an error. So one might say that Socrates represented the geometrical problem in a way that the boy's pre-existing "numerical inconsistency recognition subroutine" could be invoked, which it was not by Socrates' original query. Thus Socrates has taught at least one thing to the boy in this part of the dialogue, namely a higher-level routine for calculating area, and perhaps another, the technique for the representation of the problem of area as a problem of adding the squares within a square, which Socrates supplies and the boy instantly accepts, and which is necessary for producing the inconsistency the boy recognizes.

Described in this way, Socrates' version of the event as accepted by Menon is untrue, but Polanyi might find it more congenial, for it suggests a way for him to salvage his point against Simon, and perhaps even salvage the paradox. When the slave boy "recognizes as valid" he is doing something other than executing subroutines or stringing them together to perform a complex task, and something different from "being programmed" by Socrates: After all, the higher-level routine is being accepted as "valid," not merely as a well-formed command. Of course, one might attempt to push this description further and describe the boy's "accepting as valid routine," that is, modeling the process by which he accepts as valid and rejects as invalid the identification of the result of certain routines with certain answers, in this case answers to certain questions about the area of squares. To do this, perhaps one would model "recognition as valid" as using a successful identification of this sort as a signal to accept the routine as the determinant of area, i.e., as a step in self-programming or "learning."

But this is not quite true to the case, for the boy seems (and Polanyi has precisely this sort of thing in mind) to have a precognition of the right method and it is the fact that Socrates' suggestions match with this tacit precognition which enables him to "recognize as valid" Socrates' method of arriving at the answer. But recognition might be modeled as well, for example in terms of a preference of previously experienced patterns. And of course this process of finding discrepancies and patching the program to match additional features of the process can go on indefinitely.

One might emulate the slave boy in innumerable other ways: By beginning with a program for areas of all kinds of surfaces and blocking execution of any but the programs relating to squares, even the rules of recognition could be constructed differently, for they depend on what the learning process starts with. If we think like Socrates, we might assume that all knowledge of means calculating areas of surfaces is already present in the boy, and thus treat recognition as recollection (plus modelable error as in all mental processes) and construct a recognition subroutine such that the primary test the computer would use in "recognizing" would be to match the suggested learning with the previously blocked parts of the program and, if they match, unblock them.

The Simon-like "learning" model described earlier would be an alternative to his; Polanyi presumably would prefer another approach, perhaps the one signaled by Socrates' preliminary question to Menon, "is the boy a Greek, and does he speak our language?" One might suppose, for example, that mathematical concepts are not primary, but based on ontogenetically prior concepts and experience that may or may not be shared with persons raised differently—that there may be different paths to, and therefore different underlying inferential frameworks, onto which thinking about mathematical concepts is grafted. Some may reason visually, as the slave boy could, whereas others might find it more natural to derive their geometric results from numerical relations and to infer by operations on numbers. Indeed, there are strong reasons to believe that different cultures dispose those raised within them to different branches of mathematics, or against mathematics.

THE MEANING OF MATCHING

The sheer diversity of the kinds of models that can emulate any given cognitive process of this sort raises a question about their status. Are these models merely analogies, which may be useful for various purposes? Or is there some fact of the matter which enables us to say one analogy is right and another wrong? Does the ultimately right model also map on to features of the physical computing mechanism of the human brain? Or are there no ultimately right models, but only purpose-relative models? What is the thing called knowledge that expert systems attempt to model? What sorts of things are the "processes of scientific discovery" that Simon and his collaborators say "may be describable and explainable simply as special classes of" problem solving processes previously modeled on computers (Langley et al. 1987: 129), and in what sense do these models constitute "an empirical account"? (Langley et al. 1987: preface). It should be evident that some sort of ontic claim is being made by writers like Simon, but it is in many ways a puzzle.

Under one interpretation, the claim is simple: The cognitive processes of a Kepler were processes in the brain, and therefore the correct model of Kepler's discovery will be the model which corresponds to those processes. Claims about tacit knowledge in relation to Kepler's discovery will be settled by having the correct model, which will either contain something corresponding to tacit knowledge or will not. The mental processes of Kepler are of course irrecoverable. But the model which is constructed will inevitably represent basic cognitive processes shared by many persons and validated by empirical psychological experimentation. Thus the sense in which these are "empirical accounts" is that the models in question are empirically tested by psychology and that they match with the basic physical features of cognition that have been empirically established by neurobiologists.

The place of this last clause in the argument appears modest, but it is important to see that it is in fact central. Turning a decision between competing models of a given cognitive process, such as the slave boy's geometrizing, into an empirical question entangles us in the difficulties to which any kind of human psychological experimentation is subject. The models are ordinarily attempts to describe what are taken to be probabilistic processes, for example of arithmetic errors. The tests of the fit of these models are themselves probabilistic. Thus there is inevitably a high degree of arbitrariness in the test of the model, as various assumptions about the form of curves, about underlying distributions, and so on must be made to apply tests of fit and curve-fitting heuristics, and the like. Because the models are themselves probabilistic, many models might be generated that fit equally or almost equally well; and because sharp quantitative discriminations between them must be based on arbitrary assumptions, those that fit almost equally well cannot be nonarbitrarily rejected. Moreover, what fits in a highly controlled experimental setting may simply not generalize to the real world cognitive processes to which they are assumed to be equivalent, and the difficulties in such simple cases as arithmetic errors are compounded in cases of great complexity, such as Kepler's reasoning processes.

The reason those difficulties are usually ignored is the expectation, to quote Meehl quoting Skinner in conversation, that

> When the laws of behavior are sufficiently worked out in mathematical detail (in the next generation following me), and when the anatomy, especially the microanatomy, and the physiology of the brain are very thoroughly understood, there will be no problem of prematurely forcing a speculative translation because it will be perfectly apparent how the brain/behavior dictionary will read. (Meehl 1986: 319)

Presumably it would also be perfectly apparent which of the competing cognitive models, should any remain at the time our physiological and anatomical knowledge becomes sufficiently advanced, are to be discarded.

If we consider the problem of underdetermination apart from this expectation, matters look quite different. The case for a model's reality, or for its explanatory force, depends on the existence of match between model and process. So this expectation serves another role in making the argument plausible, that of permitting questions about the constitution of the objects, such as "processes of discovery" to be matched with the models, to be treated as non-basic—that is, as temporary or *prima facie* assumptions which one expects to replace. Again, this is an apparently small matter, with large implications. In actual cases not only are the relations between models and processes highly underdetermined—that is, the same "process" can be modeled by a variety of computer programs, each using different devices—but the gap between the *in vivo* practices of reasoning and the models of them which presently exist is usually large. In cases of expert systems consciously designed to emulate the knowledge of the expert other than fairly routine mathematical problem-solving and other very simple cases, there is a great deal of interpretation or skill which needs to be supplied by the end user (Collins et al. 1986). This implies that in these cases the expert system is not a complete emulation of the relevant expert knowledge.

The idea of "completeness" is itself puzzling. It lends itself to the line of argument that Michael Polanyi employs in his own attempts to prove the existence of tacit knowledge, as well as to attempts to show that AI programs are not "really thinking." But such arguments share a premise, or discursive practice, with their opponent, namely the idea that the description of the process to which the model or expert system is being compared has some sort of ontic significance which the model or system itself acquires or fails to acquire when it is successfully or unsuccessfully matched. The project of matching assumes that the description is itself ontically valid in some sense, or at least uniquely legitimate as a description.

There is a kind of cul-de-sac which arises in relation to these matching arguments that needs to be briefly considered. As I have suggested, the computer modeler can attempt to emulate a particular real world cognitive process, and the describer of the process can elaborate the description in ways which the computer modeler can then attempt to match. The dialectic between the modeler and the describer of features of the cognitive situation can go on indefinitely in this fashion. It is in connection with this feature of the modeling process in which the question of whether a computer really "recognizes a valid" match, really "thinks," and so forth finds a place. At each stage in the elaboration of the model the critic can say "really thinking would be when such and such," and at each stage the modeler can offer some version of such and such, only to find that it is not clear that such and such fully qualifies. Important as these questions may be for the question of man's place in the universe and for the question of the ultimate coherence of the goals of Simon-like programs of modeling human cognition, discussions of these issues do not seem to reach determinate results. Technical solutions or substitutes for such concepts as "recognition" are necessarily in part conventions or stipulations that fix the meaning of a term and consequently change it, if it is a term with an open texture such as the cognitive terms in question in discussions of scientific discovery. But this is perhaps not as decisive an issue as it might seem.

The fixing of conventions to specify one meaning of a term and allowing others to fall into disuse is one way in which language itself changes. The history of the term "*pneuma*" and its present form in the word "pneumatic" is illustrative. The association of *pneuma* with breathing and breathing with the soul has simply no part in present usage, which applies the term to suction devices and analogies with the device. This should suffice to remind us of the defective theory of language hiding behind many of these objections, namely the museum theory of meaning, and to point to a larger set of difficulties with any thesis which presumes that meanings are eternally fixed and that the laws governing the range of application of terms are there to be "found," as jurisprudential theorists say. In relation to the problem of computer modeling, the problem may be simply put: Any attempt to match meanings and claim that the computer's meaning fails to match the actual meaning of some term or mental structure predicates itself on a construction of the "meaning" to be used as a standard. Such constructions have the same difficulty as the computer modelers' technical substitutions. Like them, the constructions fix the meaning in a particular way. Hence they are always questionable when treated as a standard to which a model is matched, in much the same way that modelers' technical substitutions are questionable.

THE TACIT

We may distinguish the matching problem, where the computer program is held to the standard or a description of a process or a definition arrived at independently and taken as valid, from a kind of test which turns the problem of matching into an empirical or naturalistic problem. The Turing test is the classic strategy for "empirically" evaluating the attempt at emulation: Similar problems arise in attempts to "elicit" expert knowledge that an expert system should contain. The way in which knowledge is elicited is by a series of comparisons, in which failures to match expert judgments are "corrected" by adding new rules. These rules may be said to represent the expert's tacit knowledge, in at least this sense: Many of the rules make explicit what the expert did not think to or perhaps even could not articulate as part of his or her "knowledge."

The problem of knowledge elicitation has some familiar analogues in sociology and shares the features of a family of methods of revealing tacit aspects of an activity in which a comparison between practices that differ shows what assumptions a given practice depends on to produce the same practical results as another. The study of what Marcel Mauss called body techniques is a simple example ([1935] 1979). We assume our way of sitting is natural. It comes as a shock to us to learn that other cultures find it unnatural and "sit" quite differently. We then can see that sitting is learned, and even see how it is learned. But without the comparison we would have been hard pressed to thematize "sitting" as a technique at all. Conceivably someone would have invented, or happened upon, a full-blown alternative, that was equally "comfortable" or "natural." But when we consider how much learning (from the earliest months, when infants are praised for sitting up) has gone into sitting, we can see that this is not likely. Any other position would "feel wrong" to a person without the appropriate childhood preparation. So without an actual lived alternative, we would very likely never come to recognize it as a technique that was tacitly taken by us as natural.

The recognition of such a practice as a practice thus depends on our ability to form a contrast between this and some alternative practice, a contrast where the two practices are similar enough that a hypothesis about the character of the alternative practice can be formulated and supported by descriptions of the activity. Similarly, the recognition of something as tacit knowledge depends on a contrast. The contrast may be to an idealization, such as an expert system program, or to a divergent form of a practice or body of knowledge, or it may be, as in the case of Garfinkelian ethnomethodology, a contrast to a description of the activity that identifies some feature of the activity—some "orderliness" to it—that can be accounted for only by supplementing the usual description with some hypothesis about tacit sense-making practices of some sort.

In either case, it is contingent as to what is "revealed," and the attribution of an assumption, tacit knowledge, a skill, or a practice is relative to the project of comparison or the means of generating the alternative description. In the case of expert systems, for example, what counts as knowledge is relative to the body of decisions, or judgments chosen as the standard. "Completeness" has a sense here only relative to the comparison, and this is characteristic of attributions of tacit knowledge: There are no natural wholes here, only artifacts of comparison.

This is perhaps a banal point, but its implications are often misunderstood. Aaron Cicourel, for example, in a discussion of expert measurement systems, adds to his famous argument "that traditional social measurement must incorporate the pragmatic conditions of everyday life in order to satisfy ecological validity conditions" in "studies of problem solving or decision-making and of beliefs, attitudes, opinions and general knowledge of the world" by suggesting that the "on-line adaptive potential of computer simulation models" (Cicourel 1986: 261n18) can be used to improve social measurement. He claims that "our use of language presumes various folk models or cognitive schemata of ideas, objects, events, and action" (1986: 261–62), and that consequently "we must design our expert systems to reflect the ecological validity of problem-solving conditions that are presupposed by general reasoning processes and the use of standardized language and thus model the way everyday reasoning, language, and action enter into all attempts at social measurement or the creation of expert systems" (1986: 268).

The actual case material which Cicourel deals with involves problems users have in responding to particular queries: The solutions are attempts to get a better grip on the techniques users employ in reading the queries, so as to get better responses. The role of discussions of "presuppositions" is thus bound to a practical end and occurs within a community with shared practices, to which the problem itself is relative. In my terms, the "practices" which are hypothesized and "proved" in some sense by the removal of the difficulties are "practices" relative to this problem. Cicourel appears to think of these practices differently, and this is reflected in the way he speaks of modeling "the way everyday reasoning" enters into "all attempts at . . . the creation of expert systems" as though this were a general modeling task—that is, as though there was a class of objects, namely folk models, that could themselves be modeled, and even as though the completion of this task would result in a scheme in which "ecological validity" could itself be accounted for. If the failing of more primitive systems was the result of a failure to include "everyday" thinking, the inclusion of these models would presumably make this failure good.

This is plainly utopian, for several reasons. First, like expert systems themselves, these models would be highly underdetermined—that is, there would be a wide array of alternative models that would emulate the same results, as in the *Meno* example. So the idea that one of them corresponds to the real thing is highly problematic. It may be that each of us goes around with differently constructed models, each of which more or less emulates other persons, as in Quine's famous analogy between individuals' theories of the world and shrubs, each of which is differently structured internally, with different arrangements of branches, but all of which have been trimmed to look the same (Quine 1960). In this case even the success of some attempt to emulate the general model of common sense would tell us nothing about the total structure of individuals' reasoning practices.

Second, the leap from specific problem-frames to general claims about common sense reasoning is wholly unwarranted: Cicourel's own models, like expert systems, are also going to be subject to ecological validity limitations. Indeed, the cases are precisely parallel. The only reason Cicourel can have for believing that his overarching model would be potentially free of such limitations is that it in some sense accounts for the "ecological validity" of the expert system it improves. But its actual successes would be relative to the matching or comprehension problems of particular users of a particular expert system, which warrant no nonrelative claims whatsoever.

The ideal to which he holds expert measurement systems is global identity, or something similarly ambitious. One might say that the belief in its attainment depends on generalizing erroneously from successes in revealing parts of the tacit dimension to some nonrelative "whole." These successes, however, depend on "techniques" which assure us nothing about the possibility of an exhaustive survey of the tacit dimension, and indeed there is no whole of which the results of these analyses can be understood as parts. Worse: the tacit contents are relative to the questions we ask about them rather than a absolute themselves. Each claim about them is like a hypothesis and consequently underdetermined in its description. Absent some lucky accident by which these descriptions would be synthesized or a privileged class of true nonrelative descriptions could be selected, this underdetermination seems largely irreducible. In any case, none of the means by which the tacit is made accessible warrant claims about the "whole" of the tacit knowledge. So "global identity" between any model and the whole of tacit knowledge or any larger thing of which tacit knowledge, taken as a whole, is a part, such as "the scientific cognitive processes of community *x*," is a hopeless aim.

MODELING THE TACIT IN PRINCIPLE AND IN PRACTICE

The picture that emerges from these considerations is this: Both "artificial" matching projects, such as the Langley et al. model of Kepler's discovery (1987), in which the "process" to be watched is "constructed" such that other descriptions have equal claim to ontic validity, and "natural" matching problems, such as knowledge elicitation for an expert system, warrant claims about tacit knowledge, but these claims are very weak. First, they are highly underdetermined hypotheses: A wide range of different descriptions of the tacit practice will solve a given specific, matching problem. Second, they are relative to the particular contrast problem solved by the hypothesis: There is no sense to claims about the complete characterization of a person's or community's tacit knowledge, because the programs of comparison are all themselves necessarily limited.

With this, to paraphrase Weber's famous remark in a different context, we come to matters of faith. In view of the highly underdetermined and context-bound character of our claims about tacit knowledge and therefore the cognitive processes which employ it, a few reflections are in order about the project of a cognitive psychology of scientific discovery, and about the relation in this project between reasonable expectations for its future achievements and the element of faith. One aspect of the Simonian image of cognitive process that has been bracketed in the present discussion is the prospect that the brain behavior dictionary will be apparent once the relevant physiology and psychology is at hand. When Skinner formulated this expectation, it is evident that he envisioned a moment when there would be a much simpler body of "psychological models" than the diverse, underdetermined, and contextually limited simulations I have described here. What now can be said to remain of this article of faith?

One might retain the hope that some simulacrum of this moment might yet arrive. It might take the following form: Certain AI routines widely useful in various cognitive emulation projects might be shown to match particular neurophysiological processes, thus resolving at a stroke the problem produced by the existence of a large class of competing descriptions of cognitive processes by selecting out this class of procedures as ontically valid descriptions and frameworks for description. But even if we grant Simon's premise that the brain is a computer, there is precious little reason to believe that this day will arrive. The idea of opening up the black box and finding in it the mechanisms of mind is a powerful image. But Mill's image of a nomic social science was a powerful image as well: Its realization was foiled by underdetermination and complexity, its early successes were later seen to be very limited in scope and significance, and practical difficulties over evidence that appeared at first to be minor gradually came to be appreciated as major. Most of the false starts in the history of social sciences, and there have been many, have had these characteristics. That AI modeling of cognitive processes understood as a program of explanation and description should be so marked by each of these traits, even at this early stage in the development of the project, inspires not faith but skepticism.

2 Intelligibility without Frames
Davidson's Normativity

INTRODUCTION

Davidson's "On the Very Idea of a Conceptual Scheme" ([1973] 1984) was a powerful and influential paper. It largely ended a prolonged discussion of the rationality of other cultures (Wilson [1970] 1977), undermining particularly the claim argued at the time that there was a universal, non-culture-relative core of rationality and protocol sentence-like description that provided grounds for judging the rationality of other cultures (Hollis [1970] 1977; MacIntyre [1970] 1977a&b; Winch [1970] 1977). It blunted the impact of some of the more exuberantly relativistic interpretations of the implications of Thomas Kuhn's *The Structure of Scientific Revolutions* ([1962] 1996). But the paper introduced one of the least well-understood Davidsonian arguments, his attack on what he called "The Third Dogma of Empiricism," after Quine's "Two Dogmas of Empiricism" (Quine 1951). The third dogma was the scheme/content distinction. The paper is basic to understanding the later Davidson. Its treatment of error pointed directly toward Davidson's most controversial claims, in "A Nice Derangement of Epitaphs" ([1986] 2005), about the nonexistence of "language" as the term is usually understood: The model for the interacting language speaker correcting for error is generalized from the model of the translator in "On the Very Idea."

Davidson himself thought the implications of the argument were radical, and he specifically thought that the paper was opposed to the kind of Kantianism that was present when it was written and has since, under slightly different forms, become conventional wisdom in Anglo-American philosophy, in which normative concepts constitute the world for us. Variants of this view range from the idea that normative concepts are subject to either a small or large amount of local linguistic variation to the idea that there is a large common core of reason that anyone in any culture who is properly brought up will come to recognize as binding. The essay was directly concerned with the kind of conceptual relativity supposedly warranted by the variation in concepts between languages. But as Davidson put it in the essay, the argument showed that it was also unintelligible to say "that all mankind—all speakers of language at least—share a common scheme and ontology" ([1973] 1984: 198).

The way his paper has come to be interpreted in much of the subsequent discussion assimilates it to a form of conventional wisdom to which it was opposed. This occurred through two main steps. The first was to read Davidson as having established the necessity of some sort of logical or rational core to human thought that is transcultural or culturally invariant by showing that translatability was transitive, that is, that my translation from language *L* to language *P* would not be a translation if it did not include the translations into *L* from language *N*. This reading is based on a supposed dilemma: If the relation of translatability was not transitive, it would imply the possibility of incommensurable schemes, and if it was transitive, it would imply that our standards are the only standards (Hurley 1992: 99–101, 108n23; Nagel 1986: 92–97), which in turn implied that there was after all a universal scheme. If Davidson is consistent in rejecting the possibility of incommensurable schemes, it would mean that Davidson was in fact a scheme/content thinker himself, and his reservations about the scheme/content distinction were a matter of detail.

The detail was vaguely understood in terms of the idea of independence. What Davidson had shown was that there could be no understanding of schemes and content independently of one another. Accordingly, one interpretation was that he was proposing a novel "interdependence" model of the relation between the two (Hurley 1992). Another interpretation deradicalized it in a different direction, by suggesting that his point had to do with "the metaphors that sustain the picture of an independent scheme and worldly content" (Thornton 2004: 58) rather than the idea itself. The reinterpretation made Davidson's argument about content rather than about schemes. Davidson's explicit denial that there was "a neutral ground, or a common coordinate system" between schemes (Davidson [1973] 1984: 198; cf. Hacking 1982: 61), was taken to rule out an independent realm of "content," but it was not taken to rule out an independent realm consisting of a common "scheme." Indeed, it was reinterpreted in terms of the Kantian idea that, as John McDowell puts it, the world "cannot be constituted independently of the space of concepts, the space in which subjectivity has its being" (1998: 309). The distinction between denying our ability to step outside the conceptual—the Kantian thesis—and denying the scheme/content distinction, meaning denying common content, common schemes, and the independence of scheme and content alike—Davidson's thesis—was taken to be a distinction without a difference. The reinterpreters assumed that the languages of the conceptual and of normative reason are inescapable and ineliminable by any argument about schemes, because Davidson could not have possibly, or intelligibly, meant to challenge this foundation of contemporary philosophy.

The conventional accommodation or renormalization of Davidson's argument was made plausible through a feature of Davidson's argument in this same paper: The claim, as it became interpreted, that massive error about widely held beliefs is impossible. If this is the case, that is, if skepticism about significant ordinary beliefs is itself necessarily incoherent, this fact can in turn be taken to imply that various commonplace metaphysical views about ordinary beliefs are warranted. If the separate and autonomous existence of the world and the normative authority of reason are such facts, or are entailed by such facts, these facts, together with the idea that there is some sort of universal rationality, take us back to and support a basically Kantian picture of the metaphysical structure of the world, in which universal rationality interacts with a world that we can't be very wrong about. What Davidson saw as radical, in short, became, through these reinterpretations, validation for the default anti-naturalist philosophy of the present. Davidson, on this account, becomes the thinker who undermined Quine's arguments in "Two Dogmas of Empiricism" from within, reestablishing the synthetic a priori in the new guise of the notion of normativity. On this view, Davidson's acknowledgment that rationality, intentionality, and belief are "normative," together with his rejection of massive error, commits him to some variant of the Kantian doctrine of normativity of Sellars (1963), Haugeland (1998), Brandom (1994), and McDowell (1994), perhaps with some idiosyncratic variations with respect to the precise location of the normative, for example, or of the nature of the interaction between the normative and the nonnormative.

Davidson's own argument that meaning, intentional ascriptions, and rationality are mutually dependent, and that they arrive together in the description of intentional action, seems congenial to this reading, because it serves to make these idiosyncratic differences less significant. Davidson might locate the normative in the universal psychological properties of the interpreting agent rather than in language, as in Brandom, or in some sort of nomic realm whose normative constraining character must be recognized, as in McDowell. But meaning, intentional ascriptions, and rationality all must be there in some fashion. The rest is detail.

The oddity of this outcome is worth reflecting on. The target of the original paper was the scheme/content distinction itself. The Kantian form of this distinction was an especially visible part of this—the term "scheme" is an echo of Kant's language. The picture of the rational ordering mind organizing the Kantian manifold was transmitted to Kuhn via the neo-Kantian historians of science, such as Alexandre Koyre, whom Kuhn admired and who played a large role in the background of Kuhn's use of the notion of paradigms. So the Kantian tradition is clearly the target of Davidson's paper. What made the paper so radical, as Richard Rorty routinely pointed out in conversation, was the way in which the argument against the scheme/content distinction could be extended throughout the history of philosophy, to undermine such variants as the concept-percept distinction, the word-world distinction, and so forth. The unradical result described above—that it is taken in support of the current "idealist" variants of the scheme/content distinction—is in open conflict with Davidson's initial point.

In what follows I will try to restore this original point. I will not be concerned with the details of this "idealist" reinterpretation of Davidson, but 1 will try to show why he thought the argument of his paper had radical implications and explain what it had radical implications for. Its target, I will argue, is the whole commonplace normative conception of concepts. His approach was to show why this conception was unnecessary and deeply problematic. Explicating the argument requires more than textual analysis: The arguments to which "On the Very Idea" is now being assimilated, such as those of McDowell, Brandom, and Haugeland, were not available at the time the paper was written and were in part devised to take advantage of Davidson's claims, so the original paper does not respond directly to them and can even be construed, with effort, to support them. But the original point can, with a bit of contextualization, be reconstructed and, once reconstructed, can be seen to be the basis of the even more radical claims made in such later papers as "A Nice Derangement of Epitaphs" ([1986] 2005), "The Third Man" ([1972] 2005), and "The Social Aspect of Language" ([1994] 2005). It is an oddity of this discussion, although not an entirely mysterious one, that some of the relevant distinctions between Davidson and the normativists map onto, and are reproduced in, social theory. Brandom, at the beginning of *Making It Explicit* (1994), quotes Weber's phrase "the disenchantment of the world" and offers a project of re-enchantment in its place. Sellars' appeal to the idea of collective intentionality, which was in turn a core of his ideas about norms, was consciously echoing Durkheim. As we will see, the differences between Davidson and the normativists follow this familiar fault line between theories of obligation: those that invoke collective facts and those which rely on individualist social theory.

WHAT IS IMPOSSIBLE?

There is a kernel of truth to the conventional appropriation of the argument of "On the Very Idea of a Conceptual Scheme." The paper does rest on an impossibility argument, about intelligibility and the limits of intelligibility, and the argument has complex implications, far beyond the issue of conceptual relativism. But the implications are not congenial to the Kantian picture, as Davidson knew, and he contrasted it to the views of the main Kantian of the time, P. F. Strawson. The argument develops from an observation about incommensurability, that

> Whorf, wanting to demonstrate that Hopi incorporates a metaphysics so alien to ours that Hopi and English cannot—as he puts it "be calibrated," uses English to convey the contents of sample Hopi sentences. Kuhn is brilliant at saying what things were like before the revolution using—what else?—our post-revolutionary idiom. ([1973] 1984: 184)

Davidson's point is that it is impossible to do otherwise. If we were faced with genuine incommensurability—speakers with a truly alien conceptual scheme—we would not even be able to understand them sufficiently to say so.

Davidson's approach to the issues goes through the problem of evidence: The evidence of "different schemes" takes the form of sentences. It is normally understood that having languages is associated with having a conceptual scheme in such a way that differences in one imply differences in the other. Benjamin Whorf, for example, uses linguistic evidence from the Hopi to make claims about their conceptual schemes, and the literature on conceptual differences in science emphasizes shifts in the meanings of terms in the context of different theories. If we restate the idea of incommensurability and intelligibility at the level of the linguistic evidence, it becomes a claim about translatability, specifically about what could count as a successful translation and what follows from failures of translation. As Davidson puts it, "it seems unlikely that we can intelligibly attribute attitudes as complex as [the ones that would allow us to recognize something as speech behavior doing something as complex as making an utterance the speaker believed in] unless we can translate his words into ours" ([1973] 1984: 186). The limits of intelligibility, in short, are the limits of translation. Failure in translation makes for, and is evidence of, failure in understanding.

Davidson considers two possible kinds of failure of translatability, partial and total, and argues first "that we cannot make sense of total failure," and then examines cases of partial failure ([1973] 1984: 185). The case against total failure provides the kernel for the conventional interpretation. But the case of partial failure has the more radical implications. The impossibility argument arises in connection with purported cases of total failure of translation: The conclusion of the argument is that the only evidence in the first place that an activity is speech behavior is evidence that it can be interpreted in our language, whether directly or through translation. This turns out to have a crucial implication for the transitivity of translation: To ascribe the speech behavior "translating" to someone in translating into yet a third language requires us to translate the translation, because otherwise we would not be able to say whether we were properly translating their utterances as translation. In short, we need to know that they are not faking translation. This criterion holds for the rest of translation. This is the argument that seems to lead back to a universal core of rationality. But Davidson also makes an argument that seems to point in the opposite direction, toward the detail-oriented capacities of interpretation that are central to ordinary human interaction and understanding, as when he observes that translation requires a command of a "multitude of finely discriminated intentions and beliefs" to interpret speech as a form of human conduct. This is an important tension in his argument to which we will return. It is resolved by his normativist interpreters in the direction of normative universal rationality or the normative conceptual preconditions for language. But these options, as we have seen, seem to be ruled out by, and are indeed the target of, the argument itself.

The next step in the argument involves the contrast between mutual "contamination" of meaning and theory, that is, about what is claimed to be true—something that follows from giving up the analytic-synthetic distinction ([1973] 1984: 187). What appear to be "changes in meaning" between scientific theories, an essential element of the claim that paradigms are incommensurable, always also involves changes in what is said to be true. Failure of translation thus means failure to translate as true claims made with the same terms, so that one must say either that the meanings of the terms rather than the terms themselves must be different or that the previous claims were false. But the appeal to meanings turns out to be less than helpful, and indeed to be empty: "Meanings," in the sense of meanings in the head, are inaccessible. We don't know whether people mean the same thing as we do by the same words; we know only what they do and say. And thus the idea that truth is relative to a conceptual scheme turns out to mean nothing more than that the truth of a sentence is relative to the language in which it belongs ([1973] 1984: 189).

There is another oddity. The argument of the paper does not support the idea of a universal core of rationality common to all cultures. Indeed, it explains why the idea—promoted at the time by Martin Hollis ([1970] 1977), who was concerned with the closely related question of whether we could attribute beliefs to people who did not possess *modus ponens*—could be given no determinate content. The reasons are Quinean. Translation operates on sets of logically and semantically linked sentences, which are open to multiple interpretations, in which the truth or falsity of any given sentence is relative to the role that sentence plays in the set as a whole, a role that can be omitted or altered depending on the roles played by the rest of the sentences and their content. Consequently, "possessing *modus ponens*" is a feature not of the content of the heads of the natives whose beliefs are being interpreted, but of the translations we use to make sense of them. Whether the translations ascribe *modus ponens* to them or not reflects choices made by the translator that could have been otherwise and still have produced intelligibility. Without such universally rational content there is nothing universal for the universalizing version of the Kantian project to work with, which gives us a reason to doubt this interpretation of Davidson.

THE QUINEAN BACKGROUND

As is evident from this reference to holism, Davidson's paper, and his work in this area in general, deals with a series of problems left over from Quine. In describing his position I have used Quinean language, for the most part, and done so intentionally—separating the Quinean elements from the Davidsonian ones cannot be done without an understanding of the issues that Davidson is addressing, and avoiding, in his paper. Quine left an unresolved problem: how to reconcile the fact that (a) the data for understanding human action and language were necessarily behavioral, for the language learner as well as for the interpreter and translator learning from scratch, with (b) the widespread philosophical (and general) use of notions of intention and meaning and (c) the raw fact that people do seem to be able to interpret one another, learn one another's languages, and do so in terms of intentions and meanings.

Quine himself was willing to treat this question as a matter of what would be found in a fully naturalized scientific account of these matters. This meant that notions like "meaning" and "intention" needed to be regarded as theoretical terms in an as yet uncreated predictive theory of behavior. But in their usual form they did not work very well in this role: Behavioral evidence was insufficient to produce a reasonably determinate fact of the matter of either meaning or intention. So interpretation was left hanging by Quine. Moreover, the relativistic consequences of Kuhn seemed to follow from Quine's attack on the analytic-synthetic distinction, which undercut the idea of universal a priori rational standards by relativizing considerations previously regarded as a priori to the status of part of a "theory" that faced the evidence as a whole. This, together with the underdetermination of theory by data, implied that there might be a number of theories that had different logical elements, had different true sentences, but were equally predictive, and that this was an irreducible situation. The germs of the idea of underdetermination and the relativism of logical elements and mathematical framework were already present in logical positivism. But Quine showed that these issues could not be dealt with merely by using such notions as convention to characterize the theoretical elements in question. This left a variety of puzzles about meaning: If the truth of the sentences is relative to the theory as a whole, didn't this imply that meanings changed between theories and were thus incommensurable, making the notion of scientific progress impossible to formulate neutrally, as Paul Feyerabend pointed out (1962, esp. 74–95)?

Davidson's approach to interpretation took for granted the same evidential base. But he dealt with it in a different way. He took over from G. E. M. Anscombe the notion of "under a description" and proceeded by treating intentional and meaning questions as arising under a particular description. The description, it is important to note, is in some sense a description of choice, an option (although exactly in what sense is an important consideration to which we will return). We could describe in the language of physical or neurophysiological science instead. But if we did this the problem of interpretation would be inaccessible to us. The question for Davidson involved the conditions of interpretation, that is, of getting a reasonably determinate answer to questions about intentions and meanings using the behavioral evidence we necessarily work with. "Radical interpretation" was simply interpretation under these conditions without other background knowledge, such as prior knowledge of the meanings of utterances, which is to say interpretation with the raw behavioral evidence alone. The question was what more would be needed to make any sense of this evidence in terms of meanings and intentions, or to put it differently, the implications of the choice of description in terms of intentions and meanings.

Davidson's answer was rationality, which enabled the attribution of intentions on the basis of behavioral data and knowledge of the meanings of the utterances that are part of the behavior, if there are any. The model is this: If I can take an utterance as a sincere expression of belief, and have data about behavior, I can infer meaning; if I have knowledge of meaning and behavior, I can infer intention; and if I have knowledge of meaning and intention, I can predict—to a sufficient extent at least—behavior. But none of this inferential machinery works unless the agents being interpreted are in some sense rational, and thus behave in accordance with their intentions and beliefs. One question this raises is the status of the notion of rationality here: In what sense is it optional? If it is necessary for talk about intention and meaning, is it not necessary *simpliciter*, and thus just an example of synthetic a priori truth? Isn't the argument *a reductio* of Quine's "Two Dogmas" rather than an extension consistent with it? This reasoning is the core of the idealist interpretation of "On the Very Idea." Davidson's appeal to a "normative" notion of rationality seems like a straightforward capitulation to the notion of scheme.

The argument is superficially compelling. The idea is that the possible intransitivity of translation would be a refutation of the idea that there were no such things as incommensurable conceptual schemes. Transitivity of explanation would require that we had, so to speak, all the resources for translating all languages in advance. Only this condition for the possibility would exclude the possibility of finding a language *A* that the speakers of *B* could translate into, and a language *C*, which could be translated into *B* but could not be translated into *A*. The thought behind this is that whatever is needed to translate into *A* already has to be there in *C*. In the usual forms of this argument, this amounts to saying that "we" now must have whatever resources are necessary to translate out of *any* conceptual scheme. This in turn raises the question of whether speakers of some other language *D* might not have this capacity, specifically whether speakers of the language of a primitive society might be incapable of translating into and thus understanding our language. And because this does not seem to be an empirical question, and Davidson's argument is not at first blush an empirical argument, it must be a question not about what they could do but about what they possibly could do—justifying the Kantianization of the issue.

Davidson has a different and much more limited argument: If the speakers of *C* happen upon speakers of *B* translating *A*, if they could indeed translate *B*, they would, *ex hypothesis*, be able to translate these translations of *A* as well. Why would this follow but not necessarily imply the sufficiency of a single starting point for translation? The point is basic to Davidson's understanding of translation in this text: A translation is not merely a "translation manual" consisting of sentence correspondences. It is instead a combination of correspondences and explanations of the failures of correspondence that occur when something is accounted true in one language and false in another. These explanations take the form of what J. L. Mackie in a different context called "error theories." The example Davidson gives is a paradigmatic error explanation:

> If you see a ketch sailing by and your companion says "Look at that handsome yawl," you may be faced with a problem of interpretation. One natural possibility is that your friend has mistaken a ketch for a yawl, and has formed a false belief. But if his vision is good and his line of sight favorable it is even more plausible that he does not use the word yawl quite as you do, and has made no mistake about the position of the jigger on the passing yacht. ([1973] 1984: 196)

The hypothesis that he uses the word differently, in this particular behavioral context, requires us to attribute a whole set of correct beliefs (and norms of correspondence, as Davidson puts it) to our companion: that he or she has counted the masts and sails correctly, that he or she can count, that he or she is talking about the same boat, that he or she is not kidding, or testing our knowledge of nautical nomenclature, and so forth. This list could be extended. Davidson's point is that the number of correct beliefs we must attribute when we attribute error to the companion is high. And the more extensive the error, the larger the number of beliefs in the web of belief we must rely on to explain the error. This is why massive error is unintelligible: Making massive error intelligible would require an even more massive pool of correct beliefs to draw on to explain the error.

The significance of the interdependence of meaning and theory is that translations are like theories in that they already involve truth claims about the world, that they depend on the correctness of explanations and of the theories backing explanations of error, and that they are in this respect heir to all of the problems of theoretical explanation not only in the sciences, but in psychology and for that matter the social sciences, where they play a role in backing the explanations of error that translations inevitably involve. This means that they are also characterized by the usual infirmities of such theories: that they are underdetermined by the facts, so that alternative theories may be consistent with the facts; that new data, for example, new behavioral evidence, may require changes in the theories; and so forth. Davidson is explicit about this. The method forced on us of getting a first approximation by attributing to sentences of a speaker the "conditions of truth that actually obtain (in our opinion)" allows for meaningful disagreement. And the disagreements can emerge in a variety of ways: If we are in the position of the companion, we might find ourselves learning a lesson about the differences between ketches and yawls, and thus resolve the disagreement in favor of the hearer. But we might discover that we have a disagreement that present data cannot resolve.

If we cut this reasoning down to the basics, we get something like this: Interpretive charity is required by the economy of error explanations. The term means two things: We need to attribute rationality—in a sense yet to be defined—to the people we interpret, and we need to attribute a minimum of error. Attributing rationality is a precondition for any interpretation involving error, because attribution of error, at least of the kind relevant to Davidson, namely errors in utterances with truth-relevant content, requires an attribution of rationality: An error for Davidson is a rational but wrong response to something, and belief in this erroneous thing can be accounted for by reference to other wrong beliefs that are rationally connected to the wrong response. In constructing error explanations, one soon reaches a vague limit beyond which the error explanations are impossibly complex and insupportable, because each attribution of error requires a larger set of attributions of erroneous background belief—the beliefs that rationally support the error. Charity in interpretation avoids reaching this limit; attributing massive error is attributing something beyond this limit.

The upshot of this for everyday metaphysics can be illustrated by a simple example. Consider the Hindu belief that the world is an illusion. We have no trouble translating the relevant sentences, for the simple reason that the translation manages to preserve all our ordinary beliefs. Everything in an illusion appears just as the real thing would—otherwise it would not be an illusion. My belief that the coffee shop down the street serves espresso survives whether or not the espresso, the street, the shop, and the rest of it are illusions, because there is no difference between real and illusory espresso other than whether it is real. If we translate the terms they refer to the same thing, with the exception that we need to add an illusion operator to each sentence in the translation of the target language. But the addition does nothing beyond connecting the sentences to the belief that the world is an illusion. And what goes for illusion goes for the rest of metaphysics—the noumenal world, empirical reality, the phenomenal world, and the rest of it. There are no interesting implications of the problem of massive error for metaphysics, because in these cases there is no massive error. There is only a very economical kind of error, or alternatively a kind of underdetermination, about metaphysical facts. There is a question of whether this holds for the "fact" of normativity itself, and here there is an ambiguity. Taken by itself, it seems that the pattern with normativity mimics the pattern for "the world is an illusion." Nothing much changes whether or not we say, for example, that normativity is a fiction or that it is real. But if normativity in the requisite sense is part of the machinery that allows us to speak in this way in the first place, namely as a condition of interpretation, matters would be different.

It might seem that we ought to get more metaphysical bang out of transitivity, especially the apparent requirement that we somehow have the resources for all possible translation, in advance, so to speak. But this is not the requirement it appears to be. Focusing merely on the problem of the truth theory for a language, and ignoring the role of error, obscures important features of translation, and also obscures the reasons translation does not require us to have all the resources for all possible translations—the resources that would define the conditions for the possibility of translating all languages, in advance. Just as theories in science grow, our theories of error and our powers of translation grow in the course of translating from one language to another. This bears on the problem of transitivity. Davidson need only argue that the augmented power of translation we possess when we adequately translate *B* from *A* enables us to translate *C* from *B*, not that we can translate *C* with the resources of *A*. What his explicit argument excludes is the following case: The speakers of *C* claim that they can understand *B* perfectly, but not *A* as translated into *B*. This would mean that they couldn't understand the correspondences and the explanations of error. Davidson's point is that this would be evidence that they did not understand *B*. But without the learning and error theorizing we did when we translated, translators starting with *A* might indeed be unable to understand *C*.

This suggests that truncating the discussion of rationality and translation into a discussion of the fixed (and prefixed) "conditions for the possibility" of translation is beside the point. The conditions of translation are of a piece with and depend on our ever changing knowledge of the world. But saying this raises questions about the nature of rationality for Davidson himself and about the larger problem of normativity that the normative concept of rationality points to. For Davidson, "the concepts we use to explain and describe thought, speech, and action, are irreducibly normative" (1999: 460). What does this mean? Even if we de-Kantianize the problem of conditions for the possibility of translation, it seems, we are forced back into another form of the scheme/content distinction by the assumption of rationality and by the normativity of word-world relations. Or is there another, better, interpretation of these two things?

Davidson's actual comments are tantalizing. He does say that interpretive charity is nonoptional and also sufficient for translation, and he does refer to norms of correspondence, meaning by this something analogous to the correspondence rules of the layer cake model of scientific theories. He could have said, but does not, that interpretation requires an assumption of rationality and an assumption of certain common human norms of correspondence (1985), and that these are both nonoptional and universal. Instead, he says the following:

> The ineluctable normative element in interpretation has, then, two forms. First, there are the norms of pattern: the norms of deduction, induction, reasoning about how to act, and even about how to feel

> given other attitudes and beliefs. These are the norms of consistency and coherence. Second, there are the norms of correspondence, which are concerned with the truth or correctness of particular beliefs and values. This second kind of norm counsels the interpreter to interpret agents he would understand as having, in important respects, beliefs that are mostly true and needs and values the interpreter shares or can imagine himself sharing if he had the history of the agent and were in comparable circumstances. (1985: 92)

The norms of correspondence are norms of interpretation, but not in the sense of rules that help decide between interpretations: They are instead a feature of making intelligible interpretations in the first place. The norms of pattern correspond to the notion of rationality. But they are not quite the same as the notion of rationality, and this is where Davidson separates himself from the Kantian interpretation. Or does he? Do they constitute a scheme, or the essential normative core of a scheme? Or do they have a different status? These are the questions on which the argument against the scheme/content distinction seems to hang. And they cannot be answered directly.

Davidson might have answered them by also arguing that these two kinds of norms would be sufficient for interpretation or translation universally, that is to say, of all languages, as well as necessary, thus making them into a common scheme of a kind. He might also have said that the consideration of necessity amounts to a transcendental argument that we ourselves must be committed to these necessary elements in a metaphysical sense, that is to say, as part of our own theory of the world, and to derive from this commitment such results as a commitment to the metaphysical necessity of "normative reason" and the like. This, or some variant, is the argument that his idealist interpreters would like to read into him. But he does none of these things, and seems instead to treat the arguments about conceptual schemes as a fully sufficient alternative to these arguments. Moreover, Davidson thinks that his arguments also preclude the appeal to a universal kind of normative reason, or make it unnecessary. And because they are arguments that are assertions about necessity, about the necessity of a univocal account of normative reason construed in a certain way, showing them to be gratuitous amounts to denying them.

How does Davidson's alternative work? He says instead that interpretive charity is required to make sense of others and that interpretive charity requires something that seems to go beyond and perhaps is different from the assumptions listed above, namely the acknowledgment that most of the beliefs of others are true, which implies that most of our beliefs are also true. But it also seems that there has to be something behind this—the things that make the beliefs true and the judgments of their intentions and utterances rational. And here is the trap that the idealist interpretation relies on. If we acknowledge the necessary role of "rationality," it seems, we are back to the Kantian picture, with rationality having the status of "scheme." The issue of what is behind understanding turns out to be decisive, and Davidson, I will argue, has an answer to this question that differs from the usual normativist one and also precludes it. But it will take some background to get to this answer and explain its significance.

GETTING RID OF CONCEPTS: A BRIEF EXCURSUS

Quine's example of the translation of "Gavagai" as either rabbit or undetached rabbit part, for example, points to a central feature of translation: that the same things can be translated in multiple ways, that these ways have different ontological implications, and that some divergences, at least, are ineliminable. We can correct erroneous translations on the basis of the behavioral evidence, but we cannot eliminate all translations but one. Holism, similarly, implies that adjustments in one part of a translation explanation can be made that have the effect of preserving a given translation hypothesis. Davidson assumes all of this, and it is especially relevant in the case of error, which is not a well-developed Quinean theme, in large part because of Quine's focus on ostensive definition and willingness to give up on "meanings" as ordinarily understood. But the same considerations about the web of belief hold for Davidson. As we have seen, an error explanation is an explanation that necessarily relies on the rest of the web of belief, and if too much of this web is claimed to be erroneous, we have nothing out of which a coherent error account can be constructed.

Why is this important? Why is it anything other than an exercise in hypothetical anthropology of no philosophical interest, which is how P. M. S. Hacker (1996) dismisses it? To answer this question and to see the radical character of Davidson's argument, as well as the way in which this paper foreshadows and grounds the later papers, it is important again to see what Davidson and before him Quine did not say, and why they thought that what they did say precluded the kind of philosophy represented by Brandom and McDowell. The story can begin with Quine's systematic substitution of "sentences" for "propositions." Avoiding the language of Gottlob Frege was an attempt to avoid Platonism about concepts—the idea that concepts were out there in some sort of ether of thought, which the mind engaged, or acquired. This language was common in the "analytic" philosophy of the time and, in the specific context of Davidson's paper, the problem of other cultures, much discussed at the time, especially in the philosophy of social science. Peter Winch, in *The Idea of a Social Science* ([1958] 1990), had operated with a notion of concepts as the mental stuff of society and had imagined that one could have, and, because actions could only be understood under descriptions containing these concepts, had to have, a social science that began with the analysis of these concepts.

The metaphors that were common to all the standard figures of ordinary language philosophy at the time are telling. Concepts are possessed by people and are therefore shared, object-like things: possessions that one acquires. It was this autonomous existence that enabled them to be subject to a special kind of inquiry, conceptual analysis. The specific character of action was that it was done for reasons and therefore involved concepts, the concepts possessed by the agents that supplied the relevant stock of descriptions. Behavioral descriptions were not the descriptions of the agents themselves, did not supply reasons for action, and were thus strictly speaking irrelevant to action explanation. This same picture of concepts was the source of conceptual relativism. If concepts were possessions, different people or members of different social groups or people living in different eras had different conceptual "possessions." They would say different and incommensurable things about the world, and these different things would each be true or false under the descriptions allowed by the concepts they possessed. Concepts they didn't possess would be, by definition of the term "possession," inaccessible and unintelligible to them, that is to say, incommensurable, until they came into possession of them. The only apparent solution to this problem of relativism was to insist that somehow people really possessed, at some prelinguistic Ur-level, all the same concepts, despite the surface diversity of actual usages and for that matter beliefs about the world.

Quine did not ignore these considerations of diversity: They are central to the Sapir-Whorf hypothesis, which became the Sapir-Whorf-Quine hypothesis and revealed itself in such slogans as "ontology recapitulates philology." But Quine had already stepped off the "concepts as possessions" path by being "as behaviorist as any sane person could be." And Davidson was on the same path. But Davidson realized that to deal with meaning, rational action, and the like, it was not enough to be behaviorist. So he set about constructing an alternative account that gave as little as possible away to the picture of concepts as possessions that Quine had abandoned in favor of the language of sentences, theories, and holism. This is the motivation for his attempt to restate the slogans of the "concepts as possessions" model in terms of language. When faced with the problem of conceptual incommensurability, that is to say, the condition of possession of mutually unintelligible concepts, he asks what it means in terms of sentences and concludes that it is no more than, in terms of the evidential base, failure of translation. By moving to the behavioral level, then to sentences, then to the holistic theory-like individual webs of belief of individuals, Quine not only avoided the "concepts as possessions" model and its implications, he precluded it: The evidential base is behavioral, which is more basic than anything the concepts as possessions model operated with, and Quine could account for the diversity that was revealed in the form of this evidence without appealing to this model. The point of this argument was to make the concepts as possessions model superfluous for explanatory purposes. In Quine's exchange with Sellars, this was precisely what was at issue. Sellars wanted to show that even Quine had to accept mathematical concepts, and thus be dragged into the space of reasons, however unwillingly. Quine demurred (Quine 1980; Sellars 1980). When Davidson translates the problem of conceptual relativism into the problem of linguistic relativism, he is following Quine, with the same intent: to avoid the commitments implicit in the term "concepts" and to avoid the possessions model of concepts.

What is the significance of this? Nothing, according to the normativists: The use of "sentence" rather than "proposition" was an eccentricity that doesn't change anything. The same problem, of understanding concepts and their normative force, exists regardless of what one calls these things, because it stands behind our usages, including our usages of sentences. But something does change that is important. "Concept" in the normativists' usual sense is not only a normative concept—although it need not be, as there are plenty of naturalistic accounts of concepts as psychological facts that are not normative (see, e.g., Gallese and Lakoff 2005; Stich 1992)—it is a collective one. Concepts, in the possessions model, are out there to be shared by people, to be "possessed" by multiple people. And this is the model of concepts in Brandom, and the model of reason in McDowell as well. Indeed, this is a feature of most notions of scheme—there is nothing private about them. They are jointly held, shared, whether by a group or by all intelligences.

A behaviorist account, in contrast, is not intrinsically committed to collective objects of this sort. They may prove to be explanatory necessities, which is to say that there may be something we want to explain that cannot be explained without appealing to collective objects. But then again there may not. It may be that language itself, understood as a collective object, is a fiction that is not needed to explain anything we want to explain, such as the actual linguistic interaction between two people or between two people and the world. And this is what Davidson does in fact later argue. But this gives us another puzzle. How can anything be normative without also being collective in the requisite sense? McDowell and Brandom are fond of the metaphor of binding and being bound as a way of thinking about the normative. How can we be "bound" by the norms of rationality, for example, unless they are, to use the phrase of Durkheim, "external" and also shared? What is in common between these cases is the same idea: Each involves error and correcting for error in the course of interpretation. Understanding the centrality of this idea is our next concern.

INTELLIGIBLE ERROR

We often are compelled to translate, as Davidson points out, by treating the translation as a correct translation of a false belief: a case of explicable error. But error is not a behaviorist notion. It is "normative," and perhaps it is the root normative notion. So to say that considerations of error are inseparable from translation is to accept the role of the normative. And, of course, there is more normativity to be found in the conditions for translation or interpretation. Rationality is one of the conditions, and it is a normative notion. So to say that assumptions of rationality are necessary for interpretation seems not only to concede that some scheme-like element is necessary, but to refute Quine's "Two Dogmas" and concede the Kantian point by resuscitating synthetic a priori truth.

Or does it? One way of putting this issue is to separate two distinct aspects of "normativity," the sense of the normative as binding, as external and constraining (the Durkheimian sense), and a different sense, which can be labeled "intelligibility." As long as we are associating these as sociologists—an association that is neither accidental nor irrelevant, because both of them were drawing from neo-Kantianism, in different ways—we can call this second kind "Weberian." Durkheim was concerned with the binding character of obligation as it was experienced differently in different societies. Weber was concerned with subjectively meaningful behavior and with the problem of making the behavior of other people intelligible, something he, like Davidson, thought necessarily meant "intelligible to us in our own terms." There is a normative issue here—intelligibility is a normative notion. But it is a different kind of normative notion than correctness or rationality in the "binding" sense. Understanding a subjectively intended meaning, to use the translation of Weber's phrase, is, at least on the surface, a normative as distinct from a causal matter.

Davidson's problem, like Weber's, involves the problem of intelligibility, not the problem of supposed binding norms (cf. Hurley 1992). Explicable error is intelligible error. Translation, which incorporates a hypothesis that accounts for the error and makes it intelligible, extends the limits of intelligibility—extends them as far as they go. His argument is about the limits of intelligibility: There is no language recognizable as such beyond the intelligible. But we do not reach the limits of the intelligible without charitably extending the readily intelligible to incorporate the less readily intelligible, namely that which is not intelligible without a hypothesis about error. And these hypotheses about error necessarily rely on having already made other parts of the web of belief intelligible. As we have seen, this is the basis for the claim that massive error is not intelligible: It is not intelligible because the hypothesis of massive error amounts to denying to the constructor of explicable error accounts the material needed to construct these accounts. To explain the error of a sailor's failed attempt to keep the main from backing, we need to assume that he knows what the main is, has correctly perceived the wind, knows what the tiller is supposed to do, and so on. If we deny this, we open up the explanation of his actions to such hypotheses as these: He is communicating with Martians; he doesn't experience the wind and sea as we do but in some unknown way. And these begin to hit against the limits of the intelligible, because they are explanations of error that are themselves barely intelligible, or unintelligible to us, at least at present. The use of anthropological examples is highly relevant to the problem of the limits of intelligibility. And by considering the problem of understanding other cultures, we can see the deep differences between Davidson and the concepts as possessions model more clearly.

Anthropologists face a problem which grew into the problem that in the philosophy of social science was part of the context of "On the Very Idea." The problem was identification: We try a translation of the utterance of a member of a primitive society, and get something like this: "My blood is boiling." We are faced with the following kinds of alternatives: The members of the society actually believe that their blood is boiling; we just don't understand the utterance, meaning we have gotten the translation wrong in a way that can't be corrected, which would also mean that our translation of "blood" and "boiling" in other contexts, and therefore our translation project as a whole, is called into question; the utterance is false but metaphorical; the members of the society have a set of beliefs about blood and boiling that make it possible for them to erroneously believe that their blood could in fact be boiling. In the case of the last two explanations, there is also a significant amount of variation in possible hypotheses consistent with the facts. Metaphors can be interpreted in multiple ways, and the background belief structures about blood and boiling might also be constructed in various ways.

This seems like a methodological or epistemic problem—a real problem for anthropologists, perhaps, but not for anyone else, and in any case it is unilluminated by the considerations of hypothetical anthropology Davidson adduces, which don't tell us which to accept. But if we keep the contrast to the concepts as possessions picture in mind, we can see that there is more at stake here. The concepts as possessions picture had an answer to this problem: that concepts are the sorts of things we could ourselves come to possess or grasp, and then analyze. The problem of understanding a primitive society was thus one of grasping their concepts. Not only Kantianism but the problem of rule-following inherited from Wittgenstein lies behind this imagery, and both of these were assimilated in the form of an argument that possessing a concept consisted in grasping a rule. But as a solution to the identification problem, the grasp and possession model was a fiasco. Grasping was a primal act that operated on mysterious entities. There were no grounds for saying one was correctly grasping or not—correctness itself, knowing what accorded with the rule, presupposed grasping the rule. There is also a problem about evidence. For grasping, evidence is not so much irrelevant as insufficient. In particular, there is a mystery about the normative force of the concept or rule—if possession was no more than conformity with some set of behavioral patterns, what would be the source of its normative force? Is it some sort of mysterious added element?

Davidson's approach avoids these questions, by starting from a different point. The problem of identifying beliefs, of finding out what is believed and who believes it, in the famous formulation of Marcel Mauss, is a hypothesis-testing epistemic process, in which we employ what we know about ourselves and our beliefs to construct accounts of others' beliefs until our accounts begin to more or less match their behavior. Behavioral evidence is all we have, and all we want to explain, although we may employ nonbehavioral terms, such as "belief" itself, in order to do the explaining. Error is intrinsic to the process of hypothesis testing, in the sense that we can get the attribution of belief wrong, in which case we can't predict what others will do or say in a way that accords with the attribution of belief we hypothesize. But there is more to it than just predicting. We also want to make sense of the beliefs as beliefs—to make them intelligible. To put the point in a way that will help later, we want to be able to follow others to follow their reasoning. But this is inseparable from attributing beliefs in the first place, so it is normally not an issue. The point, however, is important: If we can't reason with others, we can't attribute belief.

Where do the possession model of concepts and the problem of rules fit in with this? In terms of interpreting other cultures, these things cannot come first. We cannot first grasp others' concepts and then come to understand their utterances. Yet the possession model has a strong bias toward this kind of formulation: If we are using a concept, it is because we have grasped the rule behind it, or the concept. Our grasp is presupposed, and it is a necessary condition for "really" using it. This is the point of the celebrated arguments about the regress problem made in the first chapter of Brandom's *Making It Explicit*. Really using it, for Brandom, amounts to being able to give justificatory reasons about its use. The chain of justifications has to end somewhere. Because justification is normative, it has to end in something normative. For Brandom it ends in the normativity of language, which is in turn made normative by our "commitments" to the score-keeping system that allows for the social regulation of error.

Davidson has none of this machinery. Why? The answer is closely related to the reason he also lacks the Brandom-McDowell imagery of constraint. For Davidson, not only does the problem of intelligibility come first and get solved by the hypothesis-testing process of translation, it ends there. The claim that the rule-following, concept-possessing model deals with something more fundamental, which is common to many of these interpretations and dismissals of Davidson, depends on showing that they are "necessary" in the first place. They are not, for Davidson. To deal with the behavioral evidence is not only enough, it is all there is. The whole machinery of the concepts as possessions model is not so much beside the point in relation to this evidence, because it is after all an attempt to account for it, as it is unnecessary to accounting for it. The accounting is done once the beliefs have been identified. There is no higher form of knowledge about these beliefs that results from "grasping" the concepts or having a normative commitment to them and the like. The only knowledge we have is this hypothesis-testing knowledge.

WHERE IS THE NORMATIVE?

For alien cultures, the normativist is inclined to say, this makes sense. We cannot penetrate their inner life, their normative commitments, their space of reasons. We can only make up hypotheses, provide error accounts, and the like. But for our own culture, we are in a different situation. Our statements about other cultures may be behavioral and explanatory. For ourselves, as Joseph Rouse argues, they are "expressivist." The reasons are our reasons; the normative commitments are ours; we have privileged access to them. Davidson is having none of this, either. One of the most visible consequences of the argument of "The Very Idea" is that the supposed distinction between cultures, that is, between our concepts, our rationality, and theirs, is eliminated. The difference is language, which is treated in a demystified way rather than as a mysterious order of shared presuppositions. But any other explanation of "their" beliefs is in terms—error—that equally apply to the people in our own culture using our own language. So there is no "ours" to go with the "theirs." There is no collective fact of shared concept possession behind their beliefs, because there is no fact of concept possession in the Kantian sense in Davidson in the first place.

The full implications of this reasoning are drawn out in Davidson's "A Nice Derangement of Epitaphs," which extends the use of the notion of error to ordinary linguistic interaction. When we deal with other people, we are constantly doing precisely what the anthropologist is doing: We are interpreting their behavior, revising our interpretations in light of our attempts to make sense of it, and attributing beliefs to them, attributions that often include error hypotheses. We could not function as language users or human beings without doing this. Making intelligible is a continuous process. Making inferences about what someone intends to mean, whether he or she is sincere, ironic, speaking metaphorically, or erroneously, is ubiquitous and a part of every human interaction. Moreover, this process is logically fundamental and perhaps ontogenetically fundamental: logically, because for the possession model to make sense, there is a two-stage process in which the interpreter of language learner first needs to identify something that is later fully grasped. In McDowell, for example, it is not until the traditional age of reason that the well-brought-up child grasps the normativity of reason (see McDowell 1994).

Learning, including language learning, is an embarrassment to the possession model. For Brandom, embracing the interdependence of inferences about rationality together with the idea of meanings as rooted in normative practices of justification underwritten by "commitment" forces him into the odd position of arguing that the prelinguistic individual does not have genuine intentions, which in turn raises the question of how he or she could have genuine commitments. Davidson avoids this problem by avoiding the possession model. Does he fall into it in another form?

For the normativist, the answer is yes. Davidson is a fellow traveler who also acknowledges the necessary role of the normative. He simply locates the normative elsewhere. But the difference is one of emphasis only: Davidson stresses one part of the triangle, the part that involves the assessment of the rationality of the intention behind utterances, which tells us whether the speaker intended to speak truly and descriptively, which enables us to infer meaning. Meaning itself, they would say, is accounted for by the normativity of the system of linguistic practices, and rationality is accounted for by the recognition of the binding character of the universal norms of rationality, a recognition that eventually comes to every well-brought-up person, regardless of his or her culture. Other normativists, in short, are filling in gaps that Davidson, by such usages as "norms of correspondence," acknowledges.

But why should Davidson accept any of this? Consider the demands and complexity of Brandom's account in *Making It Explicit*. Meanings are not something in the interactional flux, but are rooted in a complex and massive tacit system of normative score-keeping practices that we have access to in filling in the enthymemes or missing premises of ordinary speech, especially in the context of justification. We and our peers in our linguistic community are committed to this system personally and in the collective voice, as with Sellars' notion of collective intentionality. This commitment, necessarily, is a kind of blank check written by our prelinguistic and thus preintentional selves. We commit to a system in which individuals participate in a way not dissimilar to participation in Platonic Forms, that is to say, partially, because none of us has within ourselves all the meanings or inferences that are part of the concepts that make up the system. The point of Brandom's famous regression argument is to establish this: Justification has to end someplace, but the place it ends has to be normative, and thus behind each rule is a normative end point that is a commitment to a system of this sort.

For Davidson, this whole machinery of a fixed set of normative practices revealed in the enthymemes of ordinary justificatory usage is simply unnecessary. We have no privileged access to meanings which we can then expressivistically articulate, because there is nothing like this—no massive structure of normative practices—to access. Instead, we try to follow our fellow beings and their reasoning and acting, including their speaking: We make them intelligible. And we have a tool other than the normal machinery of predictive science that makes this possible: our own rationality. Rationality is normative, but not in the sense of McDowell. It is not the rationality of constraint. Our only constraint is the limit of our capacity to make intelligible. There is no gap between what we can recognize as intentional and meaningful and what we can make intelligible—that is to say, what we can follow, including intelligible error justification, which thus has no special status of the kind accorded it by Brandom. It is just another piece of behavior: Children learn that saying "why, Mommy, why?" gets a reaction. Eventually they come to follow the answers, to make them intelligible to themselves, and to provide them when elicited, but nothing about this activity of giving answers and asking questions gets beyond the behavioral facts, except for the matter of following or making intelligible.

For the normativists, this reply makes a fatal error: It falls back into a variant of the position they themselves hold, namely that normative rationality is "necessary." The fact that Davidson locates the relevant kind of normativity elsewhere, namely in the interpreting agent, is to fall back into the synthetic a priori, which has to be the source of these normative constraints. But it is worse than their own accounts, because it is mysterious, groundless, and arbitrary—the sort of thing that Quine correctly objected to. Moreover, they would say, Davidson leaves us with no account of the normativity of that which is generally recognized as normative, such as the rule-following in 2 + 2 = 4 and so forth.

What does Davidson say about this mare's nest of issues? He says something about rationality and its normative character, but not what the normativist wants to hear. For the normativist, rationality is itself a possession, an acquisition like a concept but more fundamental, more universal. Intelligibility depends on something else: the abilities we have to follow the thinking of others. The child's game of "step on a crack, break your mother's back" is intelligible—intelligible error, perhaps, but also representing a form of reasoning that we share with primitive people and indeed all peoples. And it would be hard to construct a "theory" of this kind of inference that would make it rational.

But it is also hard to construct empirical theories of human reasoning: of what "empirical" rationality, meaning how we actually infer, rather than normative rationality, actually is. Worse, there is an odd dependence of empirical theorizing on normative theories of rationality, normative theories that are false as empirical theories. This was among the lessons he learned from the experimental study of decision making in which he participated in the 1950s. Decision theory, which is usually called a normative theory in this literature, is false as an empirical theory of rationality. People do not make decisions in the way that normative decision theory defines as rational. But "normative" decision theory is indispensable in at least this sense: To study actual decision making it is needed as a starting point. Biases, errors, and the like are biases and errors in comparison to it. And there seems to be no option here. Without notions like bias we don't have a language for describing actual decision making. There is no "empirical theory" of decision-making that is an alternative to the normative account, but only one that depends on the "normative" theory in this odd way.

The normativist would argue that this is a case of a priori truth. Normativists read "indispensable" as "necessary," and "necessary" in the manner of "synthetic a priori truth." But this case doesn't fit the pattern. Empirically, it is not truth at all. But it seems to fit with other cases in which the "theory" is so deeply ingrained in our construction of empirical accounts that we can neither find an alternative to it nor dispense with it. Davidson suggests measurement theory as an example of this: It too is a case of empirical theory as classically understood, but as an empirical theory it is also literally false. The oddity has been remarked on in the literature on testing the theory of relativity: Measurements were made in accordance with the terms of the theory that relativity was to displace, rather than in relativistic terms (Laymon 1988). What confirmed the theory were the errors that appeared using the old measurement theory. But this did not displace the old measurement theory, which was as Newtonian as ever.

In the case of rationality, there is an analogous problem. The fact that the theories we have of rationality are false as empirical theories of human decision making gives us no reason to discard them as normative theory, or to stop treating them as indispensable for our various theoretical and even practical purposes. But this indispensability does not confer on them any sort of metaphysical status, much less warrant any sort of claim about the metaphysical necessity of the normative as some sort of special ideal realm equivalent and coexistent with the empirically real. And indeed, rationality has properties in relation to the task of making intelligible that point in a different direction entirely.

The different direction is to acknowledge the actual diversity of the relevant kind of rationality. The rationality needed is "rudimentary" (Davidson 1985) and the notion of reasonable belief "flexible" (Davidson [1994] 2005: 121)—very flexible. Davidson indicates how flexible in the following:

> The issue is not whether we all agree on exactly what the norms of rationality are; the point is rather that we all have such norms and we cannot recognize as thought phenomena that are too far out of line. Better say: what is too far out of line is not thought. It is only when we can see a creature (or "object") as largely rational by our own lights that we can intelligibly ascribe thoughts to it at all, or explain its behavior by reference to its ends and convictions. (Davidson [1990] 2004: 97–98)

The contraposition of this shows how flexible the notion of rationality is for Davidson. If we can recognize something as thought, it is "rational" in the relevant sense. Recognizing something as rational is a matter of being able to follow someone's thought—to simulate their thinking well enough that what they say or do that is different from what we would say or do can be either allowed for as "normal enough" or explained as error and thus made intelligible. The normative element is not rigidly fixed, unarguable, or even free from conflict, such as conflicts which arise when there are inferences that we can follow which lead to conclusions that conflict with what we believe. This is not the kind of rationality that provides the kind of constraint and ultimate justificatory ground that is the concern of Brandom or McDowell. The only constraints are interpersonal: We are constrained in our understanding by the limits of what we can follow, constrained in communicating by the limits of what others can follow, and constrained in what counts as thought by the requirement that for something to be recognized as thought, it must be the kind of thing the recognizer can follow.

What I am calling "following" is an act of imagination (Davidson 1985: 92). This is something different from "possession of a concept." The substance is frankly psychological rather than normative in the sense of Brandom, McDowell, or the rule-following literature. It is perhaps best understood in terms of the idea of simulation in cognitive science. And it is this idea that suffices to account for our capacity to make sense of others, for intelligibility as distinct from beliefs about rightness. This is what the rule-following literature stumbles over: It cannot distinguish "possession" from "following" another person's thinking. Partly this is a matter of the diet of examples: Following the idea of "addition of two" and possession, if there is such a thing, are the same; translating and possessing seem different. Davidson could simply make the point that following is basic to, and sufficient, for both. Our capacity for learning the rule of adding two is our capacity for following the teacher, and there is no additional mystery. We do not need an additional concept of possession to account for the behavioral facts. Nor do we need some notion of the intrinsic normativity of a rule, a notion of commitment, or any reference to community. The concept is "social," but only in the interactional sense of social: We are following someone else and getting feedback from our interactions that reassure us that we are following them sufficiently to say we understand them. Simulation is also not a causal idea—so it is "normative" in a specific sense unlike the Brandom or McDowell sense, not something external and constraining, but a sense linked to the agent's own capacities. These capacities are, dare I say, naturalizable, not in the sense of the reduction of intelligibility to cause, or the elimination of intelligibility, but "disenchanted": a capacity that goes with beings having brains with particular kinds of neurons, rather than souls participating in the Forms.

Part II

Critiques

Practices, Meanings, and Collective Tacit Objects

The second group of essays consists of critiques and explications of alternative discussions of tacit knowledge and frames conceptions. The key text is a critique of Harry Collins' idea of collective tacit knowledge, where it is shown that the "collective" part of Collins' conception of tacit knowledge is groundless. Arguments of this sort depend on explanatory necessity, in this case the supposed indispensability of "collective" tacit contents. But his examples can be better explained by "individual" and noncollective "social" mechanisms." The next two essays relate to "practice theory," the dominant present variant of tacit knowledge thinking. The first surveys the problem since *The Social Theory of Practices* (Turner 1994) and considers the restricted forms of the notion of practice that have appeared in the philosophical literature in response to that book. The second deals with the relation between the idea that practices have nonconceptual content and the relativism that derives from the notion that different shared practices produce different truths. It shows that the nature of nonconceptual content, and the manner in which it is acquired, individualizes content but does not share it, thus avoiding the relativism that would follow if different shared practices were the conditions of knowledge. The fourth essay deals with the attempt to use mirror neurons as a way of grounding Bourdieu's notion of *habitus* as a tacit possession. This critical discussion shows that in fact the features of mirror neurons point instead to an alternative basis for accounting for the social capacities Bourdieu attempts to explain. The fifth essay deals with Michael Oakeshott's notion of tradition and shows that it matches the decentered, individualized character of connectionist learning. The sixth essay in the group deals with "meaning." It shows that the use of frames concepts to account for meaning in the historical past is misconstrued when it is understood as a representation of historical fact—that is to say the idea that the conventions and rules it appeals to actually operated as described—but can be useful when understood as an artificial surrogate for the tacit knowledge that historical actors possessed. These critical, ground-clearing essays serve both to introduce key ideas that are presented more systematically in the final section and to show the larger contrasts between accounts of the tacit that the account in the last section is an alternative to.

3 Collins and Collective Tacit Knowledge

Starting with Tacit Knowledge, Ending with Durkheim?

Harry Collins is a science studies scholar—no other description fits without qualification—who has contributed enormously to the discussion of tacit knowledge, particularly by thinking through such things as computer-assisted surrogates for experts and the role of tacit knowledge in the building of scientific instrumentation (Collins 1974, 1990, 2001). His new book (2010) embodies the special, and somewhat strange, combination of traits for which his work generally is known: its intelligence and originality, its use of telling and interesting examples and his shrewd analyses of others' examples, its polemical character (not to say fierceness), its use of clever inversions (a practice shared with his rival Bruno Latour) along with its lack of detailed reference to the arguments of other writers, its invention of alternative language for describing familiar topics, its honesty about what is not known, and its somewhat off-key employment and reworking of philosophical topics. In this book he takes on specific rivals, particularly Hubert Dreyfus and, unusually for Collins, attaches himself to an intellectual tradition familiar to sociologists—a tribe of which he is at best only a nominal member. In addition, the book is a kind of synthesis of his work, or at least of a bunch of strands of his thinking whose connections have not always been apparent: between his critique of John Searle's Chinese Room example and his views of tacitness, for instance, and the relation between his account of types of expertise and the rest of his views. The outcome of this mélange is surprising and interesting. It advances the discussion, but perhaps not, as we will see, in the way it was intended to, and for reasons closely connected to the special qualities of Collins' work.

DEFINING "EXPLICIT"

The big idea with which the book begins is this: We cannot understand "tacit" knowledge unless we understand the binary opposite against which it is defined, namely explicit knowledge. There is a puzzle with this binary. On the one hand, explicit knowledge is parasitical on tacit knowledge. On the other, the idea of tacit knowledge is parasitical on the idea of explicit knowledge. What is it to be explicit? A traditional philosophical answer would be that it is that which is contained in sentences, or utterances. Another answer might be in terms of the distinction between conceptual and nonconceptual knowledge. Collins characteristically makes no reference to any of these distinctions, although he uses the Gibsonian-Brandomian term "affordances," a term originating in Gibsonian psychology and popularized in philosophy by Robert Brandom. Also part of the vocabulary Collins supplies are the following players: digital strings, analogue strings, causes, and interpreters.

"A string is just a physical object and it is immediately clear that whether it has any effect or what kind of effect this might be is entirely a matter of what happens to it" (Collins 2010: 9). Strings are not languages, but they "are the means by which languages are shared, and there can be no language without sharing" (2010: 10). Strings, then, are in the causal world and impact entities. But they also have inscribed properties, or patterns, although not meanings, so that they can be transformed such that these patterned or inscribed properties are preserved. But strings do more than inscriptions, in that they have causal powers: They can cause something to do something or give it new powers. Communication happens in two ways through responses to strings: with and without interpretation. He gives the case of "the Sergeant Major's shout of 'shun' to soldiers on the parade ground" (Collins 2010: 17). This should become a reflex response, a mechanical effect, needing no interpretation; but at some point in the soldier's training it is not yet a reflex and requires interpretation. Only humans, he says, interpret. Computers do not; only mechanical effects on computers are possible. Communication occurs when an entity can do something it could not do before as a result of the "transfer" of a string to it. There is a trivial sense in which one can answer a question in a game if one has memorized an answer without understanding it, but this is a kind of limit: The important sense is where you can do something with the transfer.

This becomes relevant to tacit knowledge. It is central to communication that although communication can fail, it can also often be repaired by more communication. Collins describes this in terms of longer and shorter strings. People who know the same things can often convey what they want to convey with short strings. But people who do not know the same things can often be given a longer string which enables the same effect, meaning that it enables the recipient to do something they could not do before. This turns out to be a critical part of the story for Collins, because it is in this difference that the secret of tacit knowledge lies. Whatever it means to have tacit knowledge or make tacit knowledge explicit has to do with this substitution of long strings for short strings. The fact that one can sometimes substitute communicating with long strings for failed communications with short strings suggests that all knowledge can be made explicit in this fashion. There is no guarantee, however, that substituting a longer string will result in communication. The problem can always be solved, in principle, by changing the receptor. But in practice, not every receptor can be changed.

Strings don't have inherent meanings. They get meaning by the properties and interpretive activity of the receptor. In humans, the relevant properties and capacity for interpretation are given by socialization (Collins 2010: 31). There is, he acknowledges, a bit of a mystery here: How do you transfer all this stuff unless you are fluent, meaning endowed with a capacity for interpretation and flexibility, already?

> Somehow, the ability that needs to be transferred to engender fluent language use has to be flexible—it has to be an ability to respond to social cues and contexts. To date, the only way we know how to engender such a change is through socialization. (Collins 2010: 31)

"Strings" come in two kinds: analogue (or continuous) and digital. The digital ones can be transformed easily; the analogue ones less so. Digital ones can be chopped into discrete entities, such as electronic states in a calculator, and transformed using look-up tables to produce numbers, for example. Analogue strings, such as a picture, can also be transformed, but it is harder to avoid losses.

A "language" cannot be transformed, but only translated, and translation always involves potential loss of meaning (Collins 2010: 25). Language, in contrast to strings, is something in which knowledge can be "located" (2010: 135). There is no look-up table for "meanings" (2010: 43). Translation is done by interpreters, who unconsciously add themselves to the resulting texts. But whereas strings are inert and without meaning on their own, they are prone to being interpreted in certain ways—this is what Collins means by affordances. "A photograph is just in marks on paper—a string—and in itself not 'of' anything or anybody" (2010: 34). But it is nevertheless easier to interpret a picture of Wittgenstein as that, rather than as a picture of a banana. Collins engagingly admits that terms like "afford" are "lazy terms" that "paper over deep cracks in our understanding." But he tries to do something to help. He notes that it becomes easier to interpret in certain ways with experience, that one needs to learn how to interpret a picture, and so forth.

So how does this help in defining tacit knowledge? By contrast, "explicit knowledge" now can be understood to mean "a string that, when appropriately transformed, affords, say, the Mona Lisa for those who know how to interpret it (that is those who know how to see the smile)" (Collins 2010: 46). And this definition shows why Michael Polanyi was right to claim that "all knowledge is either tacit or rooted in tacit knowledge" (Collins 2010: 46). No set of rules, no look-up table "can substitute for the ability to see the smile—one cannot explain to anyone who cannot see the smile how it is to be seen" (2010: 46). String transformation is reducible to physical processes. But where digital processes are explicable in terms of look-up tables, analogue processes are usually not.

What about the fact that computers can be constructed to do the tasks that people do using their tacit knowledge? Does that mean that we have explicated their tacit knowledge, or made it explicit? Collins says no—everything that is going on in the computer is transformation, not translation. The relevance of this to tacit knowledge becomes clear when we consider a distinction between mimeomorphic and polymorphic actions—that is, between actions that copy another action by mimicry and actions that copy the intended ends and "copy" by also achieving the end, perhaps in a way that is not physically the same (2010: 55–56). According to Collins, people can copy the motions and can also mimic intentionality, but computers and animals can only copy motions.

EXPLICITNESS, EXPLICATION, AND EXPLANATION

"Explicit," "explicable," and so on now can be seen to have a variety of meanings. "Explication" can mean describing physical processes involving strings. But this is not making something that is "usable when tacit" (namely, the neural nets or whatever supposedly contains the tacit knowledge) into something that is "usable when explicit." We do not get anything usable at all out of these explications. So it makes no sense to say that tacit knowledge is in these physical processes. The interesting issues involve the cases where we do get something usable: when people can "tell" what is "tacit" so that what is usable when tacit is also usable when explicit. What is going on when this happens?

To answer this, we need one more clarification, which is also a demystification. Polanyi says that "a wholly explicit knowledge is unthinkable." Collins wants to translate this into "strings must be interpreted before they are meaningful" (2010: 70) and for us to "forget about the word 'unthinkable.'" The point is really this: When a programmer makes a calculator do arithmetic it is doing no such thing—it is transforming strings. To do arithmetic requires a user who "has to decide what to calculate and how to use the answer," which in turn requires tacit knowledge (Collins 2010: 70). "Unthinkable" is misleading because it would be better to say this: Lengthening the string is not always a solution to problems of communication. "However long the sequence of transformations that takes place in the calculator, no arithmetic will have been afforded unless the cultural gap between the programmer and the user is not too big—the calculator is of no use to a tribesman from the Amazon jungle" (2010: 71).

There is, however, an important twist that also needs to be added, and it is one which Collins has appealed to before, in the context of asking what expert systems do. The calculator itself is not doing what people did before there were calculators. The calculator is a prosthesis. In medicine, prostheses rarely work in the same way as the part they replace. Neural nets are like calculators. The strings that make up the nets are, in principle, accessible, meaning describable, but they do not tell us anything, meaning they don't give us usable knowledge. They are just string transformers that work by cause and effect (Collins 2010: 76). Animals work in this way, but they are just machines. They don't interpret strings, as humans do (2010: 76). Of course, some human learning and action works this way as well, but not the kind that we are interested in when we are concerned with knowledge (2010: 77). The bright line is language: The way we learn language "is nothing like" this process (2010: 75).

The cases of tacit knowledge that Dreyfus and Polanyi focus on and treat as the model for all tacit knowledge are cases of embodied, or, as Collins calls it, somatic tacit knowledge. The standard example is knowledge of how to ride a bicycle, or specifically knowledge of how to keep a bicycle balanced. It is tacit because we cannot tell it. Nevertheless "it is passed on in ways which involve close contact with those who already have it" (Collins 2010: 99). So it is not the same as unrecognized knowledge, which is also passed on in this way. But the fact that we cannot tell, meaning convert our knowledge of how to balance a bike into explicit knowledge in the form of interpreted strings, is itself contingent. If "we rode our bikes on the surface of a small asteroid with almost zero gravity so everything happened much slower, we could probably use [explicit] rules to balance" (2010: 100). If our brains were faster we could do the same thing. So the tacit character of this knowledge is a consequence of what Collins calls somatic limits—the limits of our bodies and brains. Somatic limits are the source of the mystery element of tacit knowledge. In fact, machines can be programmed to do the things it involves, although they will do it in a different way (2010: 106). Human brains are complicated, but they are still just mechanisms (2010: 110). The only thing machines would lack is human somatic affordances, because they lack our bodies (2010: 109).

THE POINT

The argument so far is this: "Tacit" means not transmitted by strings; "explicit" means transmitted by strings and subject to mechanical transformation. Digital strings are easy to transform; analogue ones are harder. But in the end this difference does not mean that analogue is tacit and digital is not: Both are strings that are transformed. Interpretation is distinct from transformation and not reducible to it. There is a kind of substitution of explicit for tacit that works some of the time, so that longer strings substitute (prosthetically?) for small cultural gaps, but in the end communication depends on shortening the cultural gap. When someone "tells" what is tacit, they substitute a long string for a short one. Tacit knowledge does transfer, but not by mere imitation. Nevertheless it requires some sort of close association between persons in order to transfer. Much of what is normally called tacit knowledge is merely contingently tacit. Some is tacit because the physical conditions for making it explicit are not present: Gravity is too strong to allow writing a good bike-balancing program. Some is tacit because of the way society is organized and could be explicit if it were organized differently.

In part, Collins is writing a demystification of tacit knowledge. Much of what has been supposed to be tacit, tacit in the sense that it is irreducibly tacit, tacit in a deep or noncontingent sense, is not. Why? Apparently because we can tell that performances like bike riding that are supposedly based on it are really based on a mechanical string-transformation type process, and we know by virtue of the fact that we can substitute a mechanical process of this sort (even if the substitution requires thought experiments involving asteroids) for the supposed tacit knowledge. Once the pretenders to the title "tacit knowledge" have been sent packing, the real thing we are looking for will be revealed. The real thing is that which is irreducibly tacit. Strong tacit knowledge, "the irreducible heartland of the concept" of tacit knowledge (Collins 2010: 119), or collective tacit knowledge, "is a kind of knowledge that we do not know how to make explicit and we cannot foresee how to make explicit . . . [it] is the domain of knowledge that is located in society—it has to do with *the way society is constituted*" (2010: 85; italics in the original).

This last step of the argument is not fully spelled out. It looks like a definition, a definition of irreducibility, but it is a definition that includes the supposed cause or explanation of this kind of knowledge. Instead it is presented as a position, which Collins calls "Social Cartesianism." The core of his explication of this new position is an attack on what he calls the "bias" toward individualism.

> In Social Cartesianism, the individual is not the unit of analysis: the individual merely shares the collectivity's knowledge. The special thing about humans is their ability to feast on the cultural blood of the collectivity in the way that fleas feast on the blood of large animals. We are, in short, parasites, and the one thing about human brains that we can be sure is special is the way they afford parasitism in the matter of socially located knowledge. Neither animals nor things have the ability to live as parasites on social knowledge. (2010: 131)

The explication passes in a few short pages (2010: 119–38). Much of the discussion is devoted to claims about the differences between humans and animals. The point of the discussion is this: Human beings traffic in meanings, language, and culture, and thus are radically different from animals or machines, which do not.

> It is only humans who have the ability to acquire cultural fluency. It is only humans who possess what we call "socialness"—the ability to

> absorb ways of going on from the surrounding society without being able to articulate the rules in detail. (Collins 2010: 125)

The differences are such that we can ignore facts about how animals actually learn behavior, copy it from one another, associate in groups, and so forth (2010: 126).

A few more pages are devoted to the Chinese Room example (2010: 127–30). This thought experiment by Searle (1980) works like this: A person who does not know Chinese is in a room with a computer. Notes in Chinese are passed into the room; using the computer, the occupant runs a program that produces responses which native speakers of Chinese cannot distinguish from the responses that a real Chinese speaker would give. Searle took this as a reduction of the claim that computers understand, because, according to the premise of the experiment, the occupant did not understand. Collins notes that the occupant of the room, who gives answers according to formula, cannot respond to changes in the language: She is stuck with a look-up table that does not change. We are given a major example of collective tacit knowledge which relates to fluency, namely in the task of driving in traffic, which differs in different countries (2010: 121–24). We get a picture of the individual as a parasite on the social group, sucking up social knowledge from the super-organism; stop sucking and the knowledge gradually degrades—that is, its match with the collective's knowledge gradually weakens. But how does social knowledge pass into the individual? So far we have simply said that it happens as a result of "being immersed" in society (2010: 133).

The dependence of the individual on the group is vast, pervasive, and primary: A huge amount falls in the category of shared or collective. Collins freely concedes that there is a mystery about how it gets there, a mystery to which we have no solution but call by such names as "socialization." But we are so dependent on the social, meaning the collective, that even such research traditions as studies of child development or the project of cognitive modeling of a five year old cannot tell us how it works.

We also get a few lines on how the body serves as one of the conditions of communication (Collins 2010: 133–36) and a discussion of immersion, meaning "participating in the talk and practices of society" (2010: 133). And we get an image of the location of knowledge:

> There is nothing even remotely strange about saying that the seat of knowledge is the collectivity of brains because the collectivity of brains is just as much a "thing" as my individual brain is a "thing"; my brain is a collection of neurons separated by (if we were to examine them on an atomic scale) huge distances so the distance between brains in the collectivity is no obstacle to their comprising one "thing" between them. The collectivity of brains is just a large-scale version of my brain—it is just a bigger collection of interconnected neurons—and, as

> with synapses, the weights of the connections change whenever social and technological life is rearranged. So, if we don't like the metaphysics of the collectivity we can still accept the idea that knowledge is located in the collection of brains while remaining philosophically conservative. We can even say that the tacit knowledge that is associated with speaking language is located, not primarily in the individual brain but in the collection of brains. Interestingly, the very concept of the neural net shows us how to think about it this way without invoking anything mysterious like "collective consciousness." The metaphysically bashful can just think of all brains linked by speech as making up one big neural net. (Collins 2010: 132)

This then is the solution to the problem of irreducible tacit knowledge. It is irreducible because it is contained in collective processes, in the collective brain, on which we are parasitically dependent, so dependent that the content and extent of this dependence is beyond description. The mechanism of this dependence is socialization, which we do not understand. It has something to do with personal contact or immersion, so it operates in ways unlike the ways that ordinary explicit communication with strings operates. The result of its operation is fluency, and fluency consists in sharing collective tacit knowledge.

DURKHEIM FOR THE METAPHYSICALLY BASHFUL

The basic structure of the argument as a whole is this: Much of what passes for tacit knowledge, namely the individual part, can be done by or imagined to be done by machines; the rest cannot be done by machines, or at least machines can't be fluent at it, so this remainder must be collective. The reasoning is transparently faulty. This is why:

(a) The fact that machines can simulate something that humans do tells us nothing about how humans do it. This is a point Collins himself makes. So the entire discussion of string transformations is irrelevant: He gives us no reason to believe that what people do when they communicate has anything to do with strings, string transformations, or anything like it. This is just an analogy.
(b) There is no reason to think that "fluency" depends on anything collective, other than circular definitions of socialness—a Collins invention—in terms of fluency and fluency in terms of socialness, and both in terms of collectiveness. The driving example points in the other direction. People vary in their ease and competency in driving, but at the same time they are not uniform in their driving habits; they develop driving skills in different settings, have different driving skills, respond to others in different ways, based on their experiences and on

> other mechanisms—perhaps mirror neurons—and drive differently, while being aware of the driving of others and responding to it. Drivers in Italy may have, as an aggregate, different habits than drivers in Britain or New York, but there is nothing collective that corresponds to these differences. There are plenty of mechanisms to account for the fact that people learn to respond to others.

Therefore, both the starting point of the argument and its conclusion are groundless. So is most of what comes between. Collins concedes, repeatedly, that there is a mystery about how the collective stuff gets into individuals. The only reason to accept an explanation that depends on some causal process that is a mystery would be that the fact to be explained is so indisputable that it cannot be dismissed or given an alternative description that avoids the mystery or something similar. Instead, we get explanations that rely on terms that have more or less the same problem: practice, culture (especially as in cultural distance), society, and so forth. Crucial ideas, such as cultural affordances, are dropped into the discussion with no explanation of how they are supposed to be produced by culture. Do these get transmitted by personal contact? Is culture generally different from collective tacit knowledge and transmitted differently? Collins grants himself a free pass on these questions, but the question of transmission is not merely a mystery to be solved by someone else. It is the Achilles' heel of all collective mental concepts and anti-individualist social theories.

Collins says that he is providing an account for the ontologically bashful, meaning, presumably, that it does not carry the burdens of Durkheim's notion of the collective consciousness. But Durkheim does not just make this idea up out of ontological chutzpah. He arrives at this problematic notion because he is trying to answer the question of how something can be collective and mental and influence the individual (Turner 1986: 144–60). Collins' parallel discussions of the location of knowledge are mystifying and inconsistent on their face. In his previous discussion of individual tacit knowledge, neural nets were rejected as repositories of knowledge and dismissed as irrelevant because describing them did not result in usable knowledge. They "can do no more than the equivalent of Pavlov's dog" and "are simply string transformers whose operations merge into the ordinary world of cause and effect" (2010: 76). But in the later passages quoted above, where Collins embraces the extended mind thesis, knowledge is located in neural nets that connect multiple brains. Elsewhere we are told that knowledge is largely located in language (2010: 135)—something he also takes to be collective, but presumably in a different sense than something to be found in a neural net connecting multiple brains.

Perhaps the best case he makes for his grand claims about the specialness of humans involves meanings. The argument involves getting meanings out of jumbled words. People, he says, are very good at problems involving jumbled words and are good at unjumbling them correctly. Why? Because people can supply context that is learned through their being embedded in society (Collins 2010: 116). Machines cannot. And this is the result of the way machines learn. They can mimic human movements, as with the bicycle. But although machines can ride bikes, they cannot negotiate traffic successfully. Why? Because dealing with mistakes involves judgments of intentions, and these are social judgments (2010: 120).

This encapsulates the argument of the book: Machines cannot do something, because the something is social. "Social" means it comes from being embedded in society. Being embedded in society means it comes from a collective source. Therefore, the fact that machines cannot do something—like handle driving in traffic or decoding meanings of scrambled words—means that there is a huge collective set of tacit things. This conclusion is treated as so obviously true that we can accept the fact that we have no idea how any of this works: how being embedded in society produces these results, or transmits this collective stuff, or even what the totality of this collective stuff is. We can even dismiss child development studies, despite the fact that they tell us a lot about how this kind of "social" knowledge is acquired by children, because we are so sure that collective solutions are the right ones. But this reasoning depends throughout on equivocations, circularities, and dubious definitions. What is the cash value of "being embedded in society"? That we learn it in relation to the sayings and doings of other people? If so, it implies nothing about anything collective.

Much of what Collins claims about what humans can do, and what is collective, seems, in any case, to be simply false, or "true" only if we apply very odd standards, and then apply them inconsistently. Collins thinks the ability to read badly scrambled words is a remarkable human achievement. But machine procedures involving word games in general show that machines are in fact very good, and as good as humans, at tasks like getting the gist of a paragraph even when the words are mixed up (Bruza et al. 2009; Griffiths et al. 2007; Landauer et al. 1997). In the case of bicycle balancing, the standards allowed us to use a thought experiment about bicycling on a small asteroid to conclude that this was not really tacit knowledge, except in a contingent sense. With machines and their supposed limitations, however, the standards seem to be different. Is it really true that machines could not learn to respond to "social" cues in traffic if they were given the right inputs? Or learn what inputs to respond to, or "afford," without relying on a "culture"? Even on a large planet where cars moved very slowly and social cues were limited to smiles and screams? Why not? Why is this fantasy any different from the ones that Collins employs?

One of the great virtues of Collins' earlier writings on expert systems are his critiques, which are repeated in this book, of arguments that use the existence of a functional computer substitute for a human process as evidence that the human process is therefore something like the computer process. His point in these contexts is that functional substitutability implies nothing about similarity in underlying causal structure. This kind of argument can be readily applied to the supposed cases of tacit collective knowledge that transfix Collins. Indeed, his stress on the ineliminable role of interpretation seems to point in that direction. To understand other people, to cooperate with them in a division of labor, including the kind of distributed knowledge division that is characteristic of large-scale scientific experiments, requires functional interaction. The big question is whether there is any reason to think that there has to be anything in the way of tacit knowledge that is shared or collective, that is, whether functional substitutability is enough—that each of us can get by with sufficient tacit knowledge of our own to function in a group and generate utterances that others can interpret, without "sharing" anything tacit. Nothing Collins says implies that it is not enough. But Collins, characteristically, avoids this question in favor of his own inventions.

4 Tacitness in Practice Theory

Practices Then and Now

The concept of practice has a long history in the human sciences and in philosophy, albeit under various names. Much of the present interest in the concept, and in what has come to be called "practice theory," is a result of the failure of alternative programs of inquiry to fulfill their initial promises. These failures are related to practice ideas in an important way: Practice theories are a response to the inadequacy of theoretical or discursive summations or reductions of various activities, such as science or moral conduct. The history of modern thought, or modernity, is defined by such projects: logical positivism in the case of science, various ethical theories in the case of morals, rationalist political theory, such as Rawlsianism, and the grand narratives of social theory and history, notably Marxism.

Heidegger was the chronicler and philosopher of these failures as metaphysical doctrines, as Michael Oakeshott was of them as political doctrines, and Alasdair MacIntyre was of the project of ethical theory, which he replaced with his own practice-oriented account of the historical nature of morality. MacIntyre reduced moral doctrines from a philosophical or grounding role to the role of theoretical responses to practical conflicts that arise in moral practice within traditions of activities that are undergoing change as a result of changed social circumstances. In social theory, thinkers on the Left such as Pierre Bourdieu and Michel Foucault grasped that the traditional Marxist vision of class struggle resulting in subjective readiness for revolution, the false consciousness story, was dead. They turned to practice ideas to account for the subjective experiences in which false consciousness—or what had replaced false consciousness—was reproduced. These ideas were appropriated and developed by feminism to account for the reproduction of sexism and the failure of the modernizing projects of earlier generations, such as the suffragettes, to bring about the transformation of consciousness expected to result from women being allowed to vote.

All of the failed projects were, in part, based on explanations that proved to be inadequate. "Practice theory" was one of the explanations that remained standing after the explanations associated with the various projects were cut down. Yet, like the explanations that failed, "practice" was an explanation with distinctive properties. With "practice," the subject of practice theory, one reaches something which purports to be fundamental. Practices as usually understood are not fully articulable or capable of being fully described. There is nothing general that is beyond or behind practice that explains it. Thus the kinds of theories of practices one can have are theories that point to features of something elemental, something which cannot be reduced to the kind of object that a theory could reduce to something else or account for by something else. The attraction of practice theory is in part that it is a surrogate for the failed explanations. But it is a surrogate that can be conceived of in a variety of ways, with different properties, and different implications.

"CLASSICAL" PRACTICE THEORIES

In *The Social Theory of Practices* (1994) I identified two large families of concepts, one including notions like frames, worldviews, and paradigms, and the other including *habitus*, embodied knowledge, skills, and mores, among other things. After the book's publication (although certainly not entirely because of it!), and in part as a result of a series of conferences on practices, the discussion changed. To understand the problem of practices and its various solutions as discussed in *The Social Theory of Practices* and as the problem has evolved since then, we can start with a simple diagram of "classical" practice theories.

Begin with a box:

SOCIAL	NONSOCIAL
Cognitive/Social paradigms, *Weltanschauungen*, presuppositions, structures of consciousness or meaning, collective consciousness, systems of collective representations, tacit knowledge, the "rules" model in conversational analysis, the Searle of *Speech Acts*, etc.	*Cognitive/Nonsocial* artificial intelligence rule and symbolic representational model without sharing of rules.
Subcognitive/Social skills, *habitus*, mores," forms of life" and life-world, etc., conceived as "collective" (perhaps tradition in an Oakeshottian sense, probably in Shils' sense), Kripke's rules, collective intentions.	*Subcognitive/Nonsocial* habits, skills, etc., as the "tacit" part of an ensemble in which there are explicit parts (activities, rituals, performances, etc.) that the individual adjusts to.

The social/nonsocial divide refers to what can be thought of as location: whether a practice or worldview is understood to be located in some sort of supraindividual place such as "the social" or is no more than what exists within individual brains and bodies. A Kuhnian paradigm, presumably, is social and cognitive, because it is "shared" rather than individual, and because it consists of something like beliefs or premises or frameworks for seeing that are understood more or less on the model of premises. These distinctions are not very precise, it must be said, and in many settings not much hinges on separating, say, skills from beliefs. The families are closely related. But there are characteristically different emphases.

The "cognitive" family employs notions like rule, premise, structure of consciousness, collective representations, tacit knowledge, and so forth that involve close analogies with what can be directly articulated as roles, propositions, and so forth. What I am calling the subcognitive or "skills" family emphasizes the nonarticulable, that which may be indicated explicitly, such as the "judicial sense" of a good judge, but cannot usefully be described in terms of rules. One way of drawing this distinction is between propositional and nonpropositional knowledge (cf. Smith 1997). More recently the terminology, especially in the philosophy of cognitive science, includes conceptual and nonconceptual knowledge.[1]

The most common and familiar usages in both branches of the practice family are social, or collective, rather than individual. It is essential to the argument of Bourdieu, for example, that individual properties, such as dispositions, are constituted or produced by collective processes. One can quibble endlessly about what all these terms mean, but the basic point is this: Practices have both a causal primacy and a kind of autonomy in relation to the individual, what Emile Durkheim called externality ([1895] 1982: 38–43, 51–56). There is, however, a strong tradition of writing about practice-related concepts in which this kind of objectification or ontologization of collective notions is rejected by people who nevertheless seek to employ notions like tradition and skill and who also accord the "tacit" or the inarticulable a large and significant role. Michael Oakeshott, Gilbert Ryle, and Michael Polanyi are examples of this tendency.

The box indicates a set of possible solutions to a more or less common explanatory problem, but not the whole set. There are some, so to speak, "outside the box" solutions as well as denials of the problem itself. We can think of these as "post-classical" practice theories. Before turning to these, it will be useful to consider some of the inside the box issues that the outside the box solutions are attempting to avoid, and to explain, briefly, the argument of *The Social Theory of Practices*.

There are two basic issues about practice, which cut in different directions and divide the alternatives in the box. The first issue has to do with psychological agency, which is especially a problem for supraindividual accounts. Actions are individual, and so are brains, so there must be some individual psychological processes through which collective objects—such as practices—operate. This relation may be as simple as the following: Language is a real substantive normative structure beyond individuals that individuals internalize or habituate in order to speak, form verbal thoughts, and the like. "Internalization" and "habit" are nevertheless facts about the individual language user in whom something must happen. So the structure is not causally autonomous in its operations, nor does it exist in a different collective dimension, or in an unrelated category of reality, spirit, or "the normative." And there is a problem of linking to the psychological.

The second issue is the problem of continuity or identity, which is a problem especially for individual accounts. Whatever a tradition is, it cannot exist solely in the individual. The individual dies and the tradition goes on. But how? There is no direct continuity from brain to brain or mind to mind—only continuity mediated by speech, objects, and activities. But a tradition seems to be something more than the sum of such parts. Or is it?

The Social Theory of Practices argued against the social or "shared" solutions to these theoretical problems. To say that people "share" presuppositions or practices means that they have the same presuppositions or practices. The usual argument for this is transcendental: People do something, such as communicate; they could not communicate unless they shared the same framework; therefore they share the same framework. This argument, which shows its neo-Kantian origins, mimics a standard strategy used by Polanyi and many others to argue that explicit rules are never sufficient and need to be supplemented by something tacit. But the argument that something extra (and tacit) is needed to explain, for example, communication or scientific discovery, is not the same as the argument for a shared framework or for the possession of the same practices. The argument for "sharing" or sameness requires us to believe that there is some mechanism by which the same rules, presuppositions, or practices get into the heads of different people. But if we consider the various possible strategies for solving this problem of transmission, we soon see that it is insurmountable. The claim that the same practices, presuppositions, and the like get into the heads of many people requires a means of transmission that is little short of magical.

The details of this argument are too complex to repeat here, but the point may be seen in a simple question: Can people obtain perfect reproductions of the tacit possessions of others? In other words, can people "share" extremely complex common frameworks? If so, how? What means do they have of acquiring these frameworks that are radically less error prone than ordinary explicit communication, which is notoriously error prone? To really share they must be error free. The means in question must be much more effective than ordinary "training," which is of course imperfect. I concluded that acquiring the tacit possessions that people need is an imperfect training—like a feedback process that could not guarantee that people would "share" anything tacit, but could only, like training at its most successful, assure that people had certain habituated capacities to perform. Training of this sort only effects external similarities of performance: It tells us nothing about sameness of tacit possessions. Learning "from experience" is likely to produce an even greater diversity than formal training, because the feedback is uncontrolled rather than specifically designed to produce a specific kind of uniformity of response.

The "habituation" alternative to "sharing," once we look carefully, seems to accord better with what we know about the causal processes that actually operate in the world, especially in the brain, and with the known facts that practice theories purport to explain. This alternative account of what is going on when people learn to communicate, make scientific discoveries, and so forth, will be more plausible as an explanation because it does not appeal to any quasi-magical processes of transmission. Individual habituation (with the term being broadly construed to include all acquired learning that is tacit), I argued, does explain the same things, and we can even make some sense of such mysterious things as our common feelings by reference to the role of rituals and performances in inducing habits. This approach inverts the usual explanation of a tradition. The traditional view said that its rituals are performed because people share a common framework. I suggest that rituals are behavioral technologies that produce a certain uniformity of habits—but a uniformity that is literally superficial, a matter of external similarity, with internal or personal consequences that vary from individual to individual. Prayer, for example, has effects on those who pray. But the effects vary from person to person.

My way of thinking about this problem is summed up in the slogan I used at the end of the book, which revised Stanley Cavell's famous saying "We forget that we learn language and the world together" (1969: 19), by which he meant that the processes of learning the one were inseparable from the processes of learning the other. I said that we should add to this that "not only do we learn language and the world together, at the same time as we learn them we acquire habits that enable us to be more or less proficient in using both language and the world" (Turner 1994: 121). By this I meant that the processes of learning "objective," explicit, or public things were inseparable from tacit processes of habituation, what John Searle calls "the background." My point was that the feedback mechanisms of experience that produce habituation are personal, or individual, but at the same time bound up with learning an idiom, something "social," and experiencing the world, something "thingy."

POST-CLASSICAL PRACTICE THEORY

The arguments of *The Social Theory of Practices* were addressed primarily to what the book called "collective object" solutions to the problem of practices. The argument against these objects was that the mechanisms of transmission by which they would have to operate were so incredible and unconnected to any known psychological reality that they couldn't be taken seriously. But solutions that appear to be "outside the box" and free from these problems emerged after the book was written. These I have called "ensemble" accounts of practices, and they fall into two basic groups: "material" accounts and nonmaterial accounts.

Two of the most fully developed accounts, those of Theodore Schatzki and Joseph Rouse, discussed the book and defined their alternatives in contrast to the book's emphasis on the causal character of practices. Both quote, and reject, a statement in *The Social Theory of Practices* about "the need to connect the stuff of thought to the world of cause and substance" (Turner 1994: 37; Schatzki 1996: 222; Rouse 2002: 170). Schatzki noted common ground with the book in the idea that a practice consists of doings and sayings. But, he argued, "although doings and sayings compose a practice by virtue of expressing an array of understandings, rules, and teleoaffectivity, these items . . . do not cause the doings and sayings involved" (1996: 106). Rouse similarly denied that practice was a causal concept. "Practice" for him is a normative concept; indeed, practices and normativity are mutually explanatory: Practices are intrinsically normative, because they divide actions into correct and incorrect, and dividing into correct and incorrect is a practical activity with no further grounding. Schatzki used different language and provided a more developed account of what a practice is, as indicated by the "array" or ensemble listed above, but also shares with Rouse both the idea of normativity (1996: 160) and a generally Heideggerian picture of the problem of practices in which the core is the (normative) relation of "mattering" between us and the world we experience.

For both Schatzki and Rouse, the way in which practices relate to behavior is through the life- world as produced by this relation of mattering. As Schatzki (1996: 107) puts it,

> to which practices a behavior belongs rests on the life conditions it expresses; and which conditions these are depends on the behavior, its contexts, and understandings of life conditions. The relevant understandings are mostly those interwoven into the actor's world, into the activity or contexts to which he or she is party. For things can be standing or going only in those ways for which his or her body, activities, contexts, and practices make room. And understandings of these ways are generally interwoven into and carried by the practices involved. Actions, understandings, and practices are thus holistically related.

"Express," "belong," and so forth are noncausal terms, and our dependence on conditions here is our dependence on the world as we experience it through our normative or mattering connection to it. This is the "always already" there world that Heidegger had in mind with the notion of *Dasein*, and this is what practice theory explains (or rather explicates, as the relation between us and the world, on this account, is primordially one of mattering rather than cause and effect).

The problem of externality and continuity is solved by Schatzki with the notion of the coherence or hanging together (*Zusammenhang*) of practices, together with the idea that "integrative practices" themselves operate on practices producing coherence and "orchestration" between individuals, which in turn produces the "field of possibility" of the life-world. He acknowledged that "social theory's one-sided focus on commonality at the expense of orchestration," a failing he attributed to "Durkheim-Parsons-Habermas," makes it vulnerable (1996: 186–87). But he argued that "orchestration," or "co-existence within a practice" (1996: 187), which for him does not require complete sharing, avoids these vulnerabilities. Moreover, "a field of possibility is· not a candidate for reduction to individuals. It is emphatically the property of a practice" (1996: 186). Thus practices have a kind of distinctness from psychological cause and can be understood as noncausal, and not "shared" in a problematic sense. They are external and continuous because they are organized, and this organization, through integrative practices, is normative, and is thus, as he quotes Charles Taylor, "out there in the practices themselves" rather than "in the minds of the actors" (1996: 99–104).

A second kind of an ensemble approach shares a basic feature with this "normative" and anti-psychological approach to practices, but eliminates the normative element. Instead it identifies continuities elsewhere, namely with the objects or material culture that are shared by participants in a practice. Andrew Pickering has pioneered this approach (1995, 1997), and it has some obvious attractions. If a practice is simply an assemblage of objects which people employ, which has no inner directionality, then there is no problem of understanding its inner directionality or psychology. Continuity is simply a matter of the fact that people use or extend the use of the same assemblage of objects, or extend it by varying the assemblage by replacing one object with another without replacing them all.

This argument points to an important feature of the sociology of practices, which is that practices are often carried on around physical objects whose diffusion requires people to develop skills, habits, and so on to adapt to them. Thus the riding of horses by American Indians was certainly skilled, but perhaps owed little or nothing to European equestrian traditions, theories, and so forth. It was nevertheless a "practice," and whether there was anything borrowed along with the horses themselves from these European sources hardly matters much. The horse allowed for a new style of life, new modes of warfare, consumption, and residence—in short, a new culture. So one is tempted to get rid of the "allowed for a new culture" and the language of "field of possibility" understood in a normative way and just say, as Andrew Pickering does, that the machine consisting of the people and the objects—this cyborg—is all there is to the practice (1995).

Pickering's concern is primarily science, but the point may be generalized to the way of life of the horse-riding Indians. In its negative form, it is this: Nothing in the way of special mental content, collective or individual, is essential to the notion of practice, or for that matter "culture." In its positive form, it is this: Practices, cultures, and so on are ensembles, with no essence, whose elements change over time because people use different things together with one another, which is all the "organization" there is to a practice. The ensembles persist or have continuity by virtue of, and only by virtue of, the persistence of the elements and their joint uses themselves. John Pickstone, who has produced a (partly) parallel argument about the history of science, uses the term "the 'thinginess' of life" (2001: 20) to capture this idea of the autonomy and imperviousness of material culture to absorption into the world of thought and theory, and the requirement that this world be addressed with skills rather than words.

The Social Theory of Practices was not an attempt to provide a new theory of practices, although it closed with a chapter on the question of how we should understand the body of phenomena that collective object theories of practice had sought to understand, but in light of the arguments that the book made about transmission and sharing. In short, it was an attempt to say what kind of causal account of the continuities underlying doings and sayings could be given other than an appeal to collective objects. The basic strategy of the chapter was to invert the implicit causal reasoning of classical practice theory, which started with mind, with the supposedly shared presuppositions that formed experience, and to ask what produced the habits of mind that were directly causally involved in doing and saying.

The book pointed to many features of social life that could do the causal job of accounting for habits which produced apparent uniformity: the common performances (with objects, requiring skills) and rituals of social life; memorialization that produces what appears as collective memory; and the way in which social interaction, even the reading of a text, requires habit formation. "Habit" was perhaps the wrong word, because it led readers to think the argument was more reductive than it was, but the idea was this: Practice and the persistence of practice could be accounted for sufficiently as mental phenomena of a familiar kind and did not require any kind of collective psychology, or any mysterious process of transmission or sharing.

The replacement for traditional notions of practice, which of course were, unlike the ensemble notions discussed here, psychological, was itself psychological, but not collective. It emphasized the individual learning trajectory and thus the uniqueness of the skills and habits that each individual acquired, but argued that known mechanisms for the production of the appearance of uniformity could account for this appearance. In short, the argument was that practices consisted of learnables and that the causal effects that were distinctively those of what was formerly called "practice" were the effects of the psychological fact of learning.

There is a difference in the *kinds* of continuity that each of these approaches considered significant. The "learnables" account took up the challenge of two major strands of classical practice theory, which emphasized the problem of tradition in both science and politics, specifically liberalism. Polanyi made the point that scientific traditions were difficult to transplant—that just having the equipment and a bit of training was not enough to create a scientific tradition in a place that had none. This is a point that fits well with the practice of hiring junior scientists from labs where they had hands-on experience with particular scientific techniques: Just the equipment is not enough. The case of politics had deeper roots, in the problem that many nations had with transplanting "republican" or limited monarchy constitutions from their original Anglo-American contexts. Just having the laws was not enough. The constitutions routinely failed to produce the liberal political regimes that their drafters aspired to: Something else in the form of the relevant political culture or tradition, the practices of politics, was needed.

These particular problems of continuity pose problems for "nonpsychological" accounts of practices. But there is a sense in which choosing between the three noted successor post-classical accounts of practice is a matter of taste. As Schatzki suggests, they do not, "strictly speaking," conflict with one another except with respect to what they think needs to be explained (1996: 106). Each takes some of the material "explained" by classical practice theory and treats it as the thing that needs explanation.

These accounts do conflict with classical practice theory, although one can find many "post-classical" elements in writers like Bourdieu and Oakeshott. And they also have some different implications. Excluded accounts avoid the psychological, thereby avoiding the awkward questions about group minds that shadowed collective mentality forms of practice thinking. The identification of practices with learnables, unlike these nonpsychological accounts, leaves some hostages to fortune. It implies that practices are in some concrete sense in the brain, and this means the truth about learnability is something that goes on that fits with the actual properties of real brains, as the classical theory of practice does not. But the alternatives also leave some hostages: There are problems with "normativity." One can question whether a naturalistic explanation needs to explain nonnaturalistic facts, or even whether there are such facts to be explained. Does it commit to a dualistic metaphysics in which the normative is required, as it seems to in Rouse, some sort of noncausal, distinct realm of being? Does this dualism need to be overcome, as Rouse tries to overcome it, by a Heideggerian metaphysics of primordiality? In any event the accounts do have different implications, something that can be made clearer by considering them in the light of the problem of morality.

NEW DEVELOPMENTS IN COGNITIVE NEUROSCIENCE

After the publication of *The Social Theory of Practices*, mirror neurons were discovered. This had important implications for the argument of the book. If the issue with practice theory was the transmission of practices, mirror neurons provide an alternative to habituation or connectionist learning as a mechanism of acquisition. Moreover it is a mechanism that seems to provide an explanation of one of the puzzling cases examined in the book: Marcel Mauss's discussion of how, following the introduction of American movies in Paris after World War I, the way French women walked changed noticeably to become "American" (Mauss [1935] 1979; quoted in Turner 1994: 20–21).

The point of the example in the book was that noticing and identifying a practice depended on comparisons, in this case a comparison made possible by the expectations of French people who were familiar with women walking in a different way. Without this comparison, we would not recognize either the French or the American walk—what Mauss called *techniques du corps*—as a practice. But the example also pointed to a mode of transmission—through seeing something at the movies—that did not fit the model of connectionist learning, or indeed of any kind of learning, because it did not involve feedback. Mirror neurons provide an explanation of this: We are equipped with neurons which fire both when we perform certain bodily motions and when we see them performed. Because the neurons are the same, we are able to do what we see—to imitate without "learning" in the ordinary sense. So it seems that we have a preconceptual mode of imitation, and a mode in which we respond at the neuronal level to other people's movements and copy them for future reference.

How does this mechanism fit with the arguments of *The Social Theory of Practices*? The book, especially as I have summarized it here, hinged on an argument about sameness and transmission, and posed the following problem: How does any known mechanism of transmission produce sameness? Mirroring seems to be an answer to this question: It produces sameness by a neuronal mechanism. Or does it? There are two reasons why it does not help the older form of practice theory which made practices into collective objects that had to be reproduced in the individual. The mechanism of mirroring doesn't operate on anything collective or tacit, but rather on what someone can see or hear— paradigmatically physical movements. This relates to a point made in *The Social Theory of Practices*, that transmission must be understood to operate through "normal epistemic channels": The data for unconscious acquisitions is ordinary perceptual data—and what is seen is behavior, or "externals."

Some of the more aggressive statements of mirror neuron thinking appear to say that mirror neurons provide direct access to other minds, to motivations and intentions. If this were the case, a novel kind of copying, beyond the externals, would be taking place, and this might be a solution to the problem of transmission that could salvage some version of classical practice theory. But this is a misreading of the actual claims. Vittorio Gallese, who is often cited in support of this idea (Gallese and Metzinger 2003), doesn't say that we have actual knowledge of other people's goals via mirror neurons—just that they are the mechanisms for simulation. But simulations are like hypotheses. We can't just "read" off the goals of others, but we can "construct" them (preconsciously)—as in Gallese and Metzinger (2003: 385). The term "construct" is a cognitive term here—it shows that the mirror neuron account assumes that we can only directly apprehend externals.

The "copying" done by mirror neurons is also not the kind needed by the older kind of practice theory. There is no feedback mechanism that assures that the copies are the same. And there is evidence that what is copied depends on the physical capacities of the people doing the copying. Dancers, for example, mirror something different from non-dancers when exposed to the same images of motion. Nor is this surprising. Millions of people watch Tiger Woods' golf swing every week, but none of them have copied it exactly, or for that matter very well. In this respect, then, mirroring as a copying mechanism is analogous to connectionist learning, in that what gets acquired depends on the individual history of the person doing the acquiring. It provides a mechanism for copying that is more rapid than trial and error, but not a mechanism for excluding error or directly transferring mental content, either from one person to another or from a collective object to an individual.

ETHICS AND PRACTICE

Classical practice theory and philosophical ethics came at the problem of morality from opposed points of view. Ethics was concerned with vindicating the universality and, therefore, the binding character of moral claims, and was befuddled by the diversity of morals. Practice theory in its classical form was designed as an account of diversity: Different practices produced different moral intuitions, beliefs, dispositions, and the like. The explanatory structure was more or less the same as the Marxist theory of "the superstructure," in which an underlying and hidden causal reality with a kind of directionality produced, or rather fit with, a visible body of ideas and beliefs. There was a degree of underdetermination, or space for alternative solutions, in this model. Different beliefs and ideas could be consistent with the underlying structure, which was determinative "in the last instance" rather than directly and mechanically.

Philosophical ethics has generally had trouble giving much content to the idea of universal moral truths. Some things do seem to be more or less universal, but in a functional sense. Every society has moral ideas and rules that do things to protect the weak from the strong, to minimize conflicts, and so forth. But the doctrines and theories that surround and justify the particular moral ideas of a given society are invariably different from those of other societies, so that the moral ideas, dispositions, and so forth of a given society taken as a whole are distinctive from and even alien to those of other societies.

The message of classical practice theory to ethics, consequently, was this: Explicit ethical ideas and moral rules are only very partial representations of a deeper and more fundamental set of facts which determine the conditions of ethical thought, feeling, and so forth. Moreover, these more fundamental facts are distinctive to particular settings or forms of life, so no meaningful "universality" is possible. The parallels to the case of science are revealing. In each case, formalizations of methods or theories partially illuminate the topic, but in the end fail to fully illuminate it. Theories of scientific inference and of the nature of scientific progress, similarly, have proven to be inadequate as accounts of the historical record in science. In the case of science, these inadequacies led to Polanyi's notion of tacit knowledge as an essential element in scientific discovery (1967, [1958] 1998), to the study of tacit knowledge by the social studies of science, and to the recognition, in the economics of science, that tacit knowledge was valued and sought after in the marketplace of science.

The analogies between moral practice and science are not precise, but they are revealing. In science, new instruments and new methods allow us produce, or discover, new phenomena, that is to say, produce new possibilities, but they also constrain by providing new sources of resistance. What Pickering calls the mangle of practice—the term "mangle" is meant to evoke the wringer through which wet clothes were put in order to squeeze out the water—is the constraint that the world of tools places on our theorizing and experimenting, thus directing our practice. Moral practices, similarly, are constrained by the changing consequences of action in the world. This was one of MacIntyre's central points. The world itself changes in part through the efforts of individuals engaged in the practical business of living—of satisfying wants, including such generic wants as security and food, as well as such ideal wants, inherited from the patterns of action and satisfactions of the past, such as honor.

In both cases, then, there is what Pickering calls "resistance," by which he means the pushing back that is exhibited when tools don't work or experiments fail. In moral life, there is something about resistance and failure as well. When an individual's life strategies or choices don't work—in the manner of Sancho Panza—or produce unanticipated conflicts between two goods, such as money and respectability, that formerly could be achieved simultaneously or harmoniously, these conflicts prompt a need to theorize about the situation, or to imaginatively depict it in literature.

Even if we leave the notion of moral practice at this, at the level of coping with the resistances provided by circumstance and especially social circumstance, we have managed to say a great deal about the phenomenon of moral life. What practice means here is the external facts that persist and constrain us, that provide resistance to us. And there is a great deal that does so. If we parallel Pickering's idea that there are no constraints on our next step in science other than those provided by the tools at hand, and that the whole of the explanation of the continuity of practices is to be found in the continuity of these objects, we have successfully de-mentalized the problem of ethics.

But there is something not quite satisfactory about this notion of practice, which we can see by the same device of trying to make it into an ethical theory. As an ethical theory, it would amount to the advice "when in Rome, do as the Romans do." But the point would also provide a warning that if one does not do as the Romans do, one faces resistance and difficulty in accomplishing anything. This seems truistic, but a bit thin to mean that the would-be moral hero who promotes a new ideal or the extension of an ideal from one area of life to another—equality into familial relations, for example—needs to think about whether it works, whether it conduces to the other goals that people have and regard as "good." The idea that there is nothing to ethics but these facts of resistance has an affinity to existentialist ethics. We have a wide range of free moral choice, in the manner of existentialism, and nothing to guide us, no obligations, virtues, and the like. But we are constrained nevertheless to do most of the things we would do anyway. We cannot abandon our children or fail to pay our bills without consequences, of course. Nevertheless, we have a choice to do these things or not do them, and it is these choices that make up our moral existence.

The idea that by practice we mean something encompassing the practical business of living also fits with the alternative presented by ensemble theorists like Schatzki and Rouse. But their accounts seem closer to moral experience. Both of these thinkers have in mind, as we have seen, a notion of practice in terms of lived experience, the life-world or *Dasein*, the world of concern to us. This is an amorphous idea, more amorphous than the idea of practice itself, but one can see why it is attractive. In the hands of Rouse, as I have said, practice is associated with normativity, and the notion of normativity is applied to any relation with the world or others. The obligation to tell truth in science, for example, is rooted, for Rouse, in the normative relation we have to the world—part of our concern for the world, one might say. For this kind of practice theorist, our experience of the world, for example, the world of our familial relations, is "always already" ethical or normative in character. Ethical theory merely abstracts this experienced world, unsuccessfully, into ethical theories which are at best very partial representations.

In some sense we may choose our practices and choose to revise our practices. Rouse says he is inspired by feminist philosophy of science, which he thinks is an improvement on the naturalistic approach to practice he finds in the social study of science. Using the idea of practice to show what it is that we have or can create alternatives about, then, is the service that practice ideas can give to ethical thinking. We thought we needed to think about physics in one way; now we have more than one, and we may morally prefer the new one.

Schatzki wrote a book on the practices of the Shakers (2002) and how the physical objects in the world of the Shakers were designed to produce a practice, which is to say the kind of affective structure and experience of the world integrated externally to the individual, but which determine the individuals' experiences and thus their conduct. The message of the book to ethics is this: Our experiences of the world, and especially our experience of value, are structured by practices, not given. In this case, the construction of the life-world succeeded in producing a particular, and odd, moral outlook. One would understand the choice of a new practice in terms of the older practice that motivated the choice. One of Queen Victoria's granddaughters, a princess in the Russian royal family, chose to enter a convent, something that we can make intelligible as a royal act. And perhaps the kind of moral change in the direction of feminism of which Rouse approves can be understood in this way as well, that is to say as choices to change from one practice to another within the original practice.

The "learnables" approach to practices has a naturalistic approach to morality. Oakeshott, in "Rationalism in Politics," says that "moral ideals are a sediment; they have significance only so long as they are suspended in a religious or social tradition" (1962b: 36). The dominant moral ideologies of the present, he suggests, "are in fact the desiccated relic of what was once the unselfconscious moral tradition of an aristocracy who, ignorant of ideals, had acquired a habit of behavior in relation to one another" (1962b: 35). This puts the issue clearly; moral theories, of whatever kind, as theories, are necessarily abstractions from the rich pattern of conduct that we call ethical. They are tips of an iceberg. But the bottom of the iceberg, the religious or social tradition, is made up, at least in part, of a "habit of behavior in relation to one another." Such habits are natural facts, in the brains of people.

The learnables account also stresses the idea that learnables exist and produce their effects on our mental processes at the tacit or unconscious level. In this sense, learnables are like the furniture of the world, and like this furniture provide resistance. "When in Rome, do as the Romans" is good advice with respect to externals. But Flannery O'Connor had a point when she said, "When in Rome, do as you done in Milledgeville" (O'Connor [1979] 1988: 220). The path of least resistance is often one of less resistance to known learnings, to the internal furniture of the mind. We can think of this furniture as hard and soft. The hardest furniture is those habits of inference without which we cannot act—the most fundamental habits pointed to by Hume. This hard furniture shades off into the hardwired, into the architecture. It is an empirical question as to where the line is. The softer furniture includes such things as our moral intuitions and our sense of the good. They are acquired, as Oakeshott put it, as "a habit in relation to one another," and in relation to the world. Like the habit of causal reasoning, our intuitions are tips of icebergs, and the below water parts are inaccessible to us, even through reflection. The softest of mental furniture consists of what Oakeshott called intimations, when he spoke of politics as the pursuit of intimations, and what Polanyi thought of as the precognitions which precede scientific discovery. They fit with the learnable model of these mysterious tacit hints that direct our thought and reflect the kind of preconscious learning that Polanyian psychologists have demonstrated experimentally (Reber 1989).

This conceptual mental furniture picture fits with cognitive science. Cognitive neuroscience both supports and radicalizes the basic idea that practices operate largely as part of what Searle calls "the Background." It supports the idea first by showing how much goes on in the brain in support of our thinking and doing other than what we are conscious of or can access through theories which extend our common sense models of the mind, such as the notion that we "assume" things in order to act or reason. It provides additional support by providing evidence of the actual brain processes that occur when we think and act, for example through fMRI studies. It radicalizes the basic idea by undermining the folk psychology we use to speak of thinking and doing, such as the idea that we "assume" things, that our decisions are wholly conscious affairs, and that we have "intentions" about which we have accurate knowledge. Showing that this language is suspect, that at best it represents only a small part of the causally relevant processes, and does so inaccurately, cuts off a large class of potential objections which rely on these ideas. Even "the normative," or at least the thinking that corresponds to what is conventionally called normative, leaves distinctive traces in certain parts of the brain. The learnables model of practices coheres with this radicalization. The message to ethical theory remains the same as Oakeshott's theoretical abridgements of practices have their place as ideological tool kits to apply in new settings; they are unable to adequately represent the amorphous but real things we call practices.

Adding the resources of cognitive neuroscience also allows us to underline the plausibility of the learnables account. Learnability provides its own discipline: It is impossible to learn something that does not, in some sense, "work." Of course, the setting in which what one learns "works" well enough to learn may be very odd, and the things learned may be, from an external perspective, very strange. In the case of moral conduct, it may be as convenient to believe in the abominations of Leviticus as it is to be sickened by the betrayal of a friend. But neither would be learned, and by "learned" here we mean "connected to the parts of the brain that involve the relevant kinds of affectual responses," if they did not provide positive feedback in a given environment. Learning also involves what we may think of metaphorically as the economy of the brain itself, so that practical conflicts and contradictions can't be learned: This gives some sense to Oakeshott's idea that rationality is a matter of seeking coherence, and this allows us to account for the fact of the "organization" of practices that is central to Schatzki's account, but which he treats as necessarily external. It also gives a sense to such arguments as Max Weber's discussion of rational theodicies, that is, the consistent sets of beliefs, rare in the history of religion, that squarely faced and reconciled the omnipotence of God and the existence of evil. Weber pointed out that the rarity of the beliefs reflected the fact that the reconciliations produced so much angst that they were impossible for one to live with as a human being and were suited only to theology texts ([1915] 1946: 358–59). Angst is a constraint like the others we have discussed here, but one that in this case arises within the brain in response to unbearable truths.

Let me close with this. Morality is often a matter of reconciling, seeking coherence, as Oakeshott says—the constraints of living in Rome in actuality and living in Milledgeville in one's mind, between what is immediately convenient and workable and what one has learned in the past and learned at a very deep level. Practice ideas at their best remind us of this conflict, and remind us that there is no theory that will ever resolve it.

5 Practices and Non-conceptual Content

Practice Relativism

Relativism is an elusive notion. There are, one might say, different kinds of relativism, such as historical relativism, cultural relativism, the kind of relativism that exists between alternative fundamental theories of the world or paradigms in science, and the kind of relativism that exists between professional schemes of concepts that constitute the objects on which the professions operate in distinctive and incommensurable or not fully commensurable ways. There is also linguistic relativism, the relativism that holds between languages and results from the indeterminacy of translations between claims in different languages, and relativism of class, race, and gender, which operate with a base-superstructure or *Überbau* model. Cognitive, aesthetic, ethical, and other kinds of relativism have been seen as the consequence of hidden changes that produce new values or illuminate new values in successive historical periods. We are, in this picture, stuck with our historical starting point in terms of which we construct a worldview and constitute objects in a moral and cultural universe that is distinctive and unlike, although it may be historically connected to, past moral and cultural universes constituted by past historical personages. It was of course Thomas Kuhn who, with the concept of paradigm, extended this picture to science.

In this chapter I examine the notion of what I will call "practice relativism" as a distinct and analyzable form of relativism but with a particular question in mind: What makes a practice conception relativistic? The question is meaningful because there are a variety of concepts of practice, and a variety that are relevant to science that are not relativistic in any problematic way. So there is a question of what ingredient makes a practice concept relativistic in its implications.

WHAT ARE PRACTICES?

The concept of practices is itself, in part at least, a kind of naturalistic or "sociological" notion. It usually figures in some sort of contrast for example between theory and practice or between knowledge and practice. The term refers to something that is supposed or treated as a fact with explanatory significance. A practice is something one engages in, in many cases at least quite consciously and intentionally. The primary use of the term is, however, descriptive. A practice is something that people engage in during the course of intentional conduct or action that is not itself intended, but is a condition of the conduct. The term describes or picks out the distinctive and usually repeated features of a way of doing things. Thus if we were to talk about the practice of mathematical physics in the nineteenth century in Cambridge, one might ask questions about the distinctive mathematical training that the Wrangler competition produced and show how this was a condition for the distinctive kinds of explicit, intended, theoretical results that persons with this particular mathematical training received, as Andrew Warwick does in *Masters of Theory: Cambridge and the Rise of Mathematical Physics* (2003).

The term "practice" itself, however, is not well defined. One commonplace use of the term is found in the history of science, where the contrast is between theory, and what is in textbooks and manuals, and practice. One formulation of this usage, recently exemplified by John Pickstone (2001), equates practice to what anthropologists call material culture—practice referring literally to the tools that scientists use. This usage has some "relativistic" implications, but they are unproblematic ones. What scientists can discover is in part determined by the tools they have. So in some sense the fact accessible to them, which is to say their world of data, is determined by the tools: Different tools would mean different facts, and perhaps theories which fit or seemed plausible in the world defined by one set of tools would not in a world defined by another set. The microscope, to take a simple case, disclosed a world which changed utterly the subject matter of biology, and therefore the range of possible biological ideas. But there is no conflict in "rationality" between pre- and post-microscope biology: With the tool in hand, one would think the old biologists would have come around to the viewpoint of the microscope-possessing biologists. The situation is no different from cases involving differences in the data that scientists possess at different times, and practice in this sense is literally part of the data, the given.

Pickstone is a traditionalist, indeed, historiographically, a kind of pre-Kuhnian. He does not use the language of constructionism, which would describe the tools in relativistic terms, that is, as relative to the construction that has been placed on the tools, or in terms conceptually linked to theories which might themselves be incommensurable or otherwise "relativistic." Instead he describes the tools functionally—thus, for him, practice is more or less made up of objects with functions. He is concerned with a particular kind of problem about practice and knowledge, the question of the relations between the two and he thinks that there are historically meaningful differences. He concedes that there is a kind of knowledge associated with the tools—craft skills and knowledge of material and substances. But he wants to distinguish this kind of knowledge from scientific knowledge proper. For Pickstone a practice is thus an activity, intentionally engaged in, with particular tools, of which the paradigm case is a craft with associated skills. There is a practical issue in history to which this relates—we have material artifacts of past science, or descriptions of them. We do not have any sort of historical access to the craft skills or minds of the craftsmen themselves, and of course the same holds for the Cambridge Wranglers. We can use the archives to illuminate the coaching system, the cribs, the repeated features of explicit proofs, and so forth, but we cannot directly access the stuff in their heads.

This naive approach, which reflects the constraints on the historian of practice, is congruent with a more sophisticated version of practice theory applied to science developed by Andrew Pickering (1995), who defines practices as the assemblages of material things that are the conditions for doing science. Like Pickstone, for Pickering the objects themselves are, so to speak, inert. They do not have in themselves any sort of directionality or teleology. They are not symbols. Any meaning they have is attributed to them by their users, and the attributions and therefore the uses can change—indeed this, the novel uses of equipment, is a large part of experimental science. A scientist in possession of, or with access to, this assemblage can take it in any direction consistent with the assemblage itself. Here, as with Pickstone, theory and the substantive contents of science are not part of the concept of practice, but are a separate domain conditioned—causally—on the assemblage and the data it generates. There is a wide range of contingency in the process, and of course what happens at one stage of the process has consequences, although not determinate ones, for what happens next. The assemblage has functional relations, that is to say, there are things that one can do with a microscope and a staining solution that one cannot do with a theodolite and a staining solution. There is nothing holistic about these relations, however, except in the sense that the set of functional possibilities is limited at any given moment. One can add pieces, such as new tools or instruments, with new possible relations, and change the assemblage.

This is relativistic conception of practice in one sense—it accepts the contingent character of the historical sequences that produced present "scientific knowledge" (cf. Turner 2002: chap. 3). But it is difficult to imagine a serious account of the historical development of science where there was not, for a finite historical period, some explanatory need for the recognition of contingency. The grounds we have for thinking that we could have come to other scientific beliefs are rooted in the recognition of actual historical contingencies, not in some sort of in-principle recognition that there is a grounding element of science that is in principle arbitrary and understood in a virtual sense as a matter of nonrational "choice." It is this second sense that will take to be "relativistic" in what follows here. So my question will be "What does it take for a practice conception to be 'relativistic' in this strong sense?"

WHAT DO PRACTICE EXPLANATIONS EXPLAIN?

It becomes evident in connection with these notions of practice that one way in which concepts of practice vary is in terms of their explanatory object, that is, with respect to the questions they are designed to answer. Pickering is interested in the following problem: How do modes of doing science evolve and change in the face of the resistances they encounter in the course of their continued application to new issues and problems? Pickstone is interested in a different question. How are the possibilities of knowledge in science and technology, including its ways of thinking, limited and created by the particularities of available technologies? How, for example, are the content and ways of thinking of a geologist in the nineteenth century related to the fact that geology was done with pickaxes and theodolites? These are both quite different questions than "how is it possible for there to be consensus in science?" or "how is it possible for scientists to resolve their disagreements by reference to experiment?" which have been attributed to Kuhn or expressed by him. And these are different yet from questions like "how is communication possible?" or "how is semantic reference to the empirical world possible?" There is also an autonomous question about practice that falls in the domain of social theory that relates to the nature of practice as a natural object: What is the character of the sorts of things that, in the tradition of social theory, have been called practices or "traditions" (or mores, and so forth) and invoked as explanations of social phenomena? Are they one kind of thing, or many, and if many, how do they relate and what differentiates them? One can identify many more such explanatory objects or problems.

What is the relation between these questions and between the concepts of practice that answer them, or, put differently, what kinds of answers does one get? There is an important provisional division to be made between two kinds of answers. One kind treats practice as a gap-filling notion, which has no substantive significance other than to refer to those conditions for the thing to be explained—whether it is communication, consensus, or the course of development in science—that are not part of the explicit content. In the case of consensus the explicit content would be the publicly stated reasons and claims that went into scientific discussion. The "practices" are everything else that is part of science, the mental life of the scientists, and so forth, that make discussion leading to consensus possible. This might include the kinds of habits of mind that are inculcated by training in science, the tacit knowledge about the way the physical or biological world works that enables scientists to make discoveries and judge claims in ways that are intelligible to other scientists, and so on. But these things are invoked, or for that matter exist, not as an accessible, natural realm of autonomous facts, but as facts which function only in relation to particular explanations, so that there is no point to theorizing them as autonomous objects. "Practice," in this usage, is relative to particular, transient, explanatory situations, and its content is relative to the particular thing to be explained. When Robert Brandom (1994), for example, argues that the process of making inferential practices explicit can go on indefinitely, he is invoking this sense of practice. Different explanatory objects would require different explanatory gaps to be filled, so what counts as practice is relative to explanatory aims. From this point of view, it would be no surprise if there was nothing in common between the appeal to practices in connection with the question of whether a given constitutional form could work in a country without a political tradition of a certain kind—such as a political tradition that separated religion and politics—and an appeal to practices in connection with the question of how language is possible, or how semantic reference to the world is possible.

But there is a problem with this view of practices. In the first place, "practices" is not merely a gap-filling notion in its established uses. In the second place, it is difficult, and perhaps impossible, to consistently carry through a pure "gap-filling" conception of practices.[1] Such "practice" family terms as "tradition" have a meaning apart from these particular episodic uses, and it seems, in these cases, that there is a reasonable, autonomous question in social theory (and perhaps philosophy) as to what such things are, and indeed there are available theories or accounts of tradition, practices, and the like both in the traditions of philosophy and social theory, associated with such figures as Gadamer, Alasdair MacIntyre, and Michael Oakeshott. In each of these cases, the theory of practice or tradition distinguishes between tradition and practices and philosophy, but at the same time insists on the dependence of philosophy on tradition. Practice is thus in these cases something beyond philosophy that cannot be fully comprehended within it or replaced by it, and this implies that it is, so to speak, something substantive, something in the world and therefore governed in part by considerations of causation. Oakeshott points to one of these considerations when he argues that one of the identifying features of practices is the fact that practices must be learned. This amounts to an acknowledgment that practices are part of the natural world and that the causal processes of learning constrain our use of the term, even if practice cannot (as indeed it cannot, for Oakeshott) be reduced to these causal processes.

Oakeshott's account contrasts to Pickering's—for Pickering the assemblage of objects that makes up practice has no intellectual content—but not to Pickstone's, because Pickstone's extended conception includes skills. But Pickering's conception is unusual enough to leave aside for the moment as an interesting anomaly. Learning does seem to be a denominator common to the other available theories of practice, or a condition of what they take to define practices. Brandom's notion of accountability, for example, depends on learning something—how to recognize what sorts of things one is made accountable for by one's actions and what makes others accountable, and although Brandom does not problematize the problem of acquisition (and indeed, as we will see, has a major problem with it), the account he offers depends on the content being acquired, on something being learned or mastered, and these processes occur, indubitably, in the world of cause.

Oakeshott is the practice theorist who deals most fully with the philosophical issues here, so it is instructive to see how he proceeds. He recognizes that there is a terminology problem—that we identify and characterize practices from within the practices, through reflection. The language of description relevant to acquisition is the language of the psychology of learning. There is a gap between these languages, such that there is no way to precisely characterize practice in the language of psychology, or learning in the language of practice. Thus in our conception (or identification, as he puts it, carefully avoiding the traps of the language of conceptualism) of traditions or practices and in our application of these concepts "there is always a mystery about when it has been acquired." I will return to this later, but at the moment let me simply note the similarity between claims like this and the slogan of Michael Polanyi, "we know more than we can say" (1966a: 4). Practice theory ordinarily has proceeded by invoking the notion that there is something "non"—nonconceptual, nontheoretical, nonexplicit, or in the words of Gilbert Ryle, a kind of inarticulate "knowing how" rather than an articulate "knowing that," that lies outside, or beyond, the explicit.

One place where theories of practice divide is over the way of thinking about this "non" stuff. One approach is to conceive of it on the model of the articulable, the conscious, the intentional, the normative, and so on. The other is to deny that it can be usefully conceived in this way and to reject the analogizing implicit in the former approach, an analogizing that plays a large role in the history of the philosophy of science, in the form of such notions as framework, spectacles behind the eyes, and in contemporary philosophy in such forms as Brandom's language of commitment and scorekeeping as applied to the prelinguistic situation of the language learner. The difference between these approaches and its connection to relativism is the subject of what follows, although it is a connection that will not become clear until the end of the chapter.

WHERE DOES RELATIVISM COME IN?

The concept of framework is a good place to begin with the problem of understanding how the concept of practice becomes relativistic. The issue with conceptions of practice like Pickering's and Pickstone's is explanatory sufficiency. Do these conceptions enable us to explain what we want to explain? The usual complaint about these views of practice is that they do not. But there is a trick aspect to the question which is aggravated by a trick character in the notion of "explanation" as it applies to these cases. The problem can be put very simply. Pickering and Pickstone are concerned with more or less straightforward substantive biographical and historical facts. In Pickering's case, for example, the physicist Giacomo Morpugo's theoretical development and the expansion and standardization of operations research involve questions that ordinary historiography cannot adequately handle but which are in no sense questions that ordinary historians of science would not like to answer. The explanatory relations are typically also straightforward. The functional relations between parts of the ensemble do the explanatory work by specifying possible configurations and relations—asking what can be done with theodolites and pickaxes, for example. The explanatory objects of thinkers with richer practice conceptions are characteristically different and more abstract.

Rouse at one point in his recent book quotes Kuhn's comment that he intended not to explain scientific consensus but to explain how experiments enabled scientists to reach consensus (2002). This is a different kind of explanatory object—consensus and the conditions for the possibility of consensus are "facts" that are both abstract and collective. And there is a temptation to think that the explanations of these facts are similar in kind—collective and abstract. This is the same kind of thinking behind the idea of collective intentionality: Because norms are collective, it seems that a collective fact of some sort needs to do the explaining. Much of this literature is devoted to the problem of getting such an explanation within the limits of an ontological individualism (e.g., Searle 1995; Sellars 1963; Gilbert 1990, 1996). These kinds of collective-collective explanations contrast with a class of competing explanations in which the aggregate or collective facts are accounted for by invisible hand processes, or in which supposedly collective facts are shown not to be genuinely "collective" but merely to be aggregate-level descriptions of joint individual processes or facts.

Practice explanations can be either individual or collective. Michael Polanyi, who modeled his conception of knowledge as "per sonal knowledge" on the astronomer's "personal coefficient," had an individual conception. Science for him was an apostolic succession, in which masters trained successors; however, what the successors got was not the thing the master had, but the capacity to discover on their own, and in their own way. Discovery was individual. The process of ratification of discovery (on which he placed little stress) was public and in this sense collective, but it was only apparently so—what made science work was the interdependence of areas of science that checked one another rather than any moment in which "the scientific community" reached "consensus" which would have been a genuine collective fact.[2] For Polanyi, knowledge itself was "personal." Kuhn, to the extent that he can be considered a practice theorist, and paradigm as a practice concept, had a thoroughly collective picture of practices. Paradigms are "accepted examples of actual scientific practice which include law, theory, application and instrumentation together" (Kuhn [1962] 1996: 10), and their presence explained the collective capacity of scientists to come to agreement on the facts.

Sorting through the confusions over "paradigm" is not my purpose here but suffice it to say that Kuhn can be taken as giving a model collective-collective explanation, in which a collective fact about consensus is accounted for by a collective fact about paradigms. In this model the problem of ontological individualism is avoided by a device similar to one found in the collective intentionality literature, of treating the scientific community not as a mystical supraindividual entity which has such properties as a capacity for embodying a consensus but as a composite of individuals who "share" a paradigm and share scientific opinions. In *The Social Theory of Practices* (1994) I argued that this notion of sharing was, contrary to appearances, just as problematic as the notions of supraindividual entities it replaced, an argument I will not repeat here.[3]

Polanyi was a fallibilist and thought that issues in science could go without being settled for a long time, but that in fact they were eventually settled, although there was no principle that assured that they would be. He used the same examples as Karl Popper—Marxism and Freudianism—of circular and closed, and therefore nonscientific intellectual traditions ([1958] 1998: 288), and one suspects that if he were to have considered Kuhnian paradigms, which are circular and closed, he would have simply observed that there are often holdouts in science—people unpersuaded by the dominant theories—but that elevating this fact to claims about incommensurability and the irrationality of paradigm choice travestied the history of science. Polanyi didn't need a collective-collective explanation, because he could identify processes that produced, through various invisible hand processes, the appearance of consensus that corresponds to the historical actualities of science. But Polanyi was not, by his own lights, a relativist, and insisted on a notion of scientific truth as the goal of the tradition of science, while rejecting the idea that it could be a goal external to the tradition of science against which science could be judged.

Kuhn can be treated as a relativist. He denied that the way in which issues in science were actually settled, in conflicts between paradigms, was rational, precisely because what counted as a fact or as a good reason was paradigm relative, and the choice between paradigms could thus not be made on rational grounds. Paradigms function like ungroundable premises for arguments, and to choose between them was to accept an ungroundable premise. They function this way because, for Kuhn, scientific practice is theory-laden or paradigm-laden through and through. The effect of this reasoning is to place practice firmly inside the "theory" side of the theory/data divide. Relativism follows naturally from this step, because being theory-like means proceeding from premises or assumptions that cannot be grounded or, alternatively, tested, without circularity. The historical "fact" of alternatives implies that the alternatives cannot rationally be decided between, because the premises can't be grounded rationally, and thus must be a matter of choice or decision.

All this is familiar enough. What is more difficult is to identify the characteristic form of relativistic arguments in order to see how relativism arises as a problem. We can begin with the explanatory objects. The usual object is some sort of difference or diversity of viewpoints that cannot be accounted for in other ways. Needless to say, this "cannot be accounted for" is a problematic notion. Particular descriptions of differences may have the explanations of the differences built into them—thus a description of two groups of scientists having different paradigms, for example, de facto excludes any explanation of the differences that does not already appeal to the possession of paradigms. This dependence on description can be much more subtle, however. It is commonly thought that possessing a concept might be an object of explanation. But if this is treated as the object of explanation, and to the notion of possession of a concept we add some commonplace ideas about "concepts," the claim can be taken to imply something very elaborate. For example, if we say that concepts are normative, we find ourselves committed to the existence of a collective fact—normativity—which may seem to require an explanation with particular properties—for example, that it can account for the collective, normative character of concepts—and we will find ourselves forced to deal with the claim that normativity requires sharing and in particular sharing of the kind of collective intentionality that can produce normativity. Because a great many of the conventional descriptors of facts about science have these implications, at least in conjunction with standard claims in other areas of philosophy, taking these descriptions as having anything other than a provisional status narrows the range of possible alternative explanations. One response to this is to reject the descriptors and substitute others, as Pickering does, and as Quine did with respect to concepts by being "behaviorist," or to ignore them and style one's own problem in one's own terms, as Oakeshott and Polanyi did. The usual response to this is *tu quoque* arguments to the effect that one cannot avoid descriptions in terms of, for example, concepts and therefore normativity, an argument to which, again, I will return.

The problem of description is so closely bound up with the problem of explanation that "explanations" themselves may be little more than restatements of the descriptions. When Kuhn describes a particular historical situation in terms of the paradigms in conflict, for example, we appear to start out with normal historical facts—there is disagreement, generational conflict, and difference of opinion over key terms and over the significance of particular facts. But the evidence that establishes that there are paradigms, or that there is radical conceptual change, is the same as the evidence for the explanation. This raises the question of what it is to "account for" something in this model. The other forms of relativism with which I began—the *Überbau* model and racial relativism, for example, involve some sort of causal or at least constraint model of the relationship between base and superstructure. Here the relationship is something different, perhaps a kind of constitutive relationship.

The explanatory character of this relation is nevertheless quite puzzling. Elsewhere I have called these quasi-transcendental arguments, because they are generated from considerations of conditions of possibility. The conditionality, however, is largely definitional. Nevertheless, the argument is treated as though it has established a causal fact about the world. The peculiar character of this structure is obscured by the fact that the way in which paradigms, and for that matter practices, are usually understood, in these contexts, is generative, that is as an underlying source of many often disparate manifestations. Put differently, the explanation is one in which visible manifestations are understood to be the part or product of a constitutive whole which is not fully visible, but is nevertheless necessarily there. But the manifestations are themselves reconstructed into a unified fact, producing a kind of circularity. These should be grounds for questioning the claim that the thing—paradigm, practice, or culture—exists as a unified fact producing the manifestations at all.

Where this model turns relativistic can best be understood by seeing how it differs from the base-superstructure model. The base-superstructure model is relativistic because there is an external relativizing element in the explanation—class, race, and the like. The reason for the noncomparability of the manifestations is the noncomparability of the base. The typical resolution of the problem of relativism comes through a nonrelativistic ranking of the base—the worldview of the final class in history is thus the best view, or the view of the supreme race is the best view. How one can get a worldview-free ranking of these bases is a question that needs to be answered by other means, perhaps, but in these cases the question is blocked by the idea that race and class are second-order facts whose truth is determined in a different way than the facts that are manifested in the worldview. Even though the bourgeoisie might currently be incapable of recognizing their impending historical demise, once it happens, even they will recognize it; a master-race, similarly, is not merely a matter of race theory, it requires objective mastery.

In the case of paradigms and practices there is nothing external to rank because there is no external explainer. But there is, typically, some sort of relativizing element. To understand how this works it is perhaps simplest to start with an influential analogous case, Hans Kelsen's theory of law. Kelsen was an anti-naturalist who was concerned with the question of what makes law binding. There are, of course, different systems of law, binding on different people. So the question of the binding (or normative) character of law is a question of why *this* set of laws is binding on *these* people. Referring to the law itself—the law's own statements about its binding character—doesn't help with the question, because law cannot answer, without circularity or regress, the question of why these statements are themselves binding. Moreover, law in fact undergoes revolutionary change. Laws and systems of law cease to be binding, and new systems of law are proclaimed as binding, raising the question of what makes each of these divergent, successive, noncomparable legal systems binding.

Kelsen's general answer to this is to identify an element, which he calls the *Grundnorm*, which is simultaneously an answer to the question of what makes a legal system binding and an explanation of the distinctive binding character of the particular legal system. The notion thus has a normative role—it validates the system as law—and an explanatory one—it "accounts" for the binding character of the law, which is taken to be the explanatory object of legal theory. The *Grundnorm* is a theoretical object. Its existence—which more naturalistic legal theory denied—was claimed to result from a necessity—which naturalistic theories either failed to respond to or rejected—to explain the binding character of the law. The explanation was theoretical, because *Grundnormen* are theoretical entities not to be found or identified with actual laws. But they were by definition capable of being both justificatory and explanatory. Moreover, they have the power to produce normativity.[4] They are *Grund* because they are the final answer to the question of what makes law genuine law. They are of interest here because they also contain what I am calling relativizing elements: They "account" for the fact of difference in legal systems, something that was done naturalistically in the writings of the dominant figure in legal philosophy prior to Kelsen, Rudolph von Jhering, whose account of law in *Der Zweck im Recht* ([1877] 1968) was evolutionary and which Kelsen supplanted.

What is striking about this "explanation" is its peculiar combination of natural and normative. Rather than accounting for revolutionary change in the law "sociologically," it defines it in terms of change in the *Grundnorm*. But the idea that this hypothesized thing, the *Grundnorm*, "explains" is questionable. In the first place, there is no evidence for bindingness other than the fact of acceptance, the fact that people treat the law as binding. So the naturalistic part of the "fact" that naturalism about the law allegedly can't explain is nothing more than a fact made up and described in such a way that naturalism cannot "explain" it. Nothing new about ordinary historical facts is explained by the concept of a *Grundnorm*. It is strictly a concept necessitated in a quasi-transcendental way by the supposed normative fact of bindingness and the necessity to "account" for the multiplicity of binding legal systems. Even the claim that it "accounts" for bindingness is difficult to give much sense to: It accounts because it is asserted to account for it. There is no special evidence relative to this "accounting" and the relation is not causal (even though the *Grundnorm* would have to be a genuine historical fact with the consequence of producing bindingness) but constitutive. In this context, however, to say it is constitutive—constitutive of the bindingness of the law perhaps—is to say nothing, for the explanatory work here is being done not by some autonomously discoverable or reconstructable constitutive structure. The sole job of the *Grundnorm* is to bless the legal system as binding. So the grounds for thinking there is such a thing is the characterization of the problem of understanding the law as a problem of understanding "real" bindingness.

What one has, in short, is a concept with no empirical credentials, no explanatory value outside of this one role, which is accessible only through a kind of transcendental argument that cannot plausibly support a claim that it has causal significance, yet at the same time it has powerful consequences: It establishes or grounds claims to validity, and it does so on its own ground; i.e., it is not grounded in some further concept that tells one whether it is a valid conception of law, such as Natural Law theory attempted to provide, and it is arbitrary, thus producing relativism. It should also be noted that there is a mythical aspect to it. Of course, there is no actual historical phenomenon corresponding to creation of legality *ex nihilo*. There are revolutions, which establish accepted regimes, but acceptance is precisely the kind of "sociological" facticity that is claimed to be insufficient to "explain" legality as a normative phenomenon. Legality has to be retrospectively conferred on revolutionary regimes, in a process that has no empirical counterpart. It should be observed that there are parallels to this peculiar explanatory structure of norm-creating facts throughout the philosophical literature on normativity. For example, in the notion of collective intentionality in Sellars (1963) and Searle (1995), in H. L. A. Hart's oxymoronic surrogate for the *Grundnorm*, the notion of "authoritative reason" (cf. Postema 1987: 86), and I would argue, Brandom's use of (or as he would say, helping himself to) the prelinguistic notion of commitments as an explanation of the normativity of rules (1994). Hart's account, described here by Postema, is this:

> The key to explaining the distinctive normativity of law, while preserving the conceptual separation of law and morality, Hart now insists, lies in recognizing a special kind of normative attitude characteristic of self-identified participants in legal practices, namely the standing recognition of, or willingness to regard, certain events or states of affairs as constituting "peremptory" and "content-independent" reasons for action. Where such an attitude is widely adopted, the occurrence of events will have not only natural but normative consequences—certain actions will be made right or obligatory, others wrong or offences, by those events. (Postema 1987: 86)

How does an attitude, which is a psychological fact, make an event have normative consequences as well as causal consequences? Adding adjectival qualifiers like "normative" or "legal" to one's description of the attitude doesn't help either. The only fact here is sociological.

The constitutive version of the concept of paradigm has the same problems. The grounding nature of paradigms purportedly establishes forms of validation. What it explains is the "validity," internal to paradigms, as well as "reality" as it appears internally within paradigms. Whether Kuhn says this or not, it is a plausible extension of what Kuhn does say. The provision of an "account" of validity is what distinguishes Kuhn from a sociology of science, which would presumably limit itself to explaining acceptance, i.e., to explaining what scientists believe, or their attitudes. Sociologists would do so in terms of their beliefs about validity or attitudes rather than validity itself. Kuhn, however, tells us what validity in science is and can be, just as Kelsen tells us what legality is and can be. The fictional character of "grounding" in Kelsen—"fictional" because there is no act of grounding—is hidden by Kuhn in the fictive descriptions of radical change in conceptual schemes in science. Transcendental necessity results from narrative necessity: Because there needs to be something to ground validity and the something must change, it must historically be the case that they do change in this way. One can give many other examples of this kind of fictionalizing in other cases of relativism, such as Margaret Mead's cultural relativist image of cultures selecting their values from the bin of possible human values (1928: 13). This fiction serves the same purpose—to make the moment of arbitrariness in decision seem both plausible and necessary to understanding. But there is no empirical reason to accept these descriptions as the sole adequate descriptions, and thus no necessity to the conclusion.

Kuhn is not as explicit as Kelsen in identifying the added element that makes a paradigm into a relativizing machine, but the material he works with is different. Kelsen had explicit law, which was insufficient on its own to account for its own lawfulness. Kuhn had textbook science, which was insufficient on its own to account for its own history. "Paradigm" was a way of talking about the added element which simultaneously "accounted" for the relevant features of science, namely its conceptual diversity in history, and confirmed the relativistic character of this diversity. But it was a concept that, unlike *Grundnormen*, did more than simply add a normative element. Instead, it hid the normativizing element among the many meanings of "paradigm" (if indeed it is there). Arguably, this was at the cost of coherence, as Margaret Masterman's classic dissection of the multiplicity of meanings of the term showed (1970; cf. Kuhn 1977: 294–95).

THE THEORY/DATA DISTINCTION

Perhaps a small historical point is in order here. Kuhn cribbed most of the ideas of *Structure* from his mentor, James Bryant Conant, who was himself a promoter of the Harvard commonplace of the importance of "conceptual schemes," which outlived their usefulness and were discarded, and of the idea of radical conceptual change as a recurrent phenomenon in the history of science. But with respect to certain crucial issues, Kuhn and Conant diverged, and these issues happen to be relevant here. Conant thought of the theory-empirical relation as a continuum and thought that scientific theories or the state of scientific knowledge in a given field could be theoretical to a greater or lesser degree. He identified progress with reducing the empirical elements—the more theoretical, the better the knowledge.

Linnean botany, for example, is observational and empirical, but not very theoretical. Advance in this science would come, if it could come, in the form of making it more theoretical. He also thought that science was continuous with common sense and in this respect nonautonomous. This meant that he denied the "local holism" of Kuhn's concept of paradigm, which he disliked. But as it happens he denied it in a specific way that relates to practice.

Conant argued, consistent with this version of the theory-empirical continuum, that even in the course of radical conceptual change in science, there was considerable continuity in instrumentation and observations. In the sense of practice with which we began, there was thus no "radical change" with respect to large elements of practice and with respect to those parts of science toward the empirical end of the continuum. Kuhn's revision of this idea incorporated these elements of practice into his holistic account, a move that begins with his discussion of thermometry, in which he argues that the historical path to measurement, in this case and generally, is through theory. The point was clear: What Conant thought was largely empirical was completely theory-laden. A Bunsen burner was not an inert element of science that formed a condition of scientific activity, but a live part of a paradigmatic scheme of interpretation, subject to the same radical transformation as the rest of the paradigm.

Of course the issue is not merely historical, because the intuition behind this, namely that the bench scientist is doing something that is more or less autonomous from theory and corrects theory, is the same intuition that Ian Hacking played on in *Representing and Intervening* (1983) that ended the romance with theory-ladenness of the 1960s and 1970s that culminated in Fred Suppe's collection (1974), in which the theory-observation distinction was buried unmourned.

What is striking about the extension of "theory-ladenness" to practice is the extent to which this model appears more and more as an imposition on material that cannot be understood in this way. There is no moment of decision in relation to practices analogous to the moment of theory-choice. Pickaxes are theory-laden only in the most wildly extended sense. The situation of decision that is central to the relativistic interpretation is largely virtual rather than real—the more common case is extended discussion that eventually leads to a resolution. Kuhn's real achievement, in a sense, was to make the conflict between new theories and old theories exceptionally vivid, so that it seemed as though there were numerous cases in which scientific truth was up for grabs between mutually antagonistic and mutually uncomprehending sides. But this was an achievement of historiographic dramatics—not for nothing was it made into a novel, complete with a suicide (Russell McCormmach, *Night Thoughts of a Classical Physicist*, 1983). Even the cases on which it was based, in the didactic case studies of radical changes in conceptual schemes that Conant had created for the use of his undergraduate general education curriculum, were far less "irrational" and decisionistic. The historiographic appearance was the result of assimilating these cases to "theory-ladenness" and telling the stories in these terms rather than the cases themselves.

What the concept of practice returns us to is the mundane—the scientists who have mastered particular techniques to the point that they can get good results with them and are in demand for their skills and their capacity to pass the skills onto others. The standard examples in the science studies literature, such as Harry Collins' study of replicating the TEA laser (1985), are concerned to show how difficult it is to do certain kinds of things in science out of the book, i.e., with explicit instructions alone. In this case, some people couldn't replicate the TEA laser even with a lot of help, and those who could required continuous interaction and contact over a long period of time. The point was to show that replication was not and could not be understood as a mechanical process of taking public documents in science as sufficient for understanding a crucial process in science. The process, confirmation, is often thought to be free of the problems of accounting for discovery. Collins shows that it too depends on tacit knowledge. This kind of case is very far from the situations Kuhn describes. One can perhaps imagine that scientists trying to make a laser work are in some sense in a similar cognitive state to the scientists in a Kuhnian revolution, incapable of getting their bearing and of determining to their own satisfaction what is going on. But the solution—contact and interaction—is not the Kuhnian one of commitment and decision. Indeed there is no role for decision, virtual or otherwise, in these cases of tacit knowledge. It is more plausible to think that this kind of "practice" is fundamentally different in character from, even though curiously entwined with, the explicit, theoretical, conceptual parts of science.

If we accept, as a hypothesis, that practice in this "skills" sense might be unassimilable to the "theory" side of the divide, we are faced with a question. If the relativism that results from the Kuhnian interpretation of practice is the product of notions of nonrational decision and commitment built into the narrative structure of radical conceptual change, and practice in this sense cannot be assimilated to the theoretical, or more broadly the conceptual, is this sense of practice afflicted with the problem of relativism?

To assure that we are not merely being caught up in verbal distinctions here, it is perhaps useful to clarify what is at stake. In using the notion of theory-ladenness I was self-consciously invoking a dead vocabulary of the 1950s. But along the way I have suggested that the same problem appears under a variety of live vocabularies dealing with the classic dualisms: nature-normativity, reason and experience, with the dualism implied by the Sellarsian notion of the space of reasons, and more generally by conceptualism and the Kantian question of whether the mind infuses concepts into objects. The problem then is whether relativism arises from putting practice on one side or another of the relevant dualism.

The reasoning that places practices on the concept side goes like this: Concepts are normative in the sense of normativity that includes validity and so forth, and practices are theory-laden, meaning conceptual; therefore practices are normative in this validity-involving sense. If the normativizing element is, as in the examples I have discussed earlier, relativizing, practices is a relativizing notion, and practice relativism follows. Practices become the relativizing constitutive base, to use the Marxist locution, which is manifested in the superstructural elements of scientific fact, theory, and validity. Practices are relativizing with respect to validity because they enable validity to be established with different results in the different systems of practices based on them: What is valid in one legal system or paradigm may be invalid in another, and this is because the normative, validating element varies between them.

The general form of the problem of relativism here thus goes beyond practice. The idea is simply that the sources of normativity, namely normative attitudes, collective intentions, commitments, and so forth, vary. The Kantian story is nonrelativist. Considerations of validity apply to every intelligent being. But Kant could claim this by claiming that there is only one source of normativity. As soon as we acknowledge historical diversity with respect to fundamental constitutive presuppositions—the acknowledgment that is the gift of neo-Kantianism—we have relativism. And one can read the history of philosophy after neo-Kantianism, and indeed within neo-Kantianism, as a long series of attempted escapes from this problematic, escapes which nevertheless accepted the core picture of the production of facts through fundamental, constitutive concepts.

What happens if one dispenses with the notion that practices are conceptual, that they belong on the theory side of the dualism in question? What are the costs of doing so, or rather what about our theories of practice, validity, and so forth needs to be revised? And what are the benefits with respect to relativism? Dispensing with the relativizing elements—commitment, collective intention, normative attitudes—makes a large difference. As I suggested at the outset, differences that can be explained by reference to the data side of the theory/data distinction don't have the relativizing implications that follow from differences at the level of fundamental theoretical premises. This holds, of course, for the remaining dualisms. But the cost of dispensing with the notion that practices are, in some sense, conceptual seems high. Diversity still needs to be explained. Worse, the explanation of diversity in terms of data seems to be doomed by the problem of sufficiency. There is something more than data, or more than pickaxes, that is needed to account for the specific conditions of particular theoretical stances or subjectivities. The differences pointed to by the notion of paradigm, even if they are not to be accounted for by the notion of paradigm, still need to be explained. And it is difficult to see how there could be an account of subjective diversity that does not have its source in the subjective in notions of commitment and the like.

The problem, in a word, is content. A concept of practice sufficient for a reasonably wide range of explanatory uses must be one which allows for sufficient content to perform these tasks. The dilemma is that the best and perhaps only source of content is from the conceptual side of the dualism. The most decisive argument against a nonconceptual notion of practice would be a denial of the possibility of nonconceptual content. If by content we mean something that can be a reason for, and "reasons for" are already in the normative "space of reasons," it seems that the denial follows from the dualism: Even if there is something mental that is not conceptual, it is not "content" and not admissible in an account of practices as part of the activity of providing "reasons for" that science consists in.

There are, however, many "ifs" in this reasoning. There is also a long tradition in which different descriptions are employed, many of which evade the dualisms in question. The conceptualist description of practices, as I have suggested, is questionable. Harry Collins' examples of the problem of laser building and Michael Polanyi's example of bicycle riding as a model for the tacit knowledge needed for scientific discovery foreground cases that conceptualism can handle only by defining them as conceptual, or if conceptualism is made into a necessary truth about content that excludes the possibility of nonconceptual content. If we accept the possibility that skills, discernment in, and "senses of" such things as balance in riding a bicycle are nonconceptual, but also contentful, in that the capacities are learned or the product of learning joined with innate capacities, we have quite a different situation, in which the problem of sufficiency is potentially soluble without relativism.

It is striking that the literature on nonconceptual content, which is not motivated by examples in science, employs the same kinds of standard cases. Adrian Cuzzins gives the example of riding a motorcycle in London, being stopped by a policeman, and being asked "do you know how fast that you were traveling?" His comment is that this struck him as a deep philosophical puzzle. He did not know in the sense of knowing what the speedometer said, but he had to "know" in the sense of being able to gauge the traffic as a condition "of wiggling through and around heavy traffic and past the road dividers and traffic bollards of a London street" (1990: 156). This knowledge is different in kind.

> In the case of a novice who has to *infer* the significance-for-motorcycling of their speedometer-given speed, the characteristic functionality of conceptual knowledge interferes with the characteristic functionality of experiential knowledge. The interference can also go in the other direction. The great advantage of experiential content is that its links to action are direct, and do not need to be mediated by time-consuming—and activity-distancing—inferential work; work which may at any point be subject to skeptical challenge. Experiential knowledge

> of the kind possessed by the skilled motorcyclist may be subject to *resistance*, but not to skeptical challenge. (1990: 151)

He goes on to say that this virtue is at the same time a cognitive vice. This content is situation-specific and private, that is, it is *my* sense, so that it "cannot by itself provide what we have come to regard as the constitutive requirements on *thought* content: generality, objectivity, standardization, transportability of knowledge from one embodied and environmentally specific situation to another" (1990: 151). Cuzzins suggests that there is a nonconceptual special kind of "mundane normativity" at stake in the content, unlike that of truth and validity, which he calls "activity guidance" (1990: 159) and associates with skill and mastery.

From one point of view, this is a dead end—this kind of practical normativity, if indeed it is normativity at all, does not help with truth and validity. But several points need to be kept in mind before we give up. If my complaints about the pseudo-explanatory use of commitment, collective intentionality, and the like by conceptualism are correct, there is no viable alternative to reconsidering this apparent dead end. And there are several pressing considerations that support doing so. There is the issue of dispensability: Every serious account of legal practice acknowledges that the rules of legal construction together with written law are insufficient to produce the determinate legal outcomes that the law requires, and traditionally there has been an appeal to the notion of "judicial sense" to fill this gap; science too is through and through a skilled activity that involves knowing more than we can say, as Polanyi puts it; and in the core of semantics is the problem of rule-following, which has resisted reduction, Kripkean and otherwise, but which even in the hands of Wittgenstein needed to be supplemented by such things as "primitive reactions" (cf. Rubinstein 2004) and, it is plausible to argue, something akin to the "judicial sense" in order to account for the capacity of the rule follower to go on in a way that made sense to others. Nor is this absent from science—the "in the gut" test plays a large and, if Polanyi is correct, a necessary role in such tasks as assigning plausibilities to hypotheses and observations, a task which is itself necessary to science as it is actually practiced.

The indispensability of skills raises the question of the relation between the overt, the behavioral and explicit, and the nonconceptual. If there is such a thing as nonconceptual content, and "concepts" are theoretical constructions with explanatory purposes in the natural world or in the explanation of mind rather than Platonic entities apprehended through some sort of mystical process of participation, there is the hard question of whether nonconceptual content might do all the explanatory work that concepts were thought to do, or that concepts might be better understood in terms of the nonconceptual content that conditions performances that we interpret as "conceptual." As Robert Stalnaker puts it,

> John McDowell argued [. . .] that both kinds of information states [the contents of speech acts and contents akin to experience] are of the same kind and that content is conceptual all the way down. I am inclined to agree with McDowell that the different kinds of states have the same kind of content, but I am suggesting it is non-conceptual all the way up. (Stalnaker [1998] 2003: 106)

This point can be put in terms of practice theory in the following way. There is a huge mass of habitual inference that precedes speech, which is not articulated in speech, but that enables people to speak about the same things. Carnap wrote that the evaluation of observations "is usually carried out as a matter of habit than a deliberate, rational procedure" and said that the task of rational reconstruction was "to lay down explicit rules for the evaluation" (Carnap 1992: 73). Reading back "concepts" into this mass of habit has been a strategy of Kantians since Kant himself. But is there an explanatory necessity for doing so? It may be outside of the artificial explanatory context of a certain kind of philosophical semantics, there is no such necessity. Then the explanatory burden shifts: The problem becomes one of establishing that the problems that conceptualism solves are not artificial. I suspect that they are.

For the study of science itself, matters are even more easily resolved. The explanatory objects we choose need not involve these theories. We can explain something like the rough kind of consensus on the facts of science that leads to textbook science, for example, as distinguished from the idealized picture of a perfect consensus based on shared cognitive frameworks presented by Kuhn, by the fact that *explicit* agreement is reached by people who have attained recognized skills in laboratory work and in reasoning about science. We can say that without a convergence of skillful activity there is no science or law. If this convergence, together with other unproblematic, nonrelativizing explanations, is sufficient to establish such validity as we have in science—if it accounts for a suitably deflated notion of scientific truth, for example sufficiently accounts for such thing as successful replication, it is perhaps sufficiency enough. And if it is sufficient to account for the actual contingencies of scientific activity without involving appealing to relativizers, such as the notion of paradigm, we have the best of both worlds: a historically adequate model without relativism.

6 Naturalizing the *Habitus*

Mirror Neurons and Practices: A Response to Lizardo

Omar Lizardo has performed a useful service by opening up a question that deserves discussion, the relation of social theory to cognitive science in a category of inquiry that deserves to be enormously expanded, as I have argued elsewhere (Turner 2007a,b&e [chap. 4 in this volume]). Lizardo, however, is wrong about mirror neurons and about what they imply for Bourdieu, and misleading about the implications of the contents of *The Social Theory of Practices* (1994) and my other writings in this area. Mirror neurons, to the extent that they figure in an explanation of the surface or external similarities between people engaged in a "practice," actually undermine Bourdieu's account, by providing an alternative to the mechanism his account requires. Mirror neurons, however, fit very nicely into the account given in *The Social Theory of Practices*, which, like the mirror neuron literature, focuses on emulation (Tomasello and Carpenter 2005), and also fit with my later discussion of the implications of the simulation approach to the problem of knowledge of other minds, "Imitation or the Internalization of Norms" (2000, 2002: 58–73).

Lizardo is forced to deny the obvious affinities between *The Social Theory of Practices* and this literature in his paper, and to pretend that it has something to do with Bourdieu. The mountain he needs to climb is a high one: More than a tenth of the pages in the book are indexed to the concept of emulation and it is explicitly endorsed as a mechanism that can do the work of transmission of practices. In later work, emulation continues to be mentioned, and simulation is discussed directly in a substantial paper (Turner 2000, 2002: 58–73). In contrast, the terms and their like are not, as far as I know, to be found in Bourdieu. Lizardo, in any event, fails to cite a single instance of their use and endorses the conflicting language of "socialization." So he must find a way to discern concepts alien to Bourdieu in Bourdieu's texts and to represent *The Social Theory of Practices* in a way that ignores a large part of its content. Arguing about Lizardo's interpretation of this will not be my concern here. However, the discussion represents an opportunity to clarify some issues that are important and have not been addressed in terms of social theory, and should be.

The absence of social theory from the cognitive revolution is a topic of its own. It is an unfortunate historical accident that postmodernism, which operates with an underlying neo-Kantian conception of mind that serves as a surrogate for a concept of mind that is engaged with neuroscience, flourished at the same time that cognitive science emerged as a field. The result was a mutual lack of engagement that has disserved both. The last time that social theory was seriously engaged with the topic of the physical brain and its psychological implications was a century ago, and there is a sense in which we are now simply resuming the conversation where it left off (cf. Turner 2007b: 364–66). As it happens, the place it left off is directly relevant to Lizardo's claims about Bourdieu and about my book *The Social Theory of Practices*. So I will begin with a short historical excursus.

The earliest uses of the term "social psychology" were by Gabriel Tarde and Charles Ellwood. The term was explicitly understood at the time to contrast to the notion of "collective psychology" or in its German form *Volkerpsychologie*. Ellwood's "Prolegomena" (1899), the first serious overview of the field, was promptly denounced in Durkheim's *Année Sociologique* with the comment that he should have instead concerned himself with "collective psychology," which was the preferred Durkheimian notion (Durkheim 1900; cf. Nandan 1980: 63, 65–66). The difference was far more than a matter of semantics. Durkheim thought there was something collective that was real, causal, and produced and interacted with individual psychological facts, such as dispositions. Ellwood, agreeing with Tarde in this respect, but facing the issues in a different way,[1] considered collective usages to be metaphorical, nonexplanatory, and unnecessary to explain social life.

The issue with Bourdieu is a variation, and not a large variation, on this core issue. Bourdieu, to simplify only slightly, adheres to a form of collective psychology. For him, individual dispositions and strategies have, to a significant extent, a collective source, which is itself dispositional and strategic. This is a fancy dress form of the idea of "group will," already present in Ludwig Gumplowicz in 1883, who "depicted individual values as mere reflexes of social milieu; ethics were the code of the hegemonic classes, and the heroes of history were 'only the marionettes who carry out the will of the group'" (quoted in Crook 1994: 32). Bourdieu is more elaborate in his formulations of this core idea, and in particular allows more scope for human agency, but the logical structure of the argument is the same. It involves a dualism between the collective and the individual:

> Social reality exists, so to speak, twice, in things and in minds, in fields and in *habitus*, outside and inside of agents, and when *habitus* encounters a social world of which it is a product, it finds itself "as fish in water," it does not feel the weight of the water and takes the world about itself for granted. . . . The structuring affinity of *habituses* belonging to the same class is capable of generating practices that are convergent

> and objectively orchestrated outside of any collective "conspiracy" or consciousness. In this fashion it explains many of those phenomena of quasi-teleology which can be observed in the social world. (Bourdieu in Wacquant 1996: 216)

In short, the structuring affinity of *habituses* generates practices that produce a quasi-teleology that has the effects of a conspiracy or of collective consciousness, without being either of these things, and which have a reality both outside and inside of agents to which the agent responds as fish to water, taking it for granted and thus being controlled by it. It is thus the surrogate for the group will, which does the same thing, namely to pursue ends, for example the end of the continuing domination of a class, by directing individual behavior, through *habitus*, to produce the ends. In this respect Bourdieu is "sociological" in a familiar, functionalist sense.

In *The Social Theory of Practices*, which was not directly concerned with Bourdieu but with a form of reasoning about collective objects (1994: 100–16), I distinguished two versions of the idea that there was some sort of collective source of individual mental contents. One involved the idea of shared presuppositions (and its endless variations, such as Fleck's idea of a *Denkgemeinschaft*). The other involved embodied knowledge, skills, tacit knowledge, and the like. In a later response to my Bourdieuvian critics (especially Gross 1998), I constructed a simple 2 × 2 classification of ideas about the tacit, in which I contrasted individual and social (in the sense of collective) forms of the two families of ideas: the skills family and the presuppositions family (2002: 9).

My argument was not against the tacit as such, but against the collective forms of the idea. Skills and cognitive machinery (such as what I unfortunately called, using the language of Dewey and Hume, "habits") that were *not* collective were not only accepted as a necessary part of the explanation of the sorts of things that collective objects were held to explain, they were sufficient for the purpose, if the explanatory purpose was properly understood. Thus notions like tradition did not go to the bone yard, but could be salvaged by reinterpreting them as something other than the ontologized units I called "collective objects."

The argument itself concerned what I called "transmission." The problematic feature of all "collective object" conceptions was that they required some sort of means of getting from the collective object into the individual that preserved the sameness or unitary identity of the collective object—of what, as Bourdieu says, is taken for granted. To share a presupposition, for example, is to share the same presupposition. But what means of acquiring a presupposition guarantees sameness? There is none, I argued. We might have the same external results, such as a belief in God, but arrived at it on the basis of different "presuppositions." As with the underdetermination of theory by data, where the data cannot guarantee a unique result, the transcendental arguments used in these contexts also could not guarantee a unique result. In the case of tacit knowledge, people get different data, so their individual tacit stuff was not going to be the same anyway, at least in its fine details. Learning history matters, at the cognitive level, because something learned in one way or in one order can produce the same overt behavior as something learned in another way. But this difference does not mean that people cannot communicate, interact, and so forth.

The implications of this argument for social theory were identical to those of Ellwood's social psychology a century ago. As Ellwood put it, "as individual psychology teaches, no two psychical coordinations [a Dewey-Mead term from the 1890s] can ever be exactly alike" (1899: 663). The message here is very clear. What we acquire through interaction with others is subject to the individual variation in response that occurs in interaction. This is a social conception without being a collective one. The "social," for Ellwood, refers to the social process of interaction itself (1901: 741), not to a special realm or substance, such as the "water" to which Bourdieu refers.

Ellwood was a great user of "inter" terms, including not only "interaction," but "intercerebral" and "interlearning," among others, to characterize the social process. The resemblance to symbolic interactionism is not accidental. Ellwood was the teacher of Blumer. The difference between these terms and Bourdieu's language can be seen in the term "intersubjective agreement," which is commonly used as an alternative to notions of "objectivity." Intersubjective agreement is functional coordination, to use the Dewey-Mead term, between individual subjectivities. It does the explanatory work that appeals to objectivity do without committing us to the metaphysical implications of the language of objectivity. Applied to practice, these "social process" and "inter" conceptions mean that practices can be no more than that which is sustained through interaction subject to individual variation, and thus practices are not facts outside of individual minds.

For collective object thinkers, something unitary—the group will or its analogue (in Bourdieu's case practices which are quasi-teleological)—needs to be shared between members of the group (the water in which the fish swim) in order to explain something that is manifested in individual action, feeling, and thinking. And there is a conflict between the idea of a shared, unitary, same thing and the psychological reality of individual variation in the transmission of content between individuals. Bourdieu, with his dualism of individual fish and collective water, is a paradigmatic collective object thinker, despite his many evasive comments about whether the reality in question is subjective or objective. So *The Social Theory of Practices* could be read, correctly, as a text against Bourdieu.

BOURDIEU'S COLLECTIVISM

Bourdieu's main argument has two parts: that practices are a collective, dispositional, and strategic source of individual *habitus*, which are in turn the source of individual dispositions and strategies. The causal relation is bidirectional: up from the individual through affinities of *habituses* to the practice and down from the practice to the individual. To be quasi-teleological, the collective part needs to have some sort of feedback mechanism, as Elster pointed out, from the world to the collective thing, presumably via the individuals (1983: 70). This is a crucial problem for Bourdieu's (much criticized) larger social theoretical claims, because he wants to account for practices as part of the struggle to reproduce power and domination, that is to say the strategic properties of classes, among other groupings. This might be called the uploading problem. *The Social Theory of Practices* was concerned, as Lizardo says (2007: 324–25), with the problem I called "downloading": the problem of how something collective gets into individual heads (which is also to say bodies) to produce individual actions. There has to be such a process for Bourdieu, for the simple reason that the quasi-teleology doesn't work without it. Actions are the actions of individuals carrying out the quasi-ends and must be informed in some manner by the quasi-teleology, which is a collective fact.

Why is this such an important issue? Begin with the relation between these collective things, with their strategies for the reproduction of distinction, domination, and so forth—Bourdieu's surrogate for the idea of the class determination of consciousness. Here the problem I referred to as the downloading problem is simple: How does the consciousness of the class itself get into the heads of the individual members of the class? How does something collective get into the heads of individuals, and in such a way that the things in the individuals were in some sense the same? No one, including Lizardo, claims that the discovery of mirror neurons relates to this problem. Mirror neurons are means by which individuals relate their mental contents to those of other individuals. They have to do with individual-individual relations, not collective-individual relations.

So with respect to the crucial issue that *The Social Theory of Practices* raised with Bourdieu, mirror neurons are irrelevant. Mirror neurons might be considered to help with the problem of convergences of *habituses*, or what I called "sameness." They have nothing to do with the crucial claim that practices are themselves strategic or quasi-teleological. Lizardo implicitly concedes this, or at least does not attempt to defend anything beyond convergence produced through individuals imitating other individuals. But when one considers the point of the whole Bourdieu enterprise, which is to provide a surrogate for the Marxian theory of the *Überbau* by replacing the base-superstructure distinction with the field/*habitus* distinction, saving the convergence of *habitus* part for Bourdieu is like a Marxist saving the superstructure part of Marxism. Explaining social life by reference to superstructural elements is just explaining in terms of commonly held ideas and institutions. There is no room for the Marxian teleology in such explanations: Ideas develop and change for reasons other than some underlying cause. Practice explanations that refer only to the supposed commonality, sharedness, or sameness of practices, similarly do not help with quasi-teleologies. There is no room for Bourdieu's quasi-teleology of the reproduction of domination (which is only "quasi," presumably, because Bourdieu has abandoned the full teleology of the Marxian conception of history). Acknowledging this amounts to narrowing the difference between us to an issue that is, from the point of view of "grand narrative" social theory, negligible and without interest: sameness as such.

CHANGING THE SUBJECT: WHAT CONCEPTION OF PRACTICES ARE WE CONSIDERING?

Lizardo argues that the discovery of mirror neurons shows that my objections to sameness or sharing were wrong (2007: 320, 323–24) and that the discovery vindicates Bourdieu against my critique. A few things need to be made clear about this argument. As we have seen, sameness is an implicit but necessary claim for Bourdieu, necessary because of the role it plays in linking levels. He does not need to say that individual *habituses* are in fact identical, just that there is some core or underlying disposition producing overt behavior that is shared, because he needs this shared thing to have the quasi-teleological force that distinguishes domination from stratification that results from the aggregation of individual choices, talents, and dispositions. So there is something of a mystery about what it is exactly that is shared, just as there is a mystery about what *habituses* are. Lizardo doesn't solve any of these mysteries, and his claims about them and about Bourdieu himself, as we will see, are contradictory. But he nevertheless claims that mirror neurons are a mode of transmission that allows for the transmission of dispositions and other embodied content in the sense that Bourdieu's account requires. What mirror neurons do, Lizardo thinks, is to provide direct access to and to reproduce, in the mind, the embodied dispositions of others, in such a way as to guarantee sameness of content, and that this sameness extends to such things as concepts.

In contrast, I think the mirror neuron literature is crystal clear: that mirror neurons facilitate learning, but are part of the processes of learning in which the individualized history of learning is relevant and variation in individual mental content occurs normally. So the significance of mirror neurons is that they are just another nail in the coffin of Bourdieu's conception of practices, because they provide a mechanism that supplements and makes more powerful the processes of social learning, which I argued were already sufficient to account for practices. Collectivist practice theory has always traded on the surface or external consistency of action in groups and claimed that only collective object or collective psychology explanations can account for them. I argued that this claim required downloading from a collective object—a form of transmission that is cognitively implausible.

Here is the conflict: I say learning histories are relevant and individualized; Lizardo says they are not and that mirror neurons allow the transfer of content of the kind that practice theory has traditionally been concerned with—an important qualification—unmediated by learning history. This is a genuine disagreement which is worth discussing. There are, however, some other issues which need to be clarified before considering this one. Lizardo also thinks that we have a disagreement about the role of explicit teaching. I think this is based on a misrepresentation of my claims and ungrounded in anything I have written, so I will deal with it only in passing. I would prefer to minimize quibbling discussions of the texts—readers can trace his few direct citations for themselves.[2] Lizardo has a point of greater potential scholarly interest, when he argues that *The Social Theory of Practices* criticizes the wrong kind of practice theory: the presuppositional rather than the embodied kind. This is a more serious misunderstanding. Lizardo says, "Practice theory is not synonymous—*contra* Turner—with explanations of action by way of 'paradigms' and hidden frameworks, as long as these last are still conceptualized on the older 'cognitivist' language of classical social theory [i.e., Durkheim [1912] 1995: 214]" (Lizardo 2007: 347n1).[3] Lizardo then suggests that because Bourdieu has an embodied rather than a cognitivist conception of practices he is freed from my criticism of "shared premises" explanations.

The Social Theory of Practices deals both with "premises" and "*habitus*" reasoning, and makes constant reference to skills and other embodied "knowledge" while making clear that the use of the term "knowledge" here is metaphorical and problematic. Moreover, the book argues for an "embodied," causal explanation of practices. Habits are embodied and causal in character. This is a point that has been central to the philosophical critics of the book, who have repeatedly objected to precisely this feature of the argument, on the grounds that practices is a normative rather than a casual concept (Rouse 2002, 2007; cf. Brandom 1994). My responses to this argument have formed most of my subsequent writing on the topic of practices (1998a [included in 2002: 118–44], 2003a [chap. 7 in this volume], 2005a, 2007c [chap. 5 in this volume], 2007d).

Bourdieu, however, is another matter. Does he even have an embodied conception of practices? Consider his classic statement of the nature of practices in *Outline of a Theory of Practice*:

> The language of rules and models, which seems tolerable when applied to "alien" practices, ceases to convince as soon as one considers the practical mastery of the symbolism of social interaction—tact, dexterity, or *savoir-faire*—presupposed by the most everyday games of sociability and accompanied by the application of a spontaneous semiology, i.e. a mass of precepts, formulae, and codified cues. This practical knowledge, based on the continuous decoding of the perceived—but not consciously noticed—indices of the welcome given to actions already accomplished, continuously carries out the checks and corrections intended to ensure the adjustment of practices and expressions to the reactions and expectations of the other agents. It functions like a self-regulating device programmed to redefine courses of action in accordance with information received on the reception of information transmitted and on the effects produced by that information. (1977: 10–11)

This is quite a mouthful and explains why I didn't bother to discuss Bourdieu directly in *The Social Theory of Practices*. There is far too much going on here to produce a coherent notion of practice. But it should be evident that there is plenty of cognitive language here—"information," "decoding," "precepts," "formulae," "codified cues," and of course "games." So Bourdieu does not have a consistently "embodied" noncognitive conception of practices, restricted to "bodily automatisms" as Lizardo implies (2007: 337). Nor does he abjure the idea of rules—games have rules (2007: 344).

The very luxuriance of this list causes problems for Bourdieu with respect to transmission. For a "mass of precepts, formulae, and codified cues" to be the same in multiple heads, one would need a mechanism by which this sort of thing is reproduced exactly in these various heads. For the things in each *habitus* enabling codified cues to be continuously decoded in the same way one would have to have the equivalent of identical secret decoder rings in the brain. And these secret decoder rings would have to be specific to the practice, shared by everyone who engages in the practice, and part of its transmission, not a generalized brain capacity. This is why I called this "downloading." The only analogue I could think of to getting all this rule and rule-like material in the same way from one (collective) source to many individuals is the downloading of computer programs from a common source.

What does Lizardo do in the face of the long list of things Bourdieu puts under the heading of *habitus*? He changes the subject. He never says exactly what is left in and what is left out. He seems to want to limit it to bodily automatisms plus the concepts that arise in connection with them. This is no longer the original Bourdieu, but this switch is crucial to Lizardo's argument. His defense of Bourdieu consists of throwing a large and unspecified part of the cargo overboard. First, as we have seen, the basic point of Bourdieu's whole project, the quasi-teleological character of practices as machines of domination, gets tossed. Now the bulk of Bourdieu's notion of practices goes with it. So we are no longer looking at a defense of Bourdieu. We are looking at a defense of something quite different and possibly much more limited—limited to the sorts of things that can be transmitted with the aid of the mechanism of mirror neurons. Ironically, this quite different and much more limited thing turns out to look a lot like the alternative, "habits," picture of practices developed in *The Social Theory of Practices*, because it also, and more consistently, dispenses with cognitive language. The remaining difference is over "sameness."

SAMENESS

Lizardo argues, correctly, that my issue with the standard collective object accounts rests on the problem of sameness of mental content, that I would have no objection to a mechanism that went from one person to another, and that my objection to the sameness claim was that all the supposed mechanisms for assuring sameness were implausible. He then provides what he takes to be a mechanism that avoids all my criticisms. The mechanism, he says, possesses "precisely the neuro-cognitive capacity that according to Turner (1994) belonged in the realm of high speculation and/or logical impossibility and incoherence" (2007: 330), namely that it assures sameness of content.

Lizardo interprets my discussion to mean that I suppose (*ex cathedra*) that "'tacit presuppositions' cannot be transmitted via the practical imitation of conduct, and . . . *propose that it is only by the re-translation of practical presuppositions into 'public language' of explicit instruction that a plausible account of the transmission of the 'hidden objects' of practices can be constructed*" (2007: 333). This is simply false: My examples, including the "American walk" noted by Mauss, which forms a large part of the discussion, are not restricted to cases of explicit instruction, nor is this stressed. The term I consistently use in the text is "emulation," a term which does not imply explicit instruction, although of course explicit coaching might help someone emulate. Emulation does, however, operate through ordinary epistemic channels: One can emulate only what one can see, hear, and so forth. Lizardo then goes on to make the more interesting claims that my argument "presupposes both the conceptual informational sterility of overt conduct, and thus the strict separation of conceptual content from practical action (patterns of motor activity) and the related inability of the human neurocognitive system to gather and process the implicit conceptual information encoded in patterns of overt behavior" (2007: 333). I'll accept the first of the two things "presupposed," but the second one is so loaded and potentially misleading that it needs explanation.

The picture here is this: I say that overt behavior is conceptually "sterile"; Lizardo says that something like conceptual content—not just overt behavior—is transmitted from person to person in a medium other than overt behavior, with the aid of mirror neurons. There are two elements to this conflict: the idea of transmission and the idea of concepts and conceptual content. Conceptual content raises a large set of issues that I have, as noted earlier, discussed elsewhere, but for present purposes I would be happy to accept the notion of concepts in the Gallese and Lakoff paper (2005) on which he relies—unlike most of the current philosophical community—and dispense with the normative one. The problem of transmission, however, needs to be addressed before explaining this. My response to Lizardo's idea that conceptual content is transmitted in some fashion other than through overt behavior is that he has a wrong understanding of what goes on in the kind of imitation and emulation that is involved in mirror neurons. Moreover, I will suggest, the right understanding fits with my points about emulation: The same content is not directly transmitted, as he imagines, but mirrored, that is to say simulated from within the mind of the person doing the mirroring. To understand this requires a brief discussion of mirror neurons.

Mirror neurons activate both in the performance of actions and in the perception of actions. The dual-use character of this system suggests that "we recognize someone else's action because we manage to activate our own inner action representations using mirror neurons" (Keysers et al. 2003: 634). How do we "manage" this? According to a standard view of the matter, "converging lines of evidence strongly suggest that our keen ability to perceive the actions of other people results in part, from the massive experience we have accumulated over the years in planning and executing self-produced activities" (Blake and Shiffrar 2007: 56). The interesting implication of this view is that this capacity to perceive actions is to a great extent learned and produced, not from something like our predictive experience with other people as such, but from our own experiences of acting. There is a question, indeed, as to whether the connection between perception and action on which the mirror neuron system depends is itself learned (Hurley and Chater 2005: 11; Meltzoff 2005).

This capacity is also related to imitation and imagination. It has long been known that certain brain lesions cause individuals to imitate the bodily movements of others. This suggests—although this is still a matter of hypothesis—that the action-perception system works normally in such a way that when the system is activated by the perception of an action, the system prepares to imitate, but the imitative action is inhibited by another mechanism such that the same neurons for action are activated but without action occurring (Gallese and Goldman 1998: 499). This means of inhibition or taking the system off-line is hypothesized to be the one that allows for imagination of actions and thus simulation, understood as a brain process in which the same neurons for action (which are also those activated by perception) are activated without action taking place. Simulation is thought to be an off-line process involving the same neurons as those involved in perceiving an action of another person as "minded" or intentional which thus becomes the means by which we "mind read."

Learning, and thus learning histories, are an important part of the experimental work on the activation of the perception-action system. Much of this work has involved the difference in perception that results from people's ability to perform certain actions: Dancers can see things about dance moves that other people can't see (Cross et al. 2006); male and female ballet performers see the typical gender-specific dance moves of their own gender better (Calvo-Merino et al. 2006: 1907). There is also research on the visual cues that allow motions and emotions to be identified. What this research suggests is that the cues needed by the system are very modest and that the preconscious work of perceiving is done largely by the perceiver constructing perceptions of whole actions on the basis of very limited inputs. Even a very small set of visual cues, for example, allows someone to identify motions and emotions of certain kinds (Tomasello and Carpenter 2005: 141; Loula et al. 2005; Blake and Shiffrar 2007).

The typical problems of distinguishing what is learned from what is given as a starting point in the system arise for mirror neurons as well. Some think the whole of mirroring is learned; others think that some basics are given. If they were, they would be useful as a way to account for getting learning off the ground. But disentangling the two developmentally is tough. Consider the smile of a baby. Babies mimic the smiles of parents at a very young age (Meltzoff and Moore 1977, 1989). This would be a good start to a process of interactive learning. But of course it is also the subject of a great deal of interactive learning in which babies get tremendous amounts of feedback in interactions involving smiling, smiling back, recognizing smiles, and so forth. The problem with the idea that everything in the system is learned in this way is the one raised by Lizardo about connectionism: Can this mechanism, which depends on massive inputs, account for everything it needs to, or is it too slow and laborious to do so?

Understanding other people is more complicated yet. Mirror neurons have been recruited to support simulation theory. Simulations off-line are like hypotheses. They get tested by the results of one's actions made on the basis of the simulations or by the fulfillment or nonfulfillment of one's expectations produced by the simulation. Once the associations are established, we can simulate the feedback process itself. Consider the classic example of feedback: the thermostat. If we can tell that the level of heat that would switch off the thermostat is about to be reached, based on our simulation of the process, we can avoid overshooting the mark and waiting for the actual feedback system to kick in (Hurley 2008; Gallese 2000: 29).

We can't just "read" off the goals of others, but we can "construct" them (preconsciously) (Gallese and Metzinger 2003: 385), by a kind of retrodiction of the target's mental state, as Gallese and Goldman put it (1998: 497). We construct these retrodictions with our own capacity to simulate, which we apply to what we observe, namely overt behavior, which our simulations enable us to make sense of, or code. Learning the difference between a parental smile of approval and the bogus smile of a salesman or beauty queen is a much more sophisticated achievement, based on a lot of experience that has been assimilated. Mirror neurons are not that sophisticated, but, as Gallese and Goldman suggest, they might "represent a primitive version, or possibly a precursor in phylogeny, of a simulation heuristic that might underlie mind reading" (1998: 498).

Nothing in this story so far involves anything passing from one embodied mind to another without going through the senses, nor carbon copies of action-perception capacities passing from one mind to another. Sameness, at least with respect to things that are acquired through simulation, is not a reasonable expectation. There is plenty of room for error here, and indeed in the experiments on bodily movement imitations there is plenty of error as well, and also plenty of scope for unconscious learning that corrects errors—even by very young infants (Meltzoff and Moore 1997: 185–87).

Nothing in this account conflicts with nor excludes the possibility of imitation of the kind exemplified in brain-damaged subjects for whom the inhibitions to the discharge of action do not work (Gallese and Goldman 1998: 499). What they imitate is nevertheless determined by what they can perceive as imitable, and if this is not given universally as a starting point, it is a matter of learning, with an individual learning history. So even this imitation is not carbon copying.[4]

SHARING BASIC NEURAL FORMATS: THE ROLE OF THE UNIVERSALLY GIVEN

So what about the idea of what is universally given? Lizardo takes comfort from some quotations from Gallese about the manifold—a Kantian term—and the idea that "sameness of content" is shared with different organisms as a result of "modeling the observed behavior as an action with the help of a matching equivalence between what is observed and heard and what is executed" (Gallese 2003: 175); this is a complex claim, which doesn't support Bourdieu. The problem is with "sharing." Mirror neurons are shared by the perceptual and action systems. The question of what is shared with other organisms is a separate question. If what is shared is the Kantian manifold, i.e., some universal set of starting points, such as the act of grasping, this is an argument to the effect that underlying semantic content is a set of given starting points that are shared. But this reasoning doesn't help with practices, which are by definition not universal, or with concepts, which is a more salient issue for this literature, with similar implications.

Consider the following account of concepts in relation to the problem of learning history: "Concepts are not given to us by the world, but are products of our attempts, as a species (with a phylogenetic past) and as individuals (with a personal past), to make sense of our worlds." This is in accordance with my view of the significance of learning histories. But these are the words of Mark Turner (1991: 152), a collaborator of Lakoff, and one of the major sources of the body of ideas that Lizardo relies on to refute *The Social Theory of Practices*. This quotation sharply distinguishes two things—the universal and the individual. What interests Gallese and Lakoff is something relevant to this distinction: the claim that abstract reasoning and conceptual reasoning necessarily employ the sensory-motor system. They refer to the structuring circuits used in this system as "cogs" (2005: 473) and to the perspective as a whole as "structured connectionism." It is specifically addressed to the Kantian or universal problem of what is given:

> From the structured connectionism perspective, *the inferential structure of concepts is a consequence of the network structure of the brain and its organization in terms of functional clusters.* This brain

> organization is, in turn, a consequence of our evolutionary history—of the way in which our brains, and the brains of our evolutionary ancestors, have been shaped by bodily interactions in the world. (2005: 468; emphasis in the original)

The idea—very speculative, as they note—is that abstract thought itself employs this same universally human inferential structure and thus this same functionally clustered network structure of the brain. We can think abstractly, in other words, because we can rely on this pre-given organization. This is an answer to the following problem:

> From the perspective of neural computation, a human brain consists of a very large number of neurons connected up in specific ways with certain computational properties. How is it possible to get the details of human concepts, the forms of human reason, and the range of human languages out of a lot of neurons connected up as they are in our brains? How do you get thought and language out of neurons? (Lakoff 1999: 5)

Structured connectionism, his approach, "allows us to construct detailed computational neural models of conceptual and linguistic structures and the learning of such structures" (Lakoff 1999: 5). This is, in a sense, a response to Lizardo's worry that connectionist learning and interaction can't do the job. The way it helps is by giving learning a kind of head start. If certain concepts (or a kind of neural organization that amounts to a kind of near-concept) are given phylogenetically rather than learned, they can be a means of a kind of rudimentary human sharing, and they might continue to be used in more advanced forms of thought. But this is an appeal to human universals, not to a mechanism of transmission of the kind required by Bourdieu.

There are two elements here: learning, which is still connectionist in this model, and structure, which is phylogenetic. The sharing here is at the phylogenetic level; the rest of it is learned, and thus subject to the facts of individual learning history. The possibility of learning in such a way that we understand one another may be facilitated by the phylogenetically shared common structural elements. But, as we already know from the studies of dancers, there is plenty that is learned that is not universally shared. Nothing in this discussion tells us anything to the effect that there is any kind of collective fact that is not phylogenetic that is shared in some sort of novel way, not subject to the vicissitudes and variations of learning, and indeed of embodiment itself—bodies themselves vary.

Gallese takes a pass at some very traditional problems of social theory as a way of criticizing the monadic focus of much cognitive science on individual cognition. But he does so not by postulating some sort of collective mechanism, nor even by making the kind of assertion of identity that Lizardo makes, but rather by locating group identity in the economy of the mind:

> Identity is important within a group of social individuals because it provides them with the capacity to better *predict* the consequences of the ongoing and future behavior of others. The attribution of identity status to other individuals automatically contextualizes their behavior. This, in turn, reduces the variables to be computed, thus optimizing the employment of cognitive resources by reducing the "meaning space" to be mapped. By contextualizing content, identity reduces the amount of information our brain has to process. (2003: 518; emphasis in the original)

To be clear, he does speak, loosely, about sharing of political perspectives and other forms of empathic sharing. But the only mechanism he has in mind for this sharing is the following:

> What is common between a neonate who replies to his mother sticking out her tongue with an equivalent behavior, and the skilled repetition by an adolescent of the piano chords as demonstrated by the piano teacher? Both instances of imitative behavior are made possible only by the capacity to solve the computational difficulties inherent in any type of interpersonal mapping, due to the different perspectives of demonstrator and imitator. . . . If I want to reproduce the behavior of someone else, no matter how complex it is, or whether I understand it or not, I always need to translate my external perspective of the demonstrator into my own personal body perspective. This problem can, however, be overcome if both the actions of the demonstrator and of the imitator share a basic neural format. (2003: 519)

So the common mental stuff that makes the computational problem soluble in real time is the basic neural format, which is phylogenetically shared. This basic neural format can be used as a computational starting point and attributed to the other as one imitates, in this case, that party's action, because it is already phylogenetically shared. Everything else that is shared has to get there the old-fashioned way—it has to be learned, and in the case of things that make up interpersonal relations, learned through our use of our own bodies as a model, or through explicit teaching with feedback, or through unconscious feedback. And it works solely on overt behavior: what Gallese calls "my *external* perspective of the demonstrator," which I need to "*translate*" into "my own personal body perspective" (2003: 519; emphasis supplied).

What do these claims have to do with *The Social Theory of Practices* and the follow-up papers of mine that Lizardo cites? The book is specifically not about the *Kantian* or "universal mental content" problematic.

It is concerned, in its discussion of shared presuppositions, with the *neo-Kantian* form of the problem: with the idea that a particular epoch, society, or discipline shares presuppositions. The Kantian form of the problem can be given, as it is in these texts, a phylogenetic solution. Sharing in this case is a result of a mechanism that actually does copy, namely genes. To what mechanism does *The Social Theory of Practices* appeal to solve the neo-Kantian problem? Emulation. In short, *The Social Theory of Practices* appeals to the same kind of mechanism that the mirror neuron literature does, when it is concerned with nonuniversal mental contents, such as practices.

LIZARDO'S ALTERNATIVE MECHANISM: DOES IT EXIST?

Lizardo's critique comes down to the following: *The Social Theory of Practices* says that learning histories matter and that they individuate the mental contents of individuals. Bourdieu's theory of practice denies this; mirror neurons enable mental contents to be widely shared without individuation, so Bourdieu is right and *The Social Theory of Practices* is wrong. In fact, the mirror neuron literature makes learning history central and establishes nothing like the copying relation Lizardo claims to find there. This is, indeed, the central implication of the core fact of mirror neurons, that the networks activated by perception and action are the same: "that what we see depends, in part, on what we can do" (Blake and Shiffrar 2007: 63). Consider the dancers—or a more mundane example, such as Tiger Woods' golf swing. A professional can see things about that swing that an ordinary person cannot. The process of learning to swing a golf club correctly begins not with perceiving the swing correctly, but with perceiving it crudely and gradually improving, through a stepwise process, both one's perceptual capacity and one's capacity for action (Hodges et al. 2006: 480). Learning history is essential: Without having learned enough one cannot even see the details of the swing sufficiently to be coached to correct one's errors. Learning is slow, because one can see only a bit beyond what one can do (Ericsson 2006: 694). In this case coaching, or explicit instruction, is essential to achieving at a high level: Professional athletes are constantly coached. But proceduralizing, or encouraging conscious attention to an aspect of performance, typically causes performance to decline. And this is characteristic of expert performances. Explicit discussion, however, is part of ordinary practices of all kinds: People gossip, appraise, advise, and so forth. "Chess masters do not just play a lot of chess," as a paper in the experts literature puts it, "they read a lot of the chess literature" (Hunt 2006: 31).

Where did Lizardo's critique go wrong? Lizardo has fatally mixed up two things: the Kantian problem of universal conditions of understanding and the neo-Kantian problem of understanding within a social group. We may put this in terms of the research examples. The Kantian problem is dealt with in the discussion of physical actions like grasping and smiling that are universal and which, if we take mirroring responses to them to be rooted in the phylogenetically given features of the neural system, can be the basis of interaction. The neo-Kantian problem, however, is the one that corresponds to practices. Recognizing and distinguishing dance moves is a matter of performance, and therefore training: One cannot perceive correctly without the training. And one can of course be trained in different ways to produce the same performance. So different learning histories can produce the same overt result, as I argued in *The Social Theory of Practices*. Congruence in performance, the reduction of individual differences, results from training in the form of extended practice (Schneider and Shiffrin 1977). It may be that our imitation and conceptualization of dance "employs" the universal sensory-motor system that is the solution to the Kantian problem, and that as humans we have a limited set of shared universals to which we repeatedly recur. That is the Lakoff thesis. But this explains concepts like grasping, not ballet concepts like "*grand battement en cloche*." Even if our understanding and communication to others of these more recherché concepts "employs" the universal sensory-motor system, it cannot be reduced to it.

What does Lizardo think happens in the relevant cases? Here is the key passage: "*any social setting that acts directly on the body for a given collective will necessarily result in the sharing of similar 'practical presuppositions' about the world*," and "any ecological and/or social technologies that serve to modify the body . . . , will also result in the 'transmission' and 'embodied simulation' to other members of the group of similar bodily techniques, and thus the picking up of the embodied concepts embedded in those patterns of practice" (2007: 343). The idea is this: The same kind of sharing of neural structure that happens phylogenetically in response to the Kantian problem happens in a parallel but non-phylogenetic way for the neo-Kantian problem anytime a social setting acts on the body for a given collective. There is no role for training and experience to reduce individual difference, no role for learning or its individuating vagaries. The common water osmoses into the individual. The "social setting" as a unitary fact "acts" on the individual body to produce sameness of mental content.

This is indeed what an attempt to salvage Bourdieu as a bodily mechanism theorist would require. But it is groundless. There simply is no such mechanism. It is true that if we teach people to perform the same bodily performances and then teach them the terms that correspond to the differences they have learned in their bodies, the terminology will be more easily learned than for people who have not had the experience. Indeed, this is an implication of the close relation between learning language, learning the world, and acquiring habits that *The Social Theory of Practices* closes with (1994: 121). But this is very different from the mechanism Lizardo wants to establish.

If there were such a mechanism, it would make causal history irrelevant, replace error-prone learning, and overcome the obvious fact that individuals have very different experiences and get very different feedback even in the same social setting. But a mechanism that produces sameness simply by exposure is simply beyond plausibility. A little reflection on the ontogeny of skilled performances shows why individual learning history still matters, and produces differences at the neural-level detail even for people who are engaged in the same bodily activities—let alone cognitively complex social activities. Consider a simple example: teaching advanced Little League baseball players to bat. The professional coach typically begins by asking them to swing. This "natural" swing is what the player has learned unconsciously and with the informal feedback or advice that they have received from nonprofessionals. Each swing will be slightly different, and wrong: Batting is one of those activities that requires continuous coaching, for all but the largely mythical "naturals." The coach will advise the player on how to correct what is wrong. Again, different advice will be given for different swings and problems. Even a ten year old will have many bad habits to correct, although similar problems will crop up with player after player. The acquisition and correction are the learning history, and it will be different—in the sense that the neural connections will be built up in a different sequence and a different way. If the coaching is successful (and the successes are usually only temporary), the player will be able to produce a more or less consistently good swing. The difficulty of producing even this simple physical act, however, is enormous, for the simplicity is deceptive: Unlike grasping, there are numerous parts of the body that need to work together to produce the swing.

The same point applies to concept learning: We come to concepts in different ways, through different histories, and this is especially true for concepts understood in terms of the account given by Gallese and Lakoff, in which concepts are understood in terms of their neural connections. "Sameness" in this case is sameness only at the level of functional intersubjective understanding—not a neural fact, much less one produced by common body experiences. Even less individualized training, such as military drill, is neurally overlaid on differentiated backgrounds, such as the way recruits walked before they were disciplined by the drill sergeant.

Why would I say that mirror neurons and even the Gallese hypothesis about universal neural precursors to some limited set of embodied concepts are an aid for my account and undermine Bourdieu's? For one, as noted, the idea that communication employs the universal sensory-motor system reduces the burden of learning—so if it is true, less has to be learned in a connectionist way to produce a distinctive practice by emulation. One need not learn to identify and emulate walking, for example, but might have this capacity to code for and act already wired-in. In learning *grands battements* in ballet, then, one would not start from scratch, but have the head start given by these prewired body schema. (I omit the complexities and issues with these notions of "concepts" and "schemas," and with the whole idea of precursors, obviously). Mirror neurons make emulation a real neural process, which eliminates any sense that, like introjection or socialization (or for that matter Bourdieu's reproduction), this is a purely metaphorical substitute for a genuinely causal account. But the more profound support comes from the genuinely radical feature of the larger discussion of mirror neurons—which comes from its shift from the input side of the story of how we come to be social beings capable of understanding and getting along with others to the individual construction side.

This radical shift—a Copernican revolution in cognitive science, so to speak—is completely obscured by Lizardo's presentation, but deserves to be recognized. Consider older notions like Freud's notion of introjection, which led to the "oversocialized conception of man" in thinkers like Parsons. The introjection of the content of the superego was a case of massive input of a certain kind of data into the unconscious. According to this picture, we are, as individuals, largely constituted by stuff that is crammed into our heads by society. That is, of course, also Bourdieu's picture. The idea of simulation shifts the emphasis to the individual, who uses himself or herself as a model and means of understanding others. Dautenhahn and Nehaniv (2002) call this the agent-based perspective, which captures the implications of a shift from viewing people as imitation machines to active users of these powers.

Moreover, the idea of mirror neurons pushes this use of one's own embodied capacities as a model for understanding and imitating others to the very beginning of the human developmental process. Understanding other people is an advanced achievement produced through the building up of levels, subject to error, feedback, and so on. Except, possibly, for simple bodily motions and some as yet unknown array of other universals, it is not there at the outset of the human developmental process. The models of the development of the capacity to mind read are complex and need not be discussed here (Hurley 2008). But the processes of simulation they model are, as I have argued, sufficient to account for the uniformities of overt conduct that practice theory is an attempt to account for.

Ellwood was right about this and Durkheim and his heirs were wrong. The social process, with all its opportunities for emulation, simulation, testing, feedback, and learning, is a data-rich environment, and human beings, as cognitive science is showing, are powerful emulators and simulators who are particularly good at using simulation to fill in missing data. This feature of simulation is especially important: We can learn so quickly from our social environment because simulation allows us to fill in missing data in social situations. Because we can simulate other people more readily than we can simulate the physical world, we can thus construct, test, and assimilate complex feedback-simulative "hypotheses" about this world expeditiously. The interaction between these capacities and this environment is not one that produces clones, or puppets of the group will, nor does it produce anarchy. It produces skilled interactors with enormous capacities to anticipate, predict, and model the people with whom they interact, to adjust to them, and to learn from their adjustments. This kind of coordination, as Dewey called it, is all we need to account for "society." The burden is on the believers of collective objects to show that it cannot. And advances in our understanding of our cognitive powers such as those involving simulation and mirror neurons make doing so more difficult.

7 Connectionism and the Tacit

Tradition and Cognitive Science: Oakeshott's Undoing of the Kantian Mind

Of the ideas of Michael Oakeshott that resonate today, perhaps the most resonant are found in the passages in the essays collected with "Rationalism in Politics" (Oakeshott 1962b) and in *On Human Conduct* (Oakeshott 1975) in which Oakeshott characterized traditions and human practices in terms of their irreducibility to other notions and contrasted the moral content of traditions with explicitly formulated or formulatable moral ideals. One of the most succinct descriptions of a tradition of political behavior is found in an essay titled "Political Education" (Oakeshott 1962a). Oakeshott says that

> a tradition of behavior is a tricky thing to get to know. Indeed, it may even appear to be essentially unintelligible. It is neither fixed nor finished; it has no changeless center to which understanding can anchor itself; there is no sovereign purpose to be perceived or invariable direction to be detected; there is no model to be copied, no ideal to be realized, or rule to be followed. (1962a: 128–29)

And after this, he lists more "nots": that it is "not an abstract idea, or a set of tricks, not even a ritual"; that its "authority is diffused between past, present and future," which is to say that there is no moment at which it becomes authoritative, or permanent; that "to know only the gist is to know nothing"; that it is "flimsy and elusive but not without identity"; that none of its parts are "immune from change"; that it is neither ever wholly in motion or wholly at rest; that although everything is temporary, nothing is arbitrary; that there will always be something of a mystery about how it is learned, and no point at which learning it can properly be said to begin. By comparison, what is said in a positive way is slight: "that knowledge of it is unavoidably knowledge of its detail" and that "what has to be learned is but a concrete coherent manner of living in all its intricateness" (1962a: 128–29).

So the concepts of practice and tradition, as formulated by Oakeshott here and in many places, especially in the opening chapters of *On Human Conduct* (Oakeshott 1975), are very much defined by oppositions or contrasts. In what follows, I propose to focus on the contrast with one of the "nots," a particular model of the mind that is a pervasive part of academic common sense which I will call the Kantian mind. By this, I simply mean the very familiar model in which mental "frames" constitute objects and, when shared, enable communication and other familiar aspects of social life. Even if we give up on the epistemological project of finding the ultimate frame, it is more difficult to give up the various usages that have been found for this concept and its conceptual kin. Nevertheless, as I shall suggest here, cognitive science and the broad set of ideas associated with connectionism represent a challenge to this model of mind that may lend some support to its past critics. It has long been clear that there are affinities between connectionist approaches and the family of tradition thinkers, which includes, in addition to Oakeshott, Friedrich Hayek[1], Michael Polanyi[2], Alasdair MacIntyre and Hans Georg Gadamer, and (in some respects) Karl Popper[3]. My aim in this discussion is to explore the relationship in connection with Oakeshott, the thinker in this group whom I take to have the best account of tradition.[4]

As this list suggests, there is a strongly political undertone to the issues discussed here, with the list dominated by "liberal conservatives or conservative liberals," to use a term of Edward Shils.

Oakeshott published "Rationalism in Politics" at a time in which ideological politics dominated, and many politicians and political writers of the Left, and also those formerly of the Left, understood politics as a struggle between rival worldviews. For standard theories of ideology, ideology was a frame: A worldview, quite literally, was a view of the world from within a frame. And frames were themselves thought of in terms of analogies to the explicit—to assumptions, presuppositions, and so forth. One of the claims of Marxian sociology of knowledge was that the opponents of the proletarian ideology were themselves "ideological" and that the tacit ideological "assumptions" of their thought could be revealed. Oakeshott and other theorists of tradition of the time responded to this line of thinking, which was wholly dependent on the Kantian model of mind, by arguing that the issue was more fundamental: first, that the category of "ideological thinking" was an inadequate account of political traditions; second, that traditions were ubiquitous and not inimical to rationality but in fact a condition for it; and third, that the model of thought implied by the theory of ideology was a manifestation of a tendency rooted more deeply in the history of modern philosophy and indeed modern thought more generally that needed to be exposed and rejected.

The political passions that gave interest to these arguments at the time have of course faded. Today, however, an aspect of this argument has been given new relevance. The "ideological" systems that these thinkers opposed were, incidentally, normative. To be a Marxist was to be committed to a worldview in which the significance of ordinary facts was transformed in a way that also transformed their valuative significance. This "normative" aspect of the problem of frames has become central to the present concern with "normativity" by writers such as Robert Brandom and John McDowell. Their different views of Kant's current relevance each engage the idea that there is a normative element to what Michael Friedman (2001) characterized as the process that "injects a priori forms, constructions, or categories of our own—which, for Kant, express universal capacities of the human mind—into our experience" (11).

For Brandom (1998), "Kant's big idea is that what distinguishes judgment and action from the responses of merely natural creatures is neither their relation to some special stuff nor their peculiar transparency, but rather that they . . . express commitments of ours" (127). McDowell's view, which will be discussed in more detail below, is that children must acquire the norms of reason through ordinary processes of socialization, which they can then correctly recognize to be normatively binding. Brandom uses the term "practices" to formulate his account of the Kantian conditions; McDowell uses "tradition." The appeal to these concepts alone poses a question: What is the relationship between Oakeshott's usages and theirs? The answer, I will suggest, is that they conflict very fundamentally and do so in ways that reveal strengths in Oakeshott's conception and weaknesses in theirs. But I will also conclude that accepting Oakeshott's account is not without costs.

THE KANTIAN MIND IN COGNITIVE SCIENCE

In what follows, I propose to first deal with the contrasts in the broadest terms, and to do so, it will be important to make the conflicts more concrete. Cognitive science and many of the inquires that have been spawned from the cognitive science tradition provide a variant of the basic model of the Kantian mind that allows this to be done. The traditionally dominant cognitive science model of the mind constructed mental processes on the analogy of a rule-governed machine. Capacities were explained in terms of rules whose properties could be inferred from activities. This worked nicely for grammar and basic mathematical thinking. The strategy could be extended to other activities as well, and this seemed to suggest that the mind was a very complex computer with various preprogrammed routines.

One of the principal supports of this notion of framing, and of the "shared premises" form generally, has its origins in Kant, in the form of the kind of transcendental argument that asserts the necessary existence of these frames or shared premises on the grounds that they are the conditions for the possibility of some uncontroversial fact, such as the fact that people of a particular type with a particular background communicate with one another, whereas people of another type with another background cannot communicate. In this case, the reasoning is fairly straightforward but obviously questionable: The frame is the condition of communication that is possessed by members of the one group and absent in those who cannot communicate.

There are many reasons this line of argument represents a somewhat strange procedure, but I will point to only one. It seems as though the explanatory necessities at stake in these "conditions for the possibility" arguments are themselves as uncontroversial as the facts to which they refer, such as the fact of communication—unproblematic and uncontroversial enough to overcome the possibility that there might be an alternative explanation of the very same uncontroversial fact, which differs and has different implications. But if we think of the idea of a frame as simply a hypothesis like other scientific hypotheses, the problem becomes much clearer. Frame is a theoretical entity whose existent properties are being asserted on the basis of the appearances it explains but always with the important proviso that other theories positing other theoretical entities might very well explain the same facts.

The Achilles' heel of transcendental arguments is that they depend on a unique result—that the conditions for the possibility of something are not only specifiable but uniquely so. The appearance of "uniqueness," however, is sometimes achieved by characterizing the thing to be accounted for in ways that ensure that the explanation is unique, thus making the argument at once circular and vulnerable to an alternative description of that which is to be accounted for. These arguments, however, routinely omit any consideration of alternatives and indeed characteristically describe the phenomena to be explained in such a way that excludes alternatives. This means that transcendental arguments are commonly circular: The description is constructed so that no alternative explanation is possible.

What makes these arguments persuasive is that there are many things—concepts, the symbolic, meaning—that seem to be categorically different from the things that can be accounted for "naturalistically," and to the extent that we accept this notion of categorical difference, it seems that we are compelled to accept the transcendental arguments that go with them. If we accept that there is such a special nonnatural domain as "the social" that is irreducible to the individual, to choose one that Oakeshott himself comments on, it seems that there is no alternative to accounting for it in terms of the conditions of the possibility of the social, and these conditions turn out to be the constitutive shared premises of the objects that exist in the domain, such as society. The relation between individual and society—the traditional topic of political theory—thus is preformed by the relation of culture to cognition. The realm of the political, the explicit, and deliberation comes later and depends on "the social."

This reasoning, which is so conventional today that it is now difficult to disarticulate it into its elements, also has a form like that of a transcendental argument. Margaret Mead once expressed this in connection with culture by depicting culture as a collective choice from a basket of possible values, a story reminiscent of the founding of sovereign authority in Hobbes, and equally metaphorical. Once this act of selection occurs, the culture, values, concepts, rules governing them, and so on must be "internalized" by the members of the group, so that they act in accordance with these rules without outside coercion, or at least recognize and understand them "internally" as conceptual or normative, that is, as something other than a fact of nature to be adjusted to. "Sharing premises," or "having common categories," and "following common tacit rules" are merely different ways of characterizing these collective mental processes. Thus, the characterization itself, together with the fact that objects like the state are "social" in the sense that they occur as they do only in specific social groups, pushes us to this solution. Only through these concepts are the actions of people in this society intelligible or meaningful. They are meaningful, or in the category of meaningful; therefore, the objects that are the condition for this meaningfulness are real.

Given what I said earlier about transcendental arguments, it is good to look for the trick part of this argument in the way the facts that must be explained are characterized, and there is much to puzzle over. But the bottom line is that the requirement of explaining the level of concepts, the symbolic, the rule governed, the intelligible, and so forth limits us to a small class of solutions. These objects differ from society to society, profession to profession, and so forth. So in each case, they must be said to be in some sense constituted by these groupings, and it seems that the only way for this to occur is through some sort of collective mental or ideational act specific to the group in question—"mental" or ideational because nothing that is mental or ideational can come from the nonmental or nonideational.

What does this have to do with the symbolic processing model of cognitive science? There are two directions here—from culture to the mind and from the mind to culture—and each involves some affinities that come very close to making it seem that the rules model of the mind and the rules model of culture require one another. But consider the following:

> The serial digital computer is not a self-organizing system. It does not learn easily. Indeed, the easiest metaphor for learning in a system of this kind is programming; that is, the rules that must be applied to inputs of some kind are placed directly into the system—by man, by Nature or by the hand of God. (Bates and Elman 1993: 628)

Nature, God, and individuals, however, are not likely suspects for "programming" or placing rules into the system. The "solution" that does come to mind is "society" or rather the rules that are shared. So the idea of shared rules fills a serious lacunae in the symbolic processing model—indeed, it seems as though the social origin of cultural programming is a condition for the possibility of cultures that are distinctive to social groups. The rules model also solves the problem of congruence in mental structures between the constitutive rules and the rules that operate in the individual mind: The stuff that needs to be "internalized" fits the computational model of the mind perfectly. Internalizing norms is nothing more than having them programmed into the individual mind. So the concepts fit in both directions, and indeed each appears to be a condition for the possibility of the other: Unless culture can be internalized as rules, it is difficult to see how it can be internalized to a mind that is a symbolic processor at all, and if the mind is not a symbolic processor, it is difficult to see how it can "internalize" cultural rules.[5]

TROUBLES WITH THE KANTIAN MIND

These "conditions for the possibility of" congruences, however, are peculiar. It is not that there are well-established phenomena that are congruent but rather that the congruences result from the fact that the metaphors (or to be somewhat more polite about it, the theoretical concepts) used to describe social life and the operations of the mind come from the same source—an analogy between explicit rules and rule-following and tacit rules and rule-following. Oakeshott, as it happens, points repeatedly to the issue that provides a wedge into these arguments—learning. And the problem of learning has always been trouble for the "premises model."

The transcendental arguments point away from the problem of how the premises got into the mind, and one can see why when one considers how these arguments arose in the history of philosophy. The neo-Kantians recognized two things. The first was that frames were not historically universal. The second was that they were relative to particular disciplines or forms of activity. The activity itself was said to have presuppositions, presuppositions that participants in the activity were assumed to share and that had the effect of giving the activity itself its normative character. What is striking about this particular formulation is that the ideas of sharing, normativity, and the movement of the frame concept away from the individual cognizer as possessor of the frame occur together in one step and without any particular argument. The idea of sharing and the idea that frames were relative to an activity and to historical moments of that activity were the givens of the argument, and the conclusion that there was such a thing as a shared set of constitutive suppositions simply followed from the "transcendental" inference that the coherence of the activity itself implied the existence of the presuppositions. There was no account of acquisition, or learning. "Socialization" and "internalization" were never much more than names for a mystery, a mystery that could be studied empirically in its external aspects, that is to say, in terms of the process of training and experience. And the mysterious aspect of the process showed up particularly in connection with "normativity." The older utilitarian notion that the relevant learning was a matter of recognizing the bad consequences of, say, stealing, was not persuasive. It was convenient to ascribe the normativity to the frame itself and to say that the normative content was part of the constitutive character or derived from the constitutive character. But this simply replaced the older problem with the problem of acquiring the frame.

It might be supposed that learning is the strong suit of cognitive science and that the symbolic processing model would provide a solution to the problem. But, in fact, it is a weakness of this approach. As Bates says,

> To be sure, there is a literature on computer learning in the field of artificial intelligence. However, most of these efforts are based on a process of hypothesis testing. In such learning models, two essential factors are provided a priori: a set of hypotheses that will be tested against the data, and an algorithm for deciding which hypothesis provides the best fit to those data. This is by its very nature a strong nativist approach to learning. It is not surprising that learning theories of this kind are regularly invoked by linguists and psycholinguists with a strong nativist orientation. There is no graceful way for the system to derive new hypotheses (as opposed to modifications of a pre-existing option). Everything that really counts is already there at the beginning. And this matches up very poorly to actual learning. Because the hypotheses tested by a traditional computer learning model are discrete in nature (based on the rule and representations described above), learning (a.k.a. "selection") necessarily involves a series of discrete decisions about the truth or falsity of each hypothesis. Hence we would expect change to take place in a crisp, step-wise fashion, as decisions are made, hypotheses are discarded, and new ones are put in their place. But human learning rarely proceeds in this fashion, characterized more often by error, vacillation and backsliding. (Bates and Elman 1993: 628)

Connectionism matches up somewhat better to actual learning, at least for the kinds of things that Oakeshott describes as a tradition of behavior. But more important, the connectionist approach brings together as part of the basic learning process several of the features that are so puzzlingly separated by the older model.

CONNECTIONISM AND THE SOCIAL

Connectionism is preeminently the model of the mind that deals with thought as skilled activity, and rather than give a technical account of the models, the notions of nodes, weighting, learning rules, and so on, I will consider a typical artificial intelligence application of connectionist learning: the use of feedback into connectionist systems to enable them to interpret X-ray images of, for example, breast cancer. The systems work inductively by feeding in the images in digital form and then feeding back whether it is a tumor or not. The connectionist machine *learns*, a phrase that is in a way not dissimilar from Hegel's notion that habits are already ideational (cf. McCumber 1990), and by differentiating what is only minimally differentiated by associating differences with one another, the medical systems can learn to differentiate and indeed differentiate more skillfully than human beings. This is not an example of rule-following because the connectionist machines, like the diagnosticians, having learned from a series of actual cases, will continue to diagnose in the light of the particular set of actual experiences that have been produced by feeding the data and outcomes into them, and consequently, each will diagnose somewhat differently in the face of new experiences.

The learning in question is not to be found in a rule that is learned (although there is a basic "learning" algorithm that a connectionist system needs to start with) but is a product of the changes produced on the system as a whole—a web-like system of "connections" in which connections are built up or eroded by experience, by the particular inputs and feedback from outputs that alter the weights of the connections. What is fed in and, up to a point at least, the order in which it is fed in determine the properties of the system of connections as a whole, its skills, and its biases. And like skilled practitioners generally, they vary with respect to the degree that they get the right answer and with respect to their biases, which fits with "the rather fuzzy properties of human categorization that are so elusive in psychological models inspired by the serial digital computer" (Bates and Elman 1993: 632). This is indeed characteristic of skilled behavior, which is not merely the assimilation of some package of rules but depends on the experiences that made up the skill. We can say that the machines can diagnose "more skillfully" because we can compare skilled, unskilled, and machine diagnosticians with respect to their capacity for differentiating correctly.

This is an image that is entirely consonant with Oakeshott's view of human practitioners. The "learning" done here has a series of properties that fit the list of "nots" with which I began. The connectionist net learns not by being programmed, except with a basic learning rule, but by experience and experience produced by activity, such as the activity of identifying tumors and predicting the course of disease. It is holistic in that it is the whole net and the weightings of the myriad connections that make up the net that are modified by experience. There is no part that is fixed and unchanging. Change is continuous because learning is continuous, and the history of experience—its "authority," so to speak—is built into the weightings that are produced and thus into what is learned: The past is thus always in a sense present but as a consequence of the modifications it has produced that are retained in the weightings of the connections.

It not only appears to be essentially unintelligible, it literally is unintelligible, in the sense that the units and processes by which it operates cannot be transformed into or stated as rules or principles, the kinds of explicit things that can be said to be intelligible. It is never fixed, although it becomes quite stable, so that new experiences do not dislodge what is learned. There is no changeless center or sovereign purpose, either: As Bates and Elman put it, there is "no final arbiter, no homunculus or central executive who puts all these . . . inputs together. Rather, the 'solution' is an emergent property of the system as a whole, a global pattern produced by independent, local computations" (1993: 632). The knowledge that is built into it is unavoidably knowledge of detail. To know only the gist indeed is to know nothing. There will always be something of a mystery about how whatever is learned is learned, if by this we mean that there is no way to restate the process as a series of intelligible steps and no point at which learning a particular skill can properly be said to begin, because what we are talking about is the acquisition not of "rules" but of a capacity; it is always to some extent arbitrary to draw a line marking the point at which a capacity can be said to be possessed.

These properties may be reasonably supposed to carry through to the collective aspect of practices, at least to that aspect that is not part of the relatively fixed and public world of external symbols and artifacts—the tacit part. A practical activity can succeed with skilled practitioners whose skills are not identical but are acquired in such a way that they enable the practitioners to act cooperatively and even to improve their skilled performances in relation to one another, to adjust to one another, and to learn more generally to adjust to others, as in, for example, the joint activities of skilled practitioners and in the improvement and adaptation gained through practical cooperative activity involving other skilled practitioners. And the "inherited" condition of this activity, the tradition or practice, to the extent that it consists of the skills that the practitioners have, will also have no changeless center, no gist, and so forth.

This alternative model nevertheless allows us to account for many of the puzzles that drove the "shared premises" or "rules" model. Chief among these is the constitution of objects. In this model, there simply is no moment of constitution—no rule or concept, for example, of "tumor" that is taught to or programmed into the connectionist learning machine. Objects are not separate from, or presupposed by, the activity, but the machine learns to distinguish as a product of activity and through inputs that are neither preformed nor conceptualized. In short, it operates on the Kantian manifold itself, on experience, and not on the world of objects or sense data. This is a point congenial to the conclusion of Oakeshott's early book, *Experience and Its Modes* ([1933] 1978), especially with respect to Oakeshott's refusal to distinguish between reality and experience or to give primacy to any particular experience, and indeed gives a sense to the notion of experience as a whole (322–56).[6]

The identification of shared premises or rules with social groups was motivated by the recognition that the objects of thought that were "constituted" for people, such as the state, varied from one historical setting to another, so it was inferred that whatever categories did the constituting had to vary similarly. But this argument can now be seen to be essentially circular: It is only if we assume that objects need to be constituted by shared premises or categories that we need an explanation of this sort. The fact that differentiations of things are local and historical is better understood as a consequence of the fact that practices, joint activities, are local, and what is learned in a connectionist sense from participating in these activities is also local—not to a "group" that possesses premises or categories together but to the persons who have developed capacities through learning by participating in the same activities.

INTELLIGENT SUBSCRIPTION

I have so far said nothing about normativity, but in an important sense, the problem of normativity is paired with the problems discussed here—constitutivity and shared premises are problems with the normative. It seems as though there is something to be said about normativity that cannot be said in the replacement language of Oakeshott, although it is not so easy to say what it is. Indeed, one must suspect that the problem of the circularity of some transcendental arguments is also a problem here, and at the same point: To treat as unproblematic claims about the normativity of some shared object, such as a given social practice or rule, is already to define a particular class of solutions as "required" or as "conditions for the possibility."

One peculiar point at which this issue of circularity becomes obvious is in recent discussions of Wittgenstein's famous example in the *Philosophical Investigations* of the builders who have a language game that consists of the term "slab" and so on and whose activities insist in saying "slab" and giving a slab to another person on, one might say, command. But command, description, request, and so forth are inappropriate to these utterances because there is no additional structure to this game, no possibility of raising questions, and in particular no language for correcting or identifying error. Robert Brandom (1994), accordingly, denies that the builders had a language at all and argues that having a language is bound up with the "counting as" relation so that it is possible to not merely use the word "slab" but to count some class of uses as proper uses and therefore to distinguish others as improper uses (rather than merely as incomprehensible uses), something that seems not to be possible in the language game of the builders (1994: 172–73; see also Brandom 1999: 144–45). The question of propriety, the question of "counting as," for him comes to be seen as the beginning of normativity, and "language" in the true sense is impregnated with this normativity. Brandom then argues that normativity here consists in a "commitment" to use something to count as in the instance of a word. So the relation of constitutivity is intrinsically normative, and therefore everything conceptual is normative. Brandom goes on to say a great deal to the effect that binding ourselves in this way by these normative commitments is what allows for human freedom and associates this with the greatness of German idealism, which is to make the point that choice is always conditioned by the constitutive and also made possible by the prior normative commitments that do the work of constituting. It is this kind of reasoning that I wish to question here. The telltale sign of trouble is the use of "commitment" in such an odd context, equivalent to what I discuss here as commitment to a framework.

Begin with a puzzle. On one hand, we acquire a moral language and reason with it and within it, so the deliberations that we make are deliberations about preconstituted objects and problems. We then deliberate on our "ideology" and lose confidence in it or choose to acquire another one as a result of deliberation. But because our deliberation is within the framework of terms and constituted objects of the prior framework, we can never really "choose." This is not a happy conclusion. It is not the case that deliberation occurs, or could ever occur, in a world of unconditioned and especially conceptually unconditioned choice to which one can then apply such universal principles as truth and right. On the other hand, and this is a point that was especially important to Oakeshott, we also on occasion reflect and deliberate on our frameworks, concepts, and standards of what counts as a good reason. This is to say that there is something relatively tangible that corresponds more or less to two realms of thinking about the problem of morality and normativity. The one realm I will simply refer to as the constitutive or as the "counts as" side of the problem, and the other one I will refer to in the same kind of shorthand as the side of deliberation, choice, and truth. These are only partial representations, but they do enable us to see some of the peculiarities that arise because of the problem itself, as well as the problem of conceptualizing the problem.[7]

The question of the ultimate end of deliberation, the ultimate standard to which deliberations point, seems to be the product of the notion of deliberation itself. The question of the basis of these constitutive rules, that is to say the rules that determine whether something counts as something, seems also to require some kind of backing, some kind of basis, some kind of commitment. And this has meant that much of the discussion of the problem of normativity has taken the broad form of importing language appropriate to deliberation, the language of faith, commitment, ultimate truth, and so forth, and applying it in some peculiar extended sense to the constitutive "counts as" conceptual level. In Brandom, that has amounted to a substantial expansion of the realm of the normative, so that even the employment of a concept in inferential reasoning, by virtue of the fact that to use a concept one must count something as something, is said to represent a "commitment" in the linguistic game of inference. Oakeshott seems to be pointing to something like this when he uses the term "subscription." But what is subscribed to is quite different from a set of normative rules of the game, and to see how it is different enables us to get a much clearer sense of what Oakeshott is up to in the first part of *On Human Conduct* (1975).

As we have seen, Oakeshott is extremely sensitive to the fact that practices must be acquired and, specifically, that they must be learned. What is learned when we acquire a practice is the use of a language that is already adverbial. We do not start out with a language of "brick" and "slab" that we then add normative commitments to by employing it in uses that are in effect promises to other people of some sort, as Brandom would have it. Our learning is "intelligent" by definition because it is learning rather than "internalization." Yet this is not the end of the story. In a small way, we as deliberate agents are engaged in a continuous remaking of ourselves by learning and employing in conduct new concepts and new usages. We "subscribe" by actions as modest as a wink (Oakeshott 1975: 15), but more reflection produces more complex subscription. Subscribing is a continuous process of the exercise of intelligence and of being transformed through this exercise into a skilled, intelligent performer. "Commitment" or normative decisions are not conditions for subscription but are the products of moments of reflection and abstraction in which the practice is brought into thought as an object of evaluation.

It is evident that this is an alternative way of describing the problem that the conventional idea of normativity addresses. Does it avoid the puzzle produced by the notion of constitutivity? We can separate the problem into two parts. The first will be taken up in the next section: It involves Oakeshott's previous undoing of the Kantian mind and his elimination of the need for the supposition that anything is socially constituted by shared premises. If this holds, there simply is no problem about frameworks to be solved. The second is the problem of whether we can make sense of the kind of reflection that intelligent subscribers to a practice engage in without appealing to the problematic notion of "frameworks" about which deliberation seems to be inherently impossible. Oakeshott gives an answer to this question that distinguishes him from his peers.[8] We can come to see our own "values" as contingent but not arbitrary, and as valid. We do so in the fashion of Charles Lamb's (1888) story about the discovery of roast pig. We fall into a form of life as a result of being born into it, and it is a historical product of largely blind past choices, but once we experience its benefits, we can come to recognize and appreciate them as benefits and to improve on our achievement of them, as Lamb's characters did when they realized that they did not have to burn down the house to roast the pig.

THE SPOOKINESS OF THE NORMATIVE: MCDOWELL IN OAKESHOTTIAN TERMS

Oakeshott was an idealist by virtue of the intellectual tradition in which he can be located, in which Bradley and behind him Hegel appear. In *On Human Conduct* (1975) Oakeshott objects to the notion of subject/object relations in a way that has affinities with various forms of idealism, particularly of the nineteenth century. This is very much not the same as saying that Oakeshott is an adherent of a kind of idealism that employs variants on the metaphor of framing. But there is something of a puzzle here—how can one reject what Oakeshott rejects without accepting the Kantian model? Oakeshott's commentators have sometimes simply read him in straightforwardly Kantian terms. Consider a remark of Maurice Cowling in his chapter on Oakeshott. Cowling observes that for Oakeshott, "knowledge is experience organized according to the postulates of a 'world' which the mind has established" (Cowling 1980: 257). This, I will argue in the next section, is a fundamental misinterpretation, for this is the picture Oakeshott rejects.

The significance of Oakeshott's variation on, and rejection of, this Kantian picture can be most easily understood if we have something to contrast it to. Perhaps the most vivid contemporary version of the idea that knowledge is experience organized according to the postulates of a "world" that the mind has established is presented in John McDowell's (1994) *Mind and World* (cf. Friedman 1996). McDowell's account departs from traditional Kantianism and idealism by its focus on an Oakeshottian concern, which makes the comparison more revealing. McDowell argues that children are not born rational but have to acquire the norms of reasoning. This avoids the original Kantian mystery of how the normative schema that shape experience are acquired—a genuinely spooky process that does seem to require a God—by locating the acquisition of the norms of reason in the process of acquiring norms generally, of socialization, of acculturation, and so on. The problem with this strategy, which McDowell acknowledges, is that there is still something "spooky" about the normativity of reasons thus understood. What appears to be a natural, causal process of groping around the world by an infant and then a child produces a nonnatural, noncausal result: normativity. McDowell does not treat this problem as particularly central, even to his discussion of the spookiness of normativity, but it is a manifestation of his core problem, of how a nonnatural, noncausal phenomenon of normativity arises within and relates to the causal, natural world. His own appeal to Gadamer's (1975) *Truth and Method* as a resource for understanding tradition brings the issue into contact with Oakeshott, and the contrasts are revealing. For Oakeshott, as I have argued, learning is critical—so whatever is, in McDowell's language, "normative" has to be learned. And for Oakeshott, this constraint determines the central features of a practice: Nothing can be part of a practice that is not learned in the way practices are learned.

McDowell comes to the problem from a different direction: His aim is to show that the idea of the normative demands of universal reason is not "spooky." He draws some conclusions from Davidson's ([1973] 1984) "On the Very Idea of a Conceptual Scheme" in support of his picture of a space of reason. He supposes that Davidson has established that rationality in the normative sense is unitary and universal, that there is no genuine problem of relativism with respect to normative reason (as distinct from belief), and that, therefore, in the course of socialization into any culture a child acquires this body of norms of reason along with the rest of the inheritance. If we leave aside the question of how such a miraculous convergence on common norms of reason would emerge from the variety and contingency of human learning and "cultural" experiences, a question that McDowell believes Davidson has relieved him from answering, we can focus on the puzzle of how normativity figures in the process of acquiring culture at all—including the element McDowell identifies with the normative demands of reason.

A peculiar feature of McDowell's argument, shared with Brandom, is that a profound transition needs to occur between two stages in a child's development. In one stage, the child is prenormative and prerational in the sense that he or she has not yet acquired the norms of reason (or "normative" language as distinct from sound making in the case of Brandom) and a second stage in which the relevant norms have been acquired. The problem is how they are acquired. By definition, they cannot be assented to rationally, accepted on normative grounds, and so on, because the resources to do this have not yet been acquired. Whatever is acquired must be acquired with resources available in this beginning state. This threshold problem thus is also a bootstrapping problem. The way the threshold problem has been frequently defined, influenced by Davidson and before him Stuart Hampshire (1959: 99), is this: that normative rationality, intentionality or intentional ascription, and concept possession and belief (understood normatively) presuppose one another—they are a kind of cartel. From the point of view of acquisition, consequently, they are a common threshold. And this means that none of these elements are available as a resource for bootstrapping from the nonnormative side of the threshold to the normative one.[9]

I have not directly attacked this now commonplace thesis about the conceptual interdependence of norms, intention, and language,[10] but it is perhaps appropriate to register my extreme skepticism about it here. In the first place, the argument depends on a certain amount of redefinition. In the usual uses of the notion of "attributing intention," for example, the thesis is simply false: Psychologists of infant behavior claim that young infants (eight months old) can reason about the intentions of others. There is a similar problem with the idea of the "normativity" of language as being connected to a capacity to read intentional states. In fact, high-functioning autistics, who are unable to read the intentions of others, have been known to be linguistically gifted, able to pick up a grammar book and rapidly acquire a foreign language. One might conclude from this that the capacity to speak grammatically and acquire "rules" and the capacity to recognize intentions are independent. But the commonplace view depends on arguing that some language use, for example, that of Wittgenstein's builders and, presumably, young children, is not really "language" and that the attribution of intention to infants is not "really" interpretation of intention. These arguments serve to immunize the hypothesis and circularize the claim.

My point in what follows, however, involves a different aspect of the problem. By creating a threshold and calling it normativity, and claiming that the concepts that might be employed to explain facts about normativity, such as intention, are conceptually bound up with and indeed inseparable from normativity, explanation is made impossible. There is a transition from the prenormative infant or prenormative form of human life to the normative. But if all the explainers are on the normative side, they cannot explain the transition, and the transition becomes a mystery. My purpose here is to simply identify some forms of argument, some explainers that appear to escape this problem. Of course, one response to them is to insist that these explainers also belong to the normative side, for example, the magical or charismatic. In my view, this move simply extends the circularity mentioned above.

How does McDowell deal with this problem? In two ways: by free use of metaphor in characterizing the acquisition of reason and by insisting that it is a nonproblem:

> It is not even clearly intelligible to suppose a creature might be born at home in the space of reasons. Human beings are not: they are born mere animals, and they are transformed into thinkers and intentional agents in the course of coming to maturity. This transformation risks looking mysterious. But we can take it in our stride if, in our conception of the *Bildung* that is a central element in the normal maturation of human beings, we give pride of place to the learning of language. In being initiated into language, a human being is introduced into something that already embodies putatively rational linkages between concepts, putatively constitutive of the layout of the space of reasons, before she comes on the scene. This is a picture of initiation into the space of reasons as an already going concern; there is no problem about how something describable in those terms could emancipate a human individual from a merely animal mode of living into a full-fledged subject, open to the world. (1994: 125)

Once a language, and with it conceptual capacities and reason, is acquired, their normative character need merely to be recognized—one's eyes are opened to them.

> The idea is that the dictates of reason are there anyway, whether or not one's eyes are opened to them; that is what happens in a proper upbringing. We need not try to understand the thought that the dictates of reason are objects of an enlightened awareness, except from within the way of thinking such an upbringing initiates one into: a way of thinking that constitutes a standpoint from which those dictates are already in view. (1994: 91–92)

With this, we are very close to Oakeshott's notion that the normative or, for Oakeshott, simply what we see to be good is discovered within a practice we have already subscribed to. But there is a deep difference in their notions of how acquisition occurs, which leads to a difference in their accounts of where it leads. For McDowell, acquiring a culture leads to an awakening to the dictates of reason, a normative structure that is in some sense already there. The question of how this acquiring of a culture is possible, given the threshold and bootstrapping problems mentioned earlier, is never addressed. Oakeshott, however, does address them.

For Oakeshott (1989), there is no threshold. Learning begins neither with information nor judgment but with these two components together. They "can both be communicated and acquired, but cannot be communicated and acquired separately" (1989: 56). His idealism consists in this claim, and it has a particular significance if we understand it in the light of connectionism. All experience is, so to speak, experience through one's own abilitied body. The body is one in which inputs lead to changes in how future inputs are processed. These inputs are the "information" that combines with "judgment" to produce experience. The conjoining occurs prior to experience. And in connectionist terms, we might think of it as occurring in the synapses and the connectionist net to produce the conditions of experience. Intelligence, learning, and so forth appear at the subrational level, that is to say, prior to the point at which McDowell would say "we acquire conceptual powers" (1994: 115), as recognition and differentiation improve through repetition and feedback. Intelligence is not something superadded to this process; it is a feature of the process itself.

THE COST

In the beginning of this chapter, I said that I would explain Oakeshott's significance and the significance of the conjunction between Oakeshott's account of practice and connectionism in relation to contemporary concerns. In the briefest of terms, the interest is this: Oakeshott provides an alternative vocabulary for addressing the fundamental problems posed by idealism, such as those discussed by McDowell. The vocabulary avoids what I have called the threshold and bootstrapping problems: What for McDowell must be acquired is already, for Oakeshott, being acquired, and in a way that is intelligible "naturalistically" or at least not "spooky." It is acquired through the bit-by-bit improvement of skills modeled by connectionism. Does this "solve" the problem posed by the normative account of reason? It does not pretend to. But it might provide a vocabulary within the features of intellect we wish to understand, such as our capacity to make sense of one another, which for Oakeshott is "the ability to detect individual intelligence at work in every utterance" (1989: 61) rather than our mutual subordination to the dictates of normative reason, and which can be adequately described and within which the problems of idealism that continue to haunt us do not arise. "Intelligence" and "detecting intelligence" are a change in terms from "concepts," "intentionality," and "reason." But this is not merely a change in terms. The former avoid the threshold problem; the latter do not. And we may put the matter another way. Without an account like Oakeshott's of the process of learning as acquiring the "manifolds of abilities" that the "inheritance of human achievements" (1989: 56) consists of, we are compelled, as McDowell is, to speak metaphorically about processes, such as the acquisition of an "inheritance" of normative reason, which inevitably remain, as McDowell says, "spooky," despite his insistence that they are not. Indeed, they avoid the spooky notion of the "normativity" of reason entirely.

But this solution is not cost free. To accept it, we must accept something akin to Oakeshott's own account of the way in which objects of thought emerge from experience—the problem, to be short about it, of concepts. This problem has traditionally been held against connectionism, especially by Jerry Fodor, and for similar reasons. It seems as though conceptualized experience requires concepts; unconceptualized experience, by definition, cannot fully supply them. So they must come from some other source, possibly already resident in some sense in the mind itself.

Oakeshott's idealism rests on a rejection of the distinctions that make up this problem ([1933] 1978: 67) by arguing that the real world is the world of experience, which is also (and already) a world of ideas. Thus, for Oakeshott, what is to be accounted for is not the transformation of unconceptualized experience into conceptualized experience but something that is a matter of degree. The experiences we first have are confused, or incoherent, and we make them more coherent "when noticings become thought and when, in virtue of distinguishing and remembering likenesses and unlikenesses in what is going on, we come to inhabit a world of recognizables" (Oakeshott 1975: 3). This was done in the course of what Oakeshott describes as a "continuous and unconditional engagement of learning to understand which is well on its way in even the most exiguous acts of attention" (Oakeshott 1975: 2). Distinguishing and remembering likenesses and unlikenesses are what connectionist machines do by virtue of their capacity to associate inputs with feedback and to statistically associate elements of input with other elements. Thus, a machine comes, so to speak, to inhabit a world of recognizables through association.

Is this a good enough account? The answer to this question depends on how one understands the break between having concepts and not having them. Oakeshott employs the language of "identification" to avoid this problem, but his discussion of identification is at the same time a clear attempt to face the substance of the problem by providing a surrogate language to describe it. His argument is that the break between having concepts and having an experience is not absolute, and the process of identification, of seeking less confusion, especially by identifying the "ideal characters" in terms of which we identify something as a particular kind of thing, is a continuous process and one that operates on a world of experience that is already ideational.

> Characteristics are themselves rudimental ideal characters. Such a character is a reflective composition that may begin by being no more than a sketch. It emerges from a selection, combination, and arrangement of characteristics in which recollection has superceded remembering, in which observation is directed by anticipatory guesses, and in which the characteristics on which attention is focused cease to be recognized merely in terms of resemblances and differences and merely as indications of one another and are understood as the lines or marks that together delineate a conceptual identity. (Oakeshott 1975: 4)

Identification is not, however, as concept acquisition is usually supposed to be, a normative matter, at least in the sense that a rule is—whose normativity consists in its correct use. Identification is fallible, and "mistake is possible," but "mistake here is confusion." "Such conclusions as, 'not a boy but a dwarf', 'not a bird but a kite', 'not a court of law in session but a scene from a play', are its characteristic outcomes" (Oakeshott 1975: 5). They are also, it may be noted, the characteristic outcomes of the learning done by connectionist machines, which distinguish, for example, tumors from shadows. In the higher reaches of the understanding, in theorizing and reflecting, identifications, still fallible, can be refined and also come to have different objects, including the second-order identification of the "ideal characters" that enable identification itself (Oakeshott 1975: 5–6).

It is at this stage of questioning and refining past identifications that it makes sense to speak of assumptions and postulates—at the stage in which we abstract from what is going on and explore what Oakeshott calls a "platform of conditional understanding" (1975: 9). But to speak in this way is no more than to consider as problematic conditions of understanding that we have been treating as unproblematic. To enter into such consideration is not to reveal presuppositions resident in the mind but rather to enter into a series of novel conditional understandings, in which we treat some conditions as unproblematic in order to treat some other condition as problematic. Postulates are simply conditions of understanding treated as potential objects of inquiry. They are not something pre-given, in the original Kantian sense, through universal endowment in the mind or through the internalization of a frame. The conditions in question are established through the continuous process that leads from the initial stirrings of differentiation of experience through to identification. Thus, "identification," as Oakeshott understands it, adds nothing in the way of ideal content to what is already there in experience. To the extent that there is anything normative in our understanding, the same holds: It is produced out of what is already there—not injected, as Friedman says.

8 Against Semantic Frames
Meaning without Theory

The language that is customarily used to refer to meaning is atemporal, and determinedly so. The conventional accounts of meaning developed in response to Saul Kripke's account of the problem of following a rule (Kripke 1982). As Paul Boghossian puts it, "the idea of meaning something by a word is an idea with an infinitary character . . . there are literally no end of truths about how I ought to apply the term . . . if I am to use it in accord with its meaning" (Boghossian 1989: 509). And this is not an artifact of Kripke's example, which is from arithmetic—"it holds for any concept" (Boghossian 1989: 509). Dispositions can't account for meanings, because they are finite—or as we might put it, dispositions are part of history, limited to the mental life of actual historical persons, whereas meanings are eternal or outside of time.

Quentin Skinner relied on a similar philosophical background when he appealed to the notion that in interpreting a given author one could rely on "conventions" that could be revealed by studying normal or less prominent texts of the same period (Skinner 1970: 135). The interpreter could assume that these conventions were known to the author of the text that was originally in question and that the author relied on these same conventions to give meaning to the text, even if the point of the text was to subvert the conventions. But convention is a notion bound to something historical—to the people who observe the conventions. Nevertheless, they too are fixed, and in this sense located someplace out of the flux of actual historical persons and their acts. Skinner provides something in the way of explanation when he notes "various different concepts which have gone with various different societies" (Skinner 1969: 53). There is thus some connection between concepts and "societies," but "gone with" implies that they are separable things.

The neo-Kantian historicists, similarly, regarded historical epochs as differing in the mental structures that informed their tastes, beliefs, and the meanings that they ascribed to the world of events, facts, and artifacts. This idea soon hardened into a historiographic dogma, well expressed by Carl Becker, in his study of the Enlightenment, where he called this the climate of opinion:

> Whether arguments command assent or not depends less upon the logic that conveys them than upon the climate of opinion in which they are sustained. What renders Dante's argument or St. Thomas' definition

> meaningless to us is not bad logic or want of intelligence, but the medieval climate of opinion—those instinctively held preconceptions in the broad sense, that *Weltanschauung* or world pattern—which imposed upon Dante and St. Thomas a peculiar use of the intelligence and a special type of logic. To understand why we cannot easily follow Dante or St. Thomas it is necessary to understand (as well as may be) the nature of this climate of opinion. (Becker [1932] 1959: 5)

The climates of opinion of the past no longer "impose" themselves on anyone, but they are in some sense accessible to us as objects, fixed objects which on the one hand explain the thinking of the past and on the other enable us to interpret it.

The problem of the static character of these objects, including not only meaning-bestowing objects such as worldviews, but also the words on which meaning is bestowed, runs very deep, with various surface manifestations. These manifestations appear most familiarly in the historiography of science. In the 1960s Paul Feyerabend made the then revolutionary claim, against the idea that more advanced theories explained less advanced theories by derivation, that at least some large class of theories were not about the same thing as the theories that preceded them, because the meanings of the terms had changed in the course of the advance (Feyeraband 1962: 33). In the hands of Thomas Kuhn, this thesis became the positive theory that the meanings of scientific terms were given by paradigms, which were themselves, among other things, structures of assumptions shared by a given scientific community.

These were accounts of difference. But there was an underlying conflict between the fixed character of meaning-bestowing facts, the conventions, rules, and frameworks, and the facts of change that they were supposed to help account for. Kuhn could not conceive of these meaning-bestowing assumptions as changing in a normal way, in the way that ordinary explicit beliefs changed in the face of new evidence or new considerations. Because they were at a tacit level, and were constitutive of the meanings of the new evidence and the new considerations, they were necessarily immune to revision by new evidence or considerations, and consequently could only change holistically, by revolutions that installed new constitutive meaning-bestowing assumptions.

MEANINGS AND FRAMEWORKS: THE TEMPORAL AND THE ATEMPORAL MEET

Rules, conventions, frameworks, worldviews, and the like explain meanings, and also give us access to meanings. The means of understanding and explaining are fixed. But the "meanings" that they explain are themselves things that change. This produces two problems: one having to do with explanation, and explanatory regresses, and the other having to do with access. The problem of access takes two forms: Where do we get access to the meanings of texts or actions in history and how do we get access to the rules, conventions, assumptions, and so forth governing the meanings? The relation between these two problems of access is muddled, and so is the relation between these problems and the problem of explaining the facts of rules, conventions, and frameworks and the way they change or succeed one another.

The primary problem for the historian is access to the meanings of texts and statements by historical agents. As Skinner puts it, historians face the "obvious difficulty that the literal meanings of key terms sometimes change over time" (Skinner 1969: 31–32). Indeed, to

> discover from the history of thought that there are in fact no such timeless concepts, but only the various different concepts which have gone with various different societies, is to discover a general truth not merely about the past but about ourselves as well. (Skinner 1969: 53)

So conceptual change and conceptual variation is ubiquitous, and the presently understood "literal" meaning of a text from the past may not have had that meaning in the past. In one sense this is a gift or opportunity if, as Skinner says, the "essential philosophical, even moral, value" of "the classic texts, especially in social, ethical, and political thought," is that they "help to reveal—if we let them—not the essential sameness, but rather the essential variety of viable moral assumptions and political commitments" (Skinner 1969: 52). Indeed, the exercise can tell us something about ourselves that may have been previously hidden from us, namely the fact that we assumed and politically committed to a different framework. In either case, we are compelled, in order to understand the language as it was written, to refer to something else, something that does change, namely assumptions, commitments, conventions, and so forth. The explanation of the meaning of the literal words is referred back to the thing that did change, namely the framework.

Skinner has written much more since these arguments were originally given, and we may reasonably ask whether his views have changed in ways that make any difference.[1] The key question is this: Has Skinner abandoned the idea of meaning-bestowing facts? In an earlier replies to his critics, he was unremittingly hostile to the obvious point that in order to understand past texts, historians needed to translate into terms intelligible to present audiences, a point made by Martin Hollis and myself (Turner 1983). In my case the point was posed in more or less holistic Quinean terms, and Skinner found the argument, according to our private correspondence, utterly uncompelling. Now he seems to have embraced holism, and even treats it as his main point (Skinner 2002, Vol. 1: 4–5). But for holism there are no meaning-bestowing facts; there is rather the web of belief, and meanings are a matter of the place of a claim in the inferences making up the web of belief. Foundational accounts, in contrast, provide a meaning-bestowing fact. The two approaches are antithetical in theory and produce different kinds of historical writing in practice (Turner 2010). Skinner formerly favored "convention." His current work abounds in clichés of the same kind: "We are of course embedded in practices and constrained by them" (Skinner 2002, Vol. 1: 7). The newly favored term "vision" itself functions as a meaning-bestowing explainer. Skinner suggests, for example, that the use of normative language by the "innovating ideologist" who composes a political text "will always reflect a wish to impose a particular moral vision on the workings of the social world" (2002, Vol. 1: 182). Unless this is an empty metaphor, the vision presumably determines the meanings, and to understand the meaning we need to understand the vision that motivates the speech.

Skinner's original solution to the explanatory part of the problem of change comes at an odd price: The thing that is fixed, the meaning of the original text, is accounted for by something else that is fixed, namely a set of conventions, which is different from the one we now have, and associated in some way with a different society. This produces a conflict: The means we have for talking about meaning involve notions, such as rules, assumptions, and the like, that are fixed and atemporal. They vary, as Skinner says, between societies, but they don't themselves change. So, whereas the point of appealing to these notions is to account for meaning change, or at least meaning difference, in history, this just pushes the problem one step back to the point where change itself becomes a mystery, a mystery wrapped in the enigma of "society." The new Skinner acknowledges this problem and says that as a result of his study of "the classical theorists of eloquence" he has "come to share their more skeptical understanding of normative concepts and the fluid vocabularies in which they are habitually expressed" and to "appreciate their sense that there will always be a degree of 'neighborliness', as they liked to call it, between apparently conflicting evaluative terms" (2002, Vol. 1: 182).

Where do such claims leave us? Is there an alternative, such as a dynamic notion of meaning, which would allow for and account for meaning change as a normal historical phenomenon? Or is there no alternative to theories of meaning that depend on supposed meaning-producing facts—rules that are hidden behind usages which give them meaning, for example—that are themselves static. Skinner's language of fluidity suggests that there should be, but his continued appeal to "practices," "vision," and similar terms suggests that there is no alternative to appealing to rigid meaning-bestowing structures, be they climates of opinion or conventions. Skinner's more recent writing turns to a genealogical account of meaning change, exemplified most recently in his essay "The Sovereign State: A Genealogy" (2001). Does this provide us any clues? In one respect this essay does represent an about face: The style of argument, and its focus on the unit-idea of sovereignty and its variations, would fit comfortably into the work of his former *bête-noire*, Arthur O. Lovejoy. But Skinner's "genealogy" is largely a recounting of literal quotations: What one gets is variation, but very little understanding of the structure of inferences in which these variations were meaningful, or the problems they solved for their authors, or why one followed another. Lovejoy's learned inquiries into what he himself called "the amazing diversity of meanings" (1961: x) of such terms as "Romanticism," in contrast, are all about related ideas and the problems they produce when they are fit together, and about how this explains why one followed another and how usages changed when they got into the hands of people whose related ideas were different.

DICTIONARIES VERSUS CONVENTIONS

Do we need to appeal to meaning-bestowing structures at all? An interesting hint as to what the alternative might be is provided by Nathan Tarcov, in his review of Skinner's earlier volume of methodological writings, when he remarks that "every textualist [namely, the target of Skinner's complaints, meaning for us a literal reader] who has used a historical dictionary or learned foreign languages has implicitly agreed with Skinner" (Tarcov 1982: 695–96). This gives us an alternative way of thinking of the problem. Dictionaries are fixed documents themselves. They are not means of explaining change, and not intended to be. A definition is precisely the same kind of fixed, nondynamic thing that allows for or enables interpretation but does not correspond to the dynamic fact of meaning. But dictionaries are the kinds of documents that consciously abstract from actual usage to something standard, or even "correct." And this is useful for interpretation: To know what is taken as correct usage may help in understanding the nonconforming usage in a text as a transgression. But dictionaries do not bestow meaning. They reconstruct meanings from usages that are already there and ideas about correctness that are already there.

Tarcov's comment begins to show a way out of the muddle, by implicitly separating two things: the supposed historical facts about assumptions, climates of opinion, worldviews, conventions, and whatnot on which interpretation allegedly depends and the banal stuff of dictionary definitions, which are clearly reconstructions, approximations, and simplifications of actual semantic usage, usually, given the didactic aims of dictionary writers, with a strong whiff of the normative, not to say the snobbish. Although a dictionary definition is an aid to getting at the meaning of something, and a practically indispensable shortcut for the nonnative speaker, it can never be regarded as wholly adequate as a guide nor as a fact about something in the heads or the social world of the historical agents whose words are being interpreted. In short, assumptions, climates of opinion, and the like are doing double duty, as means of interpretation that provide access to meanings and as (perhaps bogus) explanatory concepts; in contrast, dictionary definitions are post hoc simplifications that explain nothing, but help provide access to what people mean. What people mean does not depend in any explanatory way on these definitions; rather, the construction of the definitions depends on what people mean.

This allows us to rethink the muddle with which this section began. The problem of access involves two things that need accessing: the meanings of texts or actions in history and the rules, conventions, assumptions, and so forth governing the meanings. The standard account reasons that one must first access the conventions and then use this knowledge to determine the meanings of the terms and speech acts. The dictionary model, if we can call it that, works the other way around: It proceeds from actual usage and reconstructs definitions from what is actually said and how terms are applied. The reconstructed definitions can then be reused to understand other texts. The actual process of making sense of the texts, and the material on which the interpreter works, are the same in both cases: There is no direct access to conventions, rules, assumptions, and the like—they are simply inferred from usage, just as dictionary definitions are. The only difference is in the status of these things as theoretical objects—namely as explainers. Dictionary definitions are idealizations of usage; conventions and rules are bestowers of meaning that lie behind and explain usage in its normative aspect. It doesn't matter that the dictionary definition is fixed—the definition is self-consciously retrospective, although these definitions can be taken as norms, if someone chooses to be didactic about correct speech. It does matter that meaning-bestowing rules, frameworks, and so on are fixed: They are supposed to account for an infinitude of possible applications. So the difference between the two is a matter of explanatory status.

This is not an approach that "rule" theorists of meaning will accept. For them, mere reconstruction is not enough. Their reasoning is, oddly enough, temporal. And they insist on something analogous to agentic powers. For them, there is no meaning without rules, or something like rules, which lie behind and give meaning to a sentence or concept, warranting the infinitude of its application. These have to be there in the first place, in order for a term to mean anything. Rules, or whatever assures meanings, are in the realm of fact, or at least of normative fact, and they have a special explanatory job—they explain the normative fact of a speaker's meaning. For these thinkers, the explanatory regress is central: The whole point of a theory of meaning is to provide the right kind of explanation. Dispositions are the wrong kind. Rules are the right kind. But these are odd explanations. They depend on a special kind of analogy. The terms "assumption," "presupposition," "rule," and the like are terms with an explicit sense, which is being extended to a sense which is tacit and entirely a matter of ascription by the analyst. There is no explicit rule governing usage, nor are there assumptions actually made, as one might make a stipulation in a legal proceeding, nor are there actual conventions, as there are in international law, made by entering into covenants with others. One can give a definition of a word, but the words we normally use aren't "defined" for us by anyone. Rather, these terms are all analogies, which point to supposed tacit facts that shadow and give meaning to the things they explain, rather than the kinds of rules, conventions, and assumptions that are made in historical moments, by temporal acts of enactment, agreement, or statements of what one will assume. So this analogy is odd in another way: The normal use of the term refers to an act in history; the analogical use refers to the results of an act which is outside of history.

So how do rules, conventions, and the like relate to, or enter, history? The answer, if we follow the metaphorical usages, is some variant of this: They may be adhered to or assumed by different people or groups at different times, and these acts of adherence or assumption are historical. As intellectual objects they are historically inert and changeless. Terms like "adhere" simultaneously serve as substitutes for a genuine explanation and point to the analogical character of the whole picture of concepts in society of which it is a part. To bridge the gap between the atemporal character of the explanatory concepts themselves and the fact of their historical location in groups requires some sort of analogy to the convenings that produce conventions, or the rule-givers who produce rules. But there are none. This is explanation by myth.

BEHIND THE DICTIONARY

The "rule" theorists of meaning nevertheless have a point, which can be put in the form of a question. What is it that the dictionaries reconstruct into meanings? Their answer is "rule-following speech behavior." So for them, rules have to be part of the story. Is there an alternative? A simple alternative answer, suited to the idea of dictionary definitions as reconstructions of usage, might be this: Language is "intelligible speech." We understand what people say, including the extended usages, "erroneous" usages, misapplications of terms, and so forth. Many of the extensions of application we understand are analogical or metaphorical. Sometimes we make sense of what we are told by treating it as intelligible error. Sometimes it is not so much error as a novel but intelligible extension of the application of the term. Once the extension becomes widely enough used, or used by acceptable people, it can be entered into the dictionary. The dictionary is not a framework, or at least not the kind of framework that is prior to the meaning, but it is a means of gaining access to the meaning of an expression used by a person in the historical past.

This sense of language, as what is intelligible at a given time, does enter into history, at least on occasion, as the subject matter of history. It is an explicit part of the history of law, for the simple reason that legal concepts have to be extended to apply to new cases. Sometimes these extensions have dramatic consequences. One might give as a paradigmatic and historically interesting example Max Weber's dissertation in the history of commercial law (Weber 2003). Weber's problem was to identify the processes by which the law of corporations developed, which is first and foremost a matter of making contracts that distribute liability.

A similar problem arises in terms of the history of legal personality: In Roman times, it extended to the whole of the household of the free man, including the persons of his slaves, wife, and children. Over time, this diminished to the modest "person" we have today, whose right even to self-defense is circumscribed. At the same time, more categories of people acquired these rights. This case involves another process of meaning change that applies very generally as well: Changes in the beliefs about classes of people or things lead to the extension of meaning to these things. The morality of slavery was challenged by writings like *Uncle Tom's Cabin* because they humanized the slaves, bringing them into the category of beings for whom notions of rights and human dignity could be appropriately applied. Something similar might be said for the application of the concept of the soul: When different groups were taken to have souls, the usual meanings that applied to possessors of souls also applied to the newly recognized possessors of souls.

There is an interesting literature in history itself on another kind of change, the problem of oppositions, or counterconcepts, such as civilized and barbarian, associated with Rienhardt Koselleck (2004) and plausibly derived from Carl Schmitt (Koselleck 2002: 84–99). Schmitt famously said:

> Words such as state, republic, society, class, as well as sovereignty, constitutional state, absolutism, dictatorship, economic planning, neutral or total state, and so on, are incomprehensible if one does not know exactly who is affected, combated, refuted, or negated by such terms. ([1932] 1996: 30–31)

The interesting feature of these counterconcepts is that they persist because they make some sort of useful distinction. But when we characterize something as a barbaric practice, we no longer have in mind the barbarians that the Greeks made the contrast with, nor the ones the Romans did. So the distinction persists, but the objects of the distinction change, and the intentions behind using them change as well: What sort of negation or refutation is involved is not determined by the term, but by the intelligible use to which it is put. To call one's political opponents barbarians is often merely to announce that one is not going to treat them civilly.

The mechanisms by which terms get extended and concretized in new ways are well known. Metaphors end up as mundane usages: Philosophical terms such as "true" and "norm," for example, are carpentry terms. The language of political theory and law, including notions like sovereignty, bodies, the nation, and so forth derive by more or less visible past steps of extension from the concept of the monarch, the medieval problem of the king's two bodies, and metaphors about contracts. Metaphors, metonyms, analogies, similes, synecdoches, and the like harden into abstract usages along with theories that provide a web of beliefs in which they play an inferential role, and the original uses are sometimes forgotten. The extension of terms and the invention of theories go hand in hand in this process, along with the creation of new equivalences by the adjustment of belief and the alteration of categories—categories like capable of feeling pain, possessing a soul, capable of moral conduct, rights-bearing, and so forth.

The common thread in all these cases of change is this: The novel application, extension, or usage needs to be intelligible at the time the extension is made. It must at least be intelligible to the speaker or author. And these usages are normally directed at an actual audience, which will understand them or not. To imagine otherwise is to imagine an author writing for an unknown audience. But unless the author had some idea of what the audience would understand—unless it was a hypothetical audience constructed on the model of an actual audience that would take the terms in known ways—the author would be faced with the problem of communicating with an audience which might take the words in hitherto unknown ways. Nor is this an empty fear. Nietzsche's counter-genealogies of terms were designed to illustrate this point. And there are many other cases. Terms like "objective" and "subjective" reversed meanings in the course of their history. Terms like "*propria*" and "manner" went from being descriptive terms for individual conduct to terms like "proprieties" and "manners" that came to describe abstract de-individualized normative standards. Each step in the evolution of these terms is intelligible, in the sense that we can provide a reconstruction of the way in which the extension made sense to its author and to some possible audience at the time of the extension.[2]

This leaves us with a stark and problematic opposition: between the sense of meaning bound to the ongoing process of making intelligible utterances, which is a sense of meaning in the flux of speech and understanding, and the fixed sense of meaning captured through the identification of conventions. The distinction is between this practical ability and its theoretical reconstruction. The ability is in flux; the reconstruction is fixed, but also fails to ever adequately capture the practical ability to understand and to be understood.

If we leave the issue with this contrast between the flux of meaning and the necessarily false theoretical reconstruction of meaning, however, we still face some muddles. There is a long tradition of thinking that meanings, once established, cannot be lost: Mill gave an account of this, influenced by Coleridge, and one can find similar ideas in many other writers, including Heidegger. Indeed, the nineteenth century passion for philology reflected a kind of mysticism about the recovery of meanings which implied some sort of notion of meaning as hidden in the remains of texts, which the later reader can unlock. And there is a problem here, however muddled.

We live with texts from the past. We read them, interpret them in order to appeal to them as interlocutors and, in various contexts, including the law and religious settings, as authoritative. At first blush, this is a problem that arises from the fact that there are texts: Literate societies have this problem of the ongoing transformation of intelligible speech, the flux of meaning as intended and understood by speakers, and the contrasting fixity of the written word. And indeed there is a sense in which the problem of meaning vanishes if we are in an entirely oral world, in which nothing is preserved which could have a meaning that differs from the meanings of the present. But even in the world of orality, there is an analogous problem: Epic poems that are repeated according to formula become archaic and have contents that may no longer mean, in the flux of speech, the same thing, or anything at all. But in this case the muddle is not about theoretical objects, "rules" and the like. It is about actual forms of expression—epic poems and texts—that happen to be transmitted in a different way from the ordinary flux of usage and are detached from the practical knowledge of the original users.

THE MYSTERY OF PRACTICAL KNOWLEDGE

Consider a real historical problem about the fighting ship of antiquity, the trireme. We know the Greek word from the texts. The name refers to the three levels of oars. We know from the context and what is said about them that they are ships with specific properties. We have plenty of pictures on ceramics. But we lack the practical knowledge that the Greeks themselves had of making these objects and of operating them. The knowledge was lost in late antiquity. In the 1980s, a project attempted to reconstruct a trireme based on ancient sources, which included images and a great deal of recorded "literal" information about the capabilities of the vessel, together with the present knowledge of naval architects. The vessel, the *Olympias*, was subjected to sea trials, including one with a crew of 170. The sea trials showed that the reconstructed vessel had many of the capabilities attributed to the ancient triremes, including their recorded straight-line speed and their ability to turn 180 degrees quickly. However, some things could not be duplicated, notably the bracing ropes, which had to be replaced by steel cables which did not flex with the hull as the original natural fiber rope did.

Do we now know what "trireme" really meant? And with it also know what the nautical descriptions and accounts of naval battles in the ancient world really meant? Do we know what the practical meaning of the coxswain's command to "feather," or its ancient equivalent, "means" for a trireme with a large number of oarsmen? Or do we now at least have a much better theory, and better practical knowledge, because the theory and practical knowledge which we now have do a better job than previous theories of accounting for such things as the recorded capabilities of these ancient vessels? It seems clear that the answer is that we have a better theory, as well as a good surrogate for some of the practical knowledge which was lost. The *Olympias* is an "as if" trireme, reconstructed "as if" it were the same as the ancient one. It is a functional substitute for the ancient ones, designed to have the same properties, and also to resemble the ancient images and conform to the properties in the ancient texts. It is constructed for us, by us, and with the materials available to us from the evidence available to us. Aside from these tests, we can never know if the reconstruction is correct. Our reconstructed trireme is outside of the flux of intelligible discussion and practical knowledge that ended in late antiquity. We can guess that it is close enough that it would be recognized as a trireme, but this depends on whether the theory and the practical knowledge on which the reconstruction is based is right: Another reconstruction might produce a vessel with sufficiently different features that the ancient mariner would find it acceptable and the *Olympias* an anomaly. We cannot test that meaning hypothesis.

The *Olympias* is literally a model; it is not an exact model, but a kind of ideal type of the ancient trireme, which, as it happens, we can experiment on. It uses different material for lines, and thus flexes differently. But this is a kind of difference we understand in our own terms. There is a lot about the physical act of rowing we understand as well, so we know what the differences between our experience of rowing and what that of the smaller men of the ancient world would have been. So in constructing and using this model we rely on a background that does not change and to a large extent is not a matter of theory. The physicality of the act of rowing, of the features of sea water and wind, are all part of the background that we don't need to alter or account for. We know a bit about the properties of wood in sailing vessels and have reason to think that the wood used for the model is close enough to the original, although like the bracing ropes it is not the same. But we have tested the theory with this model. And we can say that we know better what "trireme" meant as a result. We have more confidence in the meaning of ancient texts about sea battles, and we may be able to make sense of previously obscure passages and claims.

At the same time, we know that this is only a model and that we are missing a vast amount of practical knowledge and oral content—the kind that is preserved, at least partially, for the period 1800–1813 in the Aubrey-Maturin series of historical novels by Patrick O'Brian, and by the passed-down practical knowledge and vocabulary of the sailors who continue to sail the "Tall Ships" that most navies still maintain. We know that techniques and practical knowledge must have changed and varied over the millennia during which the trireme was used and among the navies that used them. This vast web of usage and knowledge, which was oral or largely so, is what is lost, and for which our model ship is a substitute of limited value. We had to import our own oral tradition, and indeed the physical experience of rowing under command and giving commands, to actually get the trireme through its sea trials—we had to use our language, and our nautical language, as a functional substitute for the one that the ancient mariners possessed, in order to sail the model trireme, along with our functional knowledge and the knowledge concealed in the tools and materials we used to create the model.

MEANING WITHOUT THEORY

The *Olympias* is a model, made with a combination of physical elements, some of which are close to those we believe to be characteristic of triremes in the ancient world, some of which are functional substitutes with different properties. Not everything is the same, nor does it need to be, for the purpose at hand. And what is this purpose? To see if the model as constructed could perform as the ancient sources said the trireme performed, and thus test our theory of trireme construction. By having the model, some of the missing links in our understanding of ancient navies could be filled in. But we also know that this is an artificial model. We think we know enough to correctly conclude that certain functional substitutes, such as the steel cables, won't affect the experience. One aspect, perhaps not the most obvious but nevertheless essential to its character as a test, was the human element of the sea trials—the test of whether actual rowers could actually make the model trireme perform the feats that the ancient texts recorded. The real rowers were of course themselves "models" in a sense: It was known that ancient rowers were smaller, and this needed to be taken into account. Nevertheless, if the test had required capacities that were physically impossible for accomplished rowers, the model as a whole would have failed the test. And we would again be unable to say that we knew any better than before what "trireme" meant in these ancient texts.

The situation with the model is similar to the situation we have with appeals to convention, presuppositions, and the like. They are as artificial as the *Olympias*. But if they work, in this case to illuminate and enable the kinds of inferences that make the texts intelligible to us, they do their job of explaining how the authors could reason as they apparently did—to come to the novel conclusions that Machiavelli and Hobbes did, for example, or to the conventional but alien conclusions of other authors. In short, we can use "as if" constructions, and we do: It is "as if" people were following conventions and had coherent worldviews, and scientists had paradigms and what not, as long as these crutches get us where we want to go—to the facts about what someone meant. Once established, these meaning hypotheses can receive additional support, by making sense of more texts, and eventually depend less on the scaffolding of "as if" statements that were needed to reconstruct the meaning in the first place. Perhaps this deepened understanding would allow us to detect nuances of change and variation that can enable us to come closer to the fluid and variable "meanings" of actual speech and communication of the historical addressees, rooted in a distinctive set of experiences, and so forth.

With this kind of knowledge, we would approximate the situation of a person who was capable of interacting with the authors in their own era and possessing the practical knowledge that gives meaning to the terms, such as "feather." And this was the goal with using actual rowers to do the work of the ancient rowers—to provide substitutes who would have to be able to do what the ancient rowers did, to not only lift the oars, but to respond to the commands. To be sure, we are limited in our ability to test our understanding. The dead cannot talk back. And we cannot be sure that the samples of material on which we are working, the texts, represent fairly the experiences we would have had if we were interacting. We are even more limited when the material itself is limited, as with the ancient world. But this is a difference of degree: Interaction with the living itself provides only a sample, and not every aspect of our understanding is subject to test in these interactions.

So what is the lesson of all this? Making historical claims about what some past thinker meant on the basis of a theory of meaning seems to make history depend on the validity of particular kind of metaphysics, at least a metaphysics of meaning, and thus to lose its independence from philosophy. There is the danger that in using such notions as convention, as Skinner does, one is elevating the (inevitably passing) philosophical language of one particular era to the status of universal historical truth. With Skinner's original writings, this has perhaps already happened: Skinner has to explain the history of speech act theory to explain his former views and what he now claims. If we are treating claims about conventions and the like as an "as if" serving our particular purposes of understanding, however, we can accept the utility of these notions, if indeed there is the payoff of an improvement in understanding over the literal reading, that is to say if the texts make more sense and reveal more connections in the web of belief and practical action. We should, however, take "literal" literally, to refer to the contrast between writing and speech. The issue of recapturing what it meant to say something at a given point in the past and a given setting is a genuinely historical one. Appeals to convention, worldviews, and the like are crutches in solving this problem. It is of course an illusion that there actually is a set of shared assumptions, a Brandom-like space of reasons composed of normative inferential linguistic relations, a system of Skinnerian conventions, and so forth lying underneath actual language and making it operate at any historical moment. But debating this is not the point for the historian. These are not historical facts. The point is to know what it meant to give a command like "feather" on an ancient vessel, or to plead for judicial independence in the wake of the English civil war, or what it meant to affirm one's patriotism in the Weimar Republic, in 1920 and in 1933. And in these cases we need a simulacrum of the practical knowledge of the world in which inferences were being made from these acts of speaking and writing. If doing this is to fall into what Skinner describes as "the discredited hermeneutic ambition of stepping empathically into other people's shoes and attempting (in R. G. Collingwood's unfortunate phrase) to think their thoughts after them" (Skinner 2002, Vol. 1: 120), perhaps it is time for Skinner to grasp that attempting this is better than uncritically relying on problematic historical fictions about practices, conventions, and the like.

Part III

The Alternative

Tacitness, Empathy, and the Other

The final section collects essays that systematically present the alternative account, by showing the major facets of the account. The first essay, "Making the Tacit Explicit," examines the central puzzle: What is happening when people articulate their tacit knowledge? Much of the confusion over the notion of tacit knowledge comes from the idea that in this situation the speaker articulates inner tacit content that is more or less the same as what is made explicit. Examples show that this is false: that the statements in question are articulated for specific audiences with particular needs and are functional substitutes for the relevant tacit knowledge, not representations of it. The psychological literature on our knowledge of our intentions and on concepts, especially work by Lawrence Barsalou (1999), suggests that we are skilled at constructing these kinds of accounts "on the fly." This shifts the problem of "making explicit" to the fact that we are making something explicit to a person whom we construct as having specific functional needs. It therefore shifts the knowledge situation to one in which we already have tacit understanding of them, through such cognitive mechanisms as empathy.

The second and third essays deal with other facets. Chapter 10, "The Strength of Weak Empathy," uses empathy and the mirror neuron literature to account for the a priori through Franz Brentano's notion of *Evidenz*. The empathy required is not, however, the full kind of empathy involved in accessing complex intentions, but a weak kind, the sort required for the phenomenon of joint attention, ostensive definition, and such things as the tacit agreement Rush Rhees had in mind in accounting for Wittgenstein on rules. For Brentano, "evident" does not mean merely subjective self-evidence, but our recognition that others also take the same things to be evident. One might ask how one has the access to "other minds" that a claim like this "presupposes." But such phenomena as joint attention already involve the necessary "access" and are prior to the kind of thought that is involved in *Evidenz*. This view of *Evidenz* has broad implications as an alternative to Kantian-inflected philosophical accounts which account for our inferential capacities by appealing to underlying structures: Nothing of this sort need be hidden behind the basic phenomenon of joint attention and minimal kinds of mutual understanding, and these are sufficient to perform the explanatory work that was thought to require fixed structures of presuppositions. The final essay explains the difference between collective and social explanations, and elaborates a "social" alternative to the commonplace and empirically unwarranted use of collective concepts in cognitive science and philosophy. This chapter also deals with the difference between psychological facts about the tacit and the attribution of "assumptions."

9 The Tacit and the Social
Making the Tacit Explicit

The term "tacit knowledge" is used in a variety of ways, but the most common motivation is this: Some activity, inference, or communicative act depends on both the user and the recipient possessing some inferential element or mechanism which allows them to understand, anticipate, cooperate, or coordinate with another. The typical sign of an element of tacit knowledge is that some people can perform the activity, including the activity of inferential reasoning, and others cannot. On encountering an activity which others can perform one hypothesizes that there is such an element, and imputes it, or asks those engaged in the activity to explain it. This explanation or imputation makes the knowledge explicit, or seems to, in the least problematic cases.

The idea that the tacit can be made explicit—that not only do we know more than we can say, but that we can "say" explicitly at least some of what is tacit—is the source of a number of deep problems. In this chapter I will make two general points: The first is that the process of making the tacit explicit is misnamed and misunderstood, and that it can be better understood as a different and commonplace kind of explanatory activity resembling translation; the second is that the standard views of the tacit stuff underlying tacit knowledge in the brain are based on faulty analogies and are groundless, but there are alternatives which deal successfully with the important problem of transmission or acquisition.

TACIT KNOWLEDGE: LOGICAL, PSYCHOLOGICAL, SOCIAL, OR COLLECTIVE?

The concept of tacit knowledge trades on an ambiguity between psychological and logical notions. The difference between the two notions of tacit knowledge can be understood through an example that is marginal to the category of tacit knowledge, but has common features. In the 1980s the following puzzle was posed:

> A man is driving his son to soccer practice. The man loses control of the car and smashes headlong into a large tree. The father is killed

> instantly; however, the son is still alive but in critical condition. He's immediately rushed in for surgery for which the hospital was prepared thanks to a police call to the ER. The surgeon takes one look at the boy and says, "I can't operate on him. He's my son!"
>
> The puzzle: Who is the surgeon?

This was presented as a test of "sexism." The correct solution was that the surgeon was the mother of the injured son. To quote from one of the comments on the web version, "This classic brainteaser works—and it worked on me—because of the hidden assumption that surgeons are male."

What is a "hidden assumption"? And what sort of claim is a "because of the hidden assumption" claim? It has the surface form of an explanation citing a fact. But what sort of fact is "the hidden assumption"? Is the "assumption" a genuine fact, or simulacrum of a fact, about something in the mind or brain of the person making the comment? Or is it merely a kind of comment on the failure of this particular inference from the situation to the correct conclusion about the surgeon, with no corresponding psychological fact that resembles an "assumption"? Or is the assumption a transcendentally required condition for the possibility of answering the question in this way, and thus entailed by the answer. In short, was this a conclusion we could not have reached without this assumption, so it was "necessarily," in a logical sense, in the mind and therefore a psychological fact.

The answer seems to be this: It is a kind of comment about the failure of the inference. But if that is all it is, the "because" is insufficiently grounded. The first grounding problem is one of indeterminacy: There needs to be some reason to think that someone has in fact failed to make the correct inference "because" of this specific assumption rather than another that would warrant the same wrong inference. This is a problem for the idea that it is transcendentally required and thus entailed: It is not "required" in the sense it is the only "assumption" that could back this inference. It is equally warranted by the assumption that parents are not allowed to perform surgery on their children, or by many more assumptions that one could make up for the purpose of justifying the inference. What if the assumption was the more complicated one with the same implications for this case, that mother is an occupational role and that mothers were never surgeons? This would have the same result—it would account for the failure to make the inference. But which would be the real assumption? If we are doing Euclidean geometry, we know how the proof works because the assumptions are explicitly stated. Without an act of assumption, why even think that there is a fact of the matter that would decide between the two explanations?

There seems to be no alternative to thinking of the "assumption" as some sort of psychological fact. But what sort of psychological facts are they? This is a little more mysterious. "Sexism" is a psychological explanation, or an explanation with psychological implications: Unless there was something corresponding to it in the mind of the puzzle-solver, the response to the puzzle would not reveal it. But there are other possible psychological explanations. Perhaps the person responding to the puzzle was "primed" by hearing the terms "surgeon" and "man."[1] Perhaps the person correctly associated the term "surgeon" with male on the basis of the empirical experience that "surgeons" usually are male, or associated the answer with a type, such as an image of a surgeon that was male. Perhaps the prototype theory of concepts is correct, and the person simply fell into the error of reasoning from a prototypical image of a surgeon as male, an error which is natural if the prototype does result from actual experiences of surgeons as predominantly male. In short, the problem of indeterminacy arises both for transcendental or logical forms of thinking about this case, and causal ones.

If the inference is "natural" for someone, and they have not consciously "assumed" it, what happens when the failure is pointed out to them and they are asked to explain themselves? Do they invent the explanation on the spot, after the problematic inference is pointed out to them? There are many known cases in which people do invent explanations in this fashion, so on psychological grounds alone this is a plausible and perhaps likely explanation (Wegner 2002: 171–86). Do they need to use the language of assumptions, or is this just a bit of common folk psychology? Suppose that this puzzle was posed in a universe in which there were no women surgeons, in which, therefore, there would never be a reason for this inference to fail. Would it make sense then to say that there was a hidden assumption? If so, would it then mean that any feature of the world that allowed for correct inference would also need to be treated as a hidden assumption?

THE PSYCHOLOGIZATION OF TACIT KNOWLEDGE

The problem with any kind of ontologization of presuppositions or "assumptions" is that eventually it must return to the hard ground of the causal world. But there are two families of "tacit knowledge," each with its own issues in relation to these problems. Both appear extensively in the literature. The first is a "collective" form of tacit knowledge. We can, for example, speak of a shared language as a necessary presupposition of communication as a form of tacit knowledge, and this case reveals some typical problems with this family. In the case of language there is the causal fact of language acquisition, and this constrains our theories of language and our claims about presuppositions. If we treat languages as more or less fixed shared presuppositional structures, for example, there is the problem of language change and how the change in the "language" understood as a shared collective fact becomes a change in the "language" of the individual speaker. To make the shared presuppositions story work, in the situation in which there is ongoing change in the presuppositions, one needs a causal story that works like this: The same presuppositional contents are downloaded into individuals and become not only transcendental but causal conditions for the things they explain, such as communication; this shared content is continually updated by some sort of downloading mechanism that assures that the downloaded material is the same for everyone (because sharing is the supposed condition for the thing to be explained, such as communication). Obviously there is nothing in the causal world that conforms to this model, which would require something like a central computer to generate the presuppositions to be shared and to assure that they were downloaded to each brain. The question of how these collective tacit things are acquired and modified is thus a central mystery for this conception.

But tacit knowledge need not be conceived of as a collective object, and neither does culture nor even language need to be understood in this way (cf. Davidson [1986] 2005). Michael Polanyi's major work was called *Personal Knowledge* ([1958] 1998). The example he gave in his earlier work ([1946] 1964) is a starting point, although only a starting point, for understanding the idea of tacit knowledge as "personal." The example is the personal coefficient of the astronomer—the time it takes an individual astronomer to record an observation of a star as it appears to move across an observation space, which is what allows the star to be located in the sky. The response time of different observers will differ. The difference between the observations by that observer and the correct location is the observer's personal coefficient.

The result of the correction is the objective position. Objectivity, of course, is the centerpiece of the Kantian picture of knowing, the possibility of which the existence of categories of space and time is supposed to explain. Here we get a different picture, or partial picture, of the problem of objectivity. It is no longer a matter of the individual observer, armed with the categories, which are not public but in some fashion built into the cognizing subject, making a correct, objective observation. It is a matter of acknowledging individual difference and correcting it to a public standard.

This is a quite different picture of tacit knowledge than the "assumptions" picture. And there is a reason for this. From his first formulations of the concept of tacit knowledge, Polanyi was determined to ground the idea in genuine psychology—the concept for him was not a metaphorical or analogical one, like the notion of presupposition and others from the neo-Kantian tradition, but one which was supposed to have actual empirical content. Precognition, focal and distal awareness, the transmission of tacit knowledge from great scientists to great scientists in apostolic succession, as well as the core idea that we know more than we can say, were things in the realm of psychological reality. Polanyi met regularly with the psychologist Donald Campbell and took this part of his thought seriously. It is thus worth re-asking whether there is in fact anything psychological that corresponds to tacit knowledge or that would make sense of the possession of tacit knowledge, and then ask how this possession could be converted into something relevant to science.

Polanyi gives some important clues to what tacit knowledge might mean that conflict with the way the term later is employed and assimilated to the notion of assumption. Much of his thinking on the subject had to do with the limitations of our own access to psychological processes—itself an important theme of cognitive science. His immediate concern was scientific discovery, and he recognized that this had something to do with precognition, with the sense that a pattern or explanation was there, a sense which had to be actualized and focused on in order to make a "discovery" that could then be articulated and presented in a publicly verifiable form. A simple and commonplace example of this would be the experience of sleeping on a problem and being able to solve it on awakening. Whatever the cognitive processes prior to the solution are, they are not accessible to us. We are not conscious of them, although we may be conscious of some sort of mental effort surrounding them. Similarly for attention. Polanyi recognized that some of what we "know" and use to think is outside of the range of things that we are attending to. So he was fascinated by the difference between distal and focused or proximal attention.

This is material that is inaccessible or poorly accessible to consciousness, even on the most generous construal of the powers of reflection on consciousness, and is indisputably "individual" or "personal." But Polanyi was also concerned with what could be transmitted, as well as the phenomenon of tradition, which for him consisted of tacit knowledge. In the case of science, he believed that personal contact was important, and especially important for great science. His slogan, "science is an apostolic succession," refers to the custom of bishops laying hands on the head of the confirmed in an unbroken chain of such acts of passing on charisma reaching back to the apostles themselves.

PRECOGNITION AND FUNCTIONAL SUBSTITUTES

This poses the problem of tacit knowledge in a different way. Polanyi thinks of "tacit thought as an indispensable element of all knowing and as the ultimate mental power by which all explicit knowledge is endowed with meaning" (Polanyi 1966a: 60). But we have only very limited access to this element of knowing through introspection, reflection, or even consciousness. Nor can much of this be articulated. Moreover, there does seem to be something passed on by personal contact, or at least some sort of experience that personal contact is important for. What is passed on may include, but not be limited to, what comes under the heading of tradition, which for Polanyi means something growing, changing, and adapting, rather than a sacralization of past habits or a set of unchanging rituals.

The issue of the occlusion of our mental processes in general is not a theme made central by Polanyi,[2] but it can be easily teased out from his remarks on tacit knowledge and precognition. Polanyi's account of discovery is not limited in its implications to discovery itself. It fits an extraordinarily large set of normal experiences in which we struggle with something—such as the problem of remembering a name or face, or figuring out how to make the next step in an argument—through a process that is not accessible to us, but which we know is a "process" rather than merely a reaction because of the time it takes and our intermittent awareness that we are bothered because we have not come up with the name or solved the problem.

In the case of scientific discovery, it seems that we normally know and come to know something in advance of our recognizing it and articulating it—some pattern is matched, locked onto, and fit with other patterns prior to our becoming conscious of it, or out of sight of our consciousness or will. There is every reason to think that this is the case more generally: that the data we work with when we do something conscious or semiconscious like "interpretation" is already largely constructed for us tacitly. Put differently, when we use the notion of interpretation broadly, in the fashion, for example, of Hans-Georg Gadamer or Charles Taylor, to cover the whole meaning-conferring activity of the mind, we are making an analogy between a more or less explicit process of providing functional substitutes for passages of text that will make sense for another person with a tacit process of doing the same thing. This is a process similar to the repairing of inferences for a specific audience that we encountered with the sexism example. And it allows for a different account of "making explicit" involving normal social interaction.

Social interaction between individuals requires, for the success of the activities in which people engage, some degree of mutual understanding. If mutual understanding for the purpose of performing particular activities—functional understanding—is not based on "shared assumptions," if this is only a misleading metaphor, what is the source of, and nature of, mutual understanding? Functional substitutability is an important issue for tacit knowledge because it provides a way of thinking about such things as machine substitutes for tacit knowledge—what Harry Collins calls prostheses (2010). But it also applies more generally. Different people may perform the "same" acts, such as driving or riding a bicycle, in different ways that are functionally equivalent. The same holds for social activities and speech. If we are concerned with such a "social" activity as driving, for example, we are faced with the fact that different drivers have different habits, different experiences, and different styles, and that they notice different things. To some extent these differences are smoothed out by training, an explicit process of learning that provides feedback. But to a large extent the feedback is "wild" and consists of actual experiences with other drivers and other situations that go beyond the book or the driving school experience, and are individualized, because the individual has different experiences.

Some, indeed many, of these experiences involve other drivers, whose actions must be understood. But understanding, recognizing, representing, and so forth are terms that relate to conscious thought. They apply to the actual processes only by analogy. And this is a point that acquires a special importance in relation to tacit knowledge, for reasons that are made clear if we reconsider the idea of precognition: There is a gap between "knowing" in the sense of working through a problem, for example recognizing a pattern, and articulating this knowledge. The gap in the case of scientific discovery is very large. We struggle with a problem, which may be a problem that we have been trying without success to articulate or which we can formulate but not solve, but our "struggle" may take place entirely or largely on the precognitive, preconscious level and with preconscious materials.

What do we do when we articulate driving advice, for example to a novice driver? Do we pull something out of a stock of previously unspoken but already tacitly present sayings, which make the tacit explicit? Or do we repair inferences in a way that provides a functional substitute for what we know tacitly for the particular audience in question, a novice driver doing something that we recognize that we would not have done—waited too long to get into the turn lane, for example—which we can then formulate as practical "knowledge" or a rule which is a functional substitute for the driving and lane-changing habits that we follow unconsciously. What we do routinely in interaction, for example, when we restate or paraphrase something that we see was not understood or which the hearer made the wrong inference from. As with explanations of our intentions, we are well equipped to invent these on the spot. They tell us nothing about psychological processes: They are not reports of introspection, nor are they cases of dragging tacit things of the same kind up from the tacit to the explicit. They are functional substitutes for specific needs, needs defined by and for the person we are speaking to, and we guess or hypothesize what saying will serve as the functional substitute, the aid, or the coaching pointer to repair the failure.

REPRESENTATIONS

This account rests very heavily on something that is of little significance in either the bicycle model of tacit knowledge or the idea of collective tacit knowledge: social interaction. And this might seem to create its own regress, back to some form of shared tacit knowledge itself. There is a tradition in social theory of thinking in this way: social phenomenology as represented by Alfred Schutz, for example, or ethnomethodology, which would stress that our capacity to invent functional substitutes is a product of pre-existing, more or less fixed, local shared rules. These accounts run into the same difficulties as those I have outlined above and are discussed at length in *The Social Theory of Practices* (Turner 1994) and elsewhere (Turner 2002), and I will not discuss them further here. As I have argued in these texts, there is no good way to convert these accounts into something that can be made consistent with actual brain processes. What is still to be explained is our capacity for the kind of recognition of the inferences and therefore inferential "errors" or differences of others which we seem to be so good at spotting and responding to with functional substitutes. More narrowly, is there a way of explaining these capacities that does not depend on common tacit knowledge or shared tacit objects? And what sort of cognitive or neuroscience reality would this account connect to?

This also a problem at the heart of the discussion of mirror neurons. Mirror neurons activate both in the performance of actions and in the perception of actions. It has long been known that certain brain lesions cause individuals to imitate the bodily movements of others. This suggests—although this is still a matter of hypothesis—that the system underlying action works normally in such a way that when the system is activated by the perception of an action, the system prepares to imitate, but the imitative action is inhibited by another mechanism such that the same neurons for action are activated but without action occurring. This means of inhibition or taking the system off-line is hypothesized to be the one that allows for imagination of actions and thus simulation, understood as a brain process in which the same neurons for action (which are also those activated by perception) are activated without action taking place. Simulation is thought to be the means by which we "mind-read," which thus becomes an off-line process involving the same neurons as those involved in perceiving an action of another person as "minded" or intentional (Iacoboni 2009: 106–83).

The processes involved here are not conscious, or, perhaps it would be better to say, they are part of what is occluded from us about our own mental processes. But the language of the explicit intrudes in the usual descriptions of this work, as does the issue of the relation between the explicit or conscious and the tacit or implicit. Work on empathy and mirror neurons suggests that "we recognize someone else's action because we manage to activate our own inner action representations using mirror neurons" (Keysers et al. 2003: 634). But the "we recognize" and "we manage" in this sentence are misleading analogical terms. This process is all tacit and unconscious, although our "recognitions" may become conscious. The process combines two mechanisms. We recognize and also improve our capacity to recognize on the basis of our own abilities to perform similar actions, and especially "from the massive experience we have accumulated over the years in planning and executing self-produced activities" (Blake and Shiffrar 2007: 56). Dancers can see things about dance moves that other people can't see (Cross, Hamilton, and Grafton 2006); male and female ballet performers see the typical gender-specific dance moves of their own gender better (Calvo-Merino et al. 2006: 1907). The two mechanisms are mirroring or empathy—understood in a very thin sense[3]—and learning by doing or habituation.

THE PROBLEM OF REPRESENTATION

But there is an issue with this way of putting the problem of what the dancers are doing that is similar to the problems we run into with the idea of shared collective tacit objects, and it has to do with the term "representation." The issue is stated by Goldman in connection with the idea of mind reading:

> Person A "directly" understands the mind of person B if A experiences a mental event that matches one experienced by B, and A's mental event is caused by B's mental event, via a brain mechanism that can reproduce such matches on similar occasions. (Goldman 2005: 83)

Goldman asks the pertinent question:

> Do babies who experience upsetness as a consequence of hearing another's cry *represent* the latter *as* upset? As undergoing a matching state? That is debatable. If not, then I don't think it's a case of either mindreading or interpersonal understanding. For these to occur, the receiver must *represent* the sender as a subject of a similar state, must *impute* such a state to the sender. No such requirement is included in [this description of mirroring]. (Goldman 2005: 84; emphasis in the original)

At what point does "interpersonal understanding" occur? For Goldman, it is not at the point of making explicit statements about them, or even of mentally rehearsing statements about them, each of which would be "social" or refer to a prospective audience, but before this point: at the point of possessing a "representation" of something that can then be matched to something else coming from another person, producing understanding.

It is a short step from this use of the notion of matching representations to the idea of collectively shared representations. This step is implicitly made when the term "concept" is substituted for "representation." As a philosophical term, the origins of the term "concept" are in the idea of an object of thought that is shared in the sense that it is accessible or can be "possessed" by many people. But are there such things as representations—or imputations of mental states, for that matter? And even if there are—if the baby has a picture that corresponds to the thing being recognized—does it play a role in this kind of interaction? This is at least one site which allows us to think about the relation between social interaction and shared objects, and to make the relevant distinctions. The larger issue is this: What sorts of mental things are needed to account for interaction? Do we need at least something substantial that could be shared or matched—a proto-collective concept of some sort—or does this talk add nothing to what other mechanisms, for example mirror neurons plus our capacity to invent functional substitutes in speech—already provide?

The "contagion" described by Goldman seems to involve some sort of response in kind: The baby cries in response to the cry of the other baby, rather than responding in some other way. But this, Goldman thinks, is not matching because there is no "representation" made by the responding baby. The idea of a matching representation, however, involves a mysterious process applying to representations. For Goldman, a similar intuition governs the use of the term "empathy": Contagion is not empathy because the baby is not taking the other baby as an object to empathize with. The hint that empathy, or imitation, or imputation, must be a process modeled on or very similar to conscious, intentional, and explicit versions of the same thing is never far from the surface of these discussions, and this should not be surprising: These are analogies, and making the analogy convincing requires that as many elements are in common between the analogized objects as possible. But we have just seen in connection with tacit knowledge that this analogy can be completely misleading about the relevant mental processes.

In the case of the baby one sees that there is a serious difficulty in making the "matched representations" picture plausible. Somehow, the baby needs to develop in such a way that eventually the "in kind" responses transform into representations and imputations. For Goldman these are strictly mental things—they imply nothing about explicit speech or language. The acts of imputing and representing, however, are "explicit": Attributing them to mental objects is analogical, with all the problems that kind of analogizing produces. Nevertheless, the analogizing allows us to build a picture. The picture is that babies respond in kind first, perhaps via mirror neurons, and later pass into a stage in which they represent, impute, and thus can be said to understand. Later yet they can articulate this understanding. But what would a representation be made of and how would the baby come to have the same kinds of representations as others? If we are talking about cultural differences, this representation-making activity of the brain seems to require some sort of mechanism that not only constructs mental representations, but matches them to the representations in the minds of others. It is a short step from this way of thinking to the idea, as Durkheim famously put it, that society is made of representations, by which he meant precisely these kinds of shared, or as he called them, "collective" representations ([1895] 1982: 108–42).

There is no reason, however, to take this path, that is, to require that the baby develop in such a way that representations are constructed (somehow) out of in-kind responses and then synchronized to the culture at large, and then articulated (or perhaps in some other order). The only thing compelling us to do so is the analogy between actual explicit representation and a supposed mental act of representation that is supposed to serve as the mental backing for articulated speech. This is a way of construing the problem that, as Wittgenstein said, is like thinking that there is painted steam inside the painted pot ([1953] 2009: 107, §297). A simpler account would be this: The baby responds, through the mirror neuron system, in kind, as "contagion," and subsequently responds, perhaps through the same mirroring mechanism, to articulated speech, which is "understood" as intended when the baby comes to connect speech with intention and responds through the mirror neuron system to intentional actions as a kind. The use of speech serves to stabilize or crystallize the mirror neuron systems' in-kind responses, and to add to them, as experience adds to the dancers' ability to discern distinctions. This in turn produces more or less standardized usages in speech that can be constructed by an observer as a language.

What work could mirror neurons do in this? The current evidence is that the mirror neuron system is not limited to motion-related parts of the brain, but that mirror neurons are widely distributed in the brain. There is also evidence that the kind of imitation occurring through the mirror neuron system is not limited to motions, but that imitation of goal seeking works in the same way. Moreover, there is a great deal of evidence about how early in the developmental process babies become attuned to intentions. So it is plausible to think that a great deal of tacit knowledge is acquired before children speak and that the system is activating "action" neurons as well as allowing for feedback. In short, they know something, and perhaps a lot, about action and understanding others, tacitly. This has an effect on our way of thinking about action. Representation is traditionally understood to be a precondition of action—the act is an attempt to achieve the represented goal. But if goal-oriented action is already imitated (unconsciously) through the mirror neuron system, it does so before representations, or shared representations, play a role. The explanatory need for "representations" and the problem of explaining how the representations got there disappears.

The interesting problem then becomes explicitness. The developing child lives in a world of people whose conduct, including goal seeking, is mirrored in the child's mind, in a tacit way. What happens when the child begins to speak about mental life? The developmental evidence here is compelling: Children apply this language to themselves and to others at the same time and begin to use the words that relate to mental life in stages. At each stage the situation is the same: They begin to explicitly impute states to others at the same time they explicitly impute them to themselves. This is at least suggestive: Imputation is something that is learned socially, and the words are applied in the context of mirroring, a situation of mutual in-feeling which provides a basis for understanding the mentalistic words.

Polanyi's notion of precognition in scientific discovery provides a model for this situation of language learning. For Polanyi, in the course of discovery the scientist already "knows" or has tacitly made the discovery in advance of being able to articulate it or represent it. Making a discovery involves a struggle to articulate. But it is a struggle to articulate something that is already there, or has already been arrived at in thought, in a precognitive form. The situation is similar to Goldman's contagion: The babies know what crying is and that others are doing the same thing. They cannot yet articulate it or "represent" it. But when they are presented with the term "cry" in the context of joint attention to the act of crying, they can learn to articulate their inchoate knowledge. So in language learning they do not need to rely solely on trial and error to learn the correct words. They can rely on precognition produced by the experience of mirroring others and "know" that they are talking about the same things.

Which of these accounts of the acquisition of common competence to communicate is more plausible? The implausible account is this: that there is "contagion" and other mirror-like responses first, then representation, then the matching of representations with objects, all of which is tacit, and then some sort of additional matching of representations to articulate speech, which allows the mental things that are tacit to become explicit. The implausibility comes in at a familiar point: the matching of representations in one head with those in another head, or in the collective head in which these shared representations are stored, ready to be downloaded. The more plausible account, although of course only a sketch, is that the kind of nonmatching response Goldman calls "contagion" comes first, gets refined through feedback, and then, in this more advanced state, gets engaged with the intentional act of speaking, which in turn, through repeated interactions with others who provide feedback, produces regularized habits of speech which copy the goal-seeking or intentional aspects of the speech that the child is exposed to and the inferences that others are seen to make. These patterns become regularized between people by the same discipline: To understand and to be understood one must perform the kinds of speech acts that others understand, and in this way "mean what one says." They get knit together into a "whole" within the individual by virtue of the inferential connections, and, because this whole is in rough but imperfect correspondence to others, there is a loose sense in which there is an external "shared" thing, a concept or representation, that corresponds to the individual's habituated patterns. But only a loose sense, because the mechanism is not one which downloads exact copies, but rather downloads matches in behavior that are good enough for the purposes of interaction, including such things as joint attention and making oneself understood.

REPRESENTATIONS AND "CONCEPTS" RECONSIDERED

In this sketch, representations are superfluous. But of course there is a whole range of thinking in which representations do perform explanatory work, and they do so, as Eduard Machery notes, in connection with "the cognitive processes underlying categorization, induction, deduction, analogy-making, planning, or linguistic comprehension" (2009: 110). Moreover, representations or concepts are the sorts of things we can "make explicit." And these other cognitive functions raise questions about whether we can ignore representations as part of our explanatory account of tacit knowledge and its transmission. The literature in this area, nicely summarized in Machery (2009), is complex and problematic: It does not yield a clear picture of "concept" as a psychological phenomenon that integrates the various roles that the concept of "concept" has played in past literatures. It specifically fails to provide any support for the idea of "matching" representations. The alternative is an even more speculative and groundless idea: that there is a common pre-established language of thought that assures that each of us possesses the same stock of representations, which would enable matching.

But this idea, even if it was substantiated, would be useless in explaining the highly specific and differentiated kind of mental contents that the term "tacit knowledge" is used to describe.

The work of a school known as neo-empiricism supports a certain view of the cognitive processes that employ representations and need to be fitted with a psychology of tacit knowledge. As Machery explains it, the "central insight" of this school (Barsalou 1999: 586; Prinz 2002: 148; Stein 1995) is that "these cognitive processes involve tokening and manipulating perceptual representations" and that "retrieving a concept from long-term memory during reasoning or categorization consists of tokening some perceptual representations. For example, retrieving the concept of dog consists of tokening some visual, auditory, etc., representations of dogs" (Machery 2009: 110). This amounts to a form of "simulation" or "reenactment" which produces an experience like the original perceptual experience (Machery 2009; see also Barsalou 1999: 578; Barsalou et al. 2003: 85; Prinz 2002: 150).

The key to this account, however, is the process of retrieval and what it consists of. What does one retrieve? A concept? And is a concept a stable object in memory, or something else? An experiment by Barsalou and his students (Barsalou, Solomon, and Wu 1999; Wu 1995)

> involves making a tacit concept explicit by listing the properties of the concept. Subjects are presented with a word, for instance, "dog," and are asked to list the properties that are typically true of the denoted objects. Psychologists of concepts assume that in this task, subjects retrieve their concepts from their long term memory and use the knowledge stored in the concept to solve the task. (Machery 2009: 112)

The results of these experiments, however, show that subjects list different things when they list the properties of dogs, that what they list is dependent on the context, that is to say on such things as the expectations of others. This is not a dramatic finding, but it is suggestive: Presumably it means that what is in the subjects long-term memory about dogs, that is to say something tacit they are making explicit, is personal, a collection of their perceptual experiences, rather than collective, and certainly not collective in the sense implied by philosophical theories of concepts as shared objects of thought which one either possesses or not, and that the "concept" that comes to mind for them, exhibited in lists of properties, is constructed on the fly out of these materials, rather than sitting in the brain in some fixed form.

"Matching" is not a part, or not yet a part, of this account. Indeed, there is a problem with matching and the idea of shared concepts that appears with experiments. As Machery summarizes the findings,

> on two occasions (two weeks apart), subjects were asked to describe bachelors, birds, chairs, and so on (a feature production task). Overlap

> in the properties mentioned by different subjects on a given occasion and by the same subject across the two occasions was calculated. Barsalou and colleagues found that only 44 percent of the properties mentioned by a given subject were mentioned by another subject and that only 66 percent of the properties mentioned by a subject on a given occasion were mentioned by this very subject on the other occasion. (Machery 2009: 23)

Thus there is nothing like "matching" between subjects with respect to concepts, but rather more or less overlap in properties made explicit and instability between occasions for the subjects themselves.

Nevertheless, as Machery notes, "Barsalou's own findings show that the variability of the knowledge we bring to bear in different contexts is small and is thus consistent with the existence of bodies of knowledge being retrieved by default from long-term memory" (Machery 2009: 23). These considerations led Barsalou to argue that "instead of being default bodies of knowledge in long-term memory, concepts are temporary bodies of knowledge in working memory. According to his proposal, concepts are constructed on the fly so that we can reason, categorize, and so on, in a context-sensitive manner" (Machery 2009: 21). As Barsalou puts it,

> a concept is a temporary construction in working memory, derived from a larger body of knowledge in long-term memory to represent a category, where a category, roughly speaking, is a related set of entities from any ontological type. . . . Across contexts, a given person's concept for the same category may change, utilizing different knowledge from long-term memory, at least to some extent. (Barsalou 1993: 29; quoted in Machery 2009: 22)

This applies to much of what falls under the heading of tacit knowledge: not perhaps the evanescent precognitions that the scientist attempts to articulate in the course of scientific discovery, but to the process of articulation itself, which is a matter of constructing an articulation, on the fly, that is sensitive to context.

The effect of this line of argument is to shift the problem of understanding others from one of matching representations in order to enable understanding to one of responding to the other as a another thinking, acting being and using one's empathic capacity to guess successfully how to articulate interventions, explanations, and the like (prostheses which are functional equivalents) in order to facilitate interaction, repair inferences, and so forth. The former requires a set of common representations which can be matched. And this hypothesis requires an answer to the questions of how these representations are acquired and transmitted, how they are kept stable, and more generally how a process like downloading from a common server can be mimicked by the kinds of processes of learning, habituating, remembering, and interacting that humans actually engage in. As I have argued elsewhere, there is no good answer to these questions. But there is no need for an account of concepts, or tacit knowledge, that requires this kind of "collective object" hypothesis.

TACIT KNOWLEDGE RECONSIDERED

What does all this have to do with tacit knowledge as it is normally understood? If we think of the problem of mutual understanding in terms of mind reading, there would be no need to convey tacit knowledge. The ideal mind reader would already have access to it. Prostheses, such as claims about assumptions or about what someone knows or believes, have a place where empathy fails. When we explain ourselves to an audience, we guess or hypothesize what it is that would make our actions or claims intelligible. We are guessing at what prostheses will enable them to understand us, or us to understand them. We may guess wrong: This is an act akin to discovery or invention. But we are good at doing this, and especially good at it among people with whom we have learned about language and the world, because we can rely on our mostly successful ability to think as they do and can identify what we would have had to think to draw the conclusions they draw.

To say this is to radically separate the explicit from the tacit: It is not a matter of saying what is in the mind. What happens when one makes an assumption "explicit" is simply to say, to a specific audience with specific knowledge and inferential habits for whom this is useful, that whatever the psychological facts of the matter are, the people in question are reasoning as if they assumed *x*. The "as if" assumption statement, the prosthesis, is audience specific and an invention. We will be unable to construct this kind of invention, except by lucky accident, unless we have some prior understanding of the thinking of the audience that needs the prosthesis.

This leaves the question of the psychological or neuroscience facts of the matter themselves. But when we add mirror neurons to the story, these facts are already, implicitly, facts about social interaction. Who we are, our skills, competencies, capacities to discern and distinguish, which is to say the conditions of our conscious thought, are a matter of whom we have interacted with and from whom we acquired, through the twin mechanisms of mirroring and feedback, skills, competencies, and capacities to discern and distinguish. The dancers mentioned earlier are who they are for this reason, but the point is more general. It is a traditional idea in the tacit knowledge literature, as noted earlier, that tacit knowledge passes from person to person in the course of close interaction. To the extent that this is true, we, as tacit knowers, are the product of our interactions.

But the boundaries of tacit knowledge are not so precise. We know more, or different things, than the things we get simply through interaction. As with the dancers, there is mirror knowledge and there is feedback. Each works together to form the individual's unique set of skills, competencies, capacities to distinguish, and so forth. Some of these may be novel and distinctive—a new dance move invented consciously and then learned and embodied as a skill, for example—and can be conveyed to others by the same mechanisms of mirroring and feedback. But there are also skills that we develop without interaction, through feedback alone, through invention and feedback, and so forth. Of course even these things may have elements from the world of interaction with others. As tacit knowers we are not simply products of our interactions, or of mirroring: There is learning, too.

A few final thoughts of larger significance than the issue of tacit knowledge itself might be added. The "as if" character of assumptions talk extends to the problems that are generated by this language, such as the regress problem. In psychological reality, there is no regress problem, and nothing for transcendental reasoning to reach: There are, rather, inferences that a person makes without reference to any conscious or introspectively accessible source. Jerome Bruner commented that "when things are as they should be, the narratives of Folk Psychology are unnecessary" (1990: 40). The same point applies to the term "assumptions." They repair communication and facilitate understanding. They are a crutch that gets one to the point of empathic understanding. To describe one's own "assumptions" or those of others is merely to engage in an "as if" exercise, in the language of a special kind of folk pseudo-psychology, for an audience for whom the addition of the "assumption" makes the actions, sayings, or attitudes of the person intelligible to the other person. But they can only repair communication against the background of other things that are tacitly understood in a way that is functionally equivalent for both parties. This is as much "empathy" as we need. Bruner's point turns the problem of assumptions on its head: The baseline is not the individual knower with a problem of grounding experience, which he or she discovers can only be done on the basis of assumptions and communicated only when there are shared assumptions. For Bruner, the problem is communicating and understanding others. The baseline is not the individual groping for the intersubjective or collective conditions of understanding, but the fact that we do understand each other, that we know what the other person is doing when they act, and so forth—not always, but much of the time, and without a process of conscious or introspectable reasoning of the sort analogized as the making of assumptions. This "knowledge" is a product of mirror neurons—a neurophysiological "natural" fact, and not a mysterious invented fact, such as a collective tacit object or transcendental conditions of reasoning.

As I have suggested, the problem with tacit knowledge is explaining how it is transmitted. Explicit knowledge is transmitted through explicit means: speech, texts, and so forth. To the extent that tacit knowledge is transmitted, it requires, by definition, other means. The problem arises from the analogy between the "knowledge" that is tacit and the knowledge that is articulated when what is tacit is made explicit. If we think that these are the same thing, or more or less the same thing, the knowledge will come in the form of articulable assumptions and the like. And we will need an account of transmission that transmits these kinds of things tacitly. This is where the argument runs into a wall, for there are no such means. The reason, however, is that the explicit statements that people make to enable themselves to be understood, or construct to enable them to understand others, do not correspond to tacit knowledge. They are, rather, functional substitutes for bits of tacit knowledge for particular audiences and particular purposes, invented on the fly.

The idea of tacit knowledge contrasts to this. One cannot read a book to learn how to read. What one learns in the course of learning to read, perhaps largely through some process of mirror neuron imitating and understanding together with feedback, is tacit, and it is knowledge of a "knowing how" kind. One can provide many partial functional substitutes for this knowledge in the course of teaching a child to read, for example in the form of coaching pointers about how to see words or associate sounds and letters. But the tacit skill of reading as a matter of psychological fact cannot consist in the memorization and application of these pointers. A reader who "read" in this way would be unable to read at the speed of genuinely skilled readers. As the bicycle riding example suggests, this is a matter of individual learning. The mystery aspect of tacit knowledge is entirely a product of the mistaken analogy between explicit functional substitutes with an "as if" character and the actual content of the brain.

10 *Evidenz*

The Strength of Weak Empathy

ARGUMENT

This chapter builds on a neglected philosophical idea, *Evidenz*. Max Weber used it in his discussion of *Verstehen*, as the goal of understanding either action or such things as logic. It was formulated differently by Franz Brentano, but with a novel twist: that anyone who understood something would see the thing to be understood as self-evident, not something dependent on inference, argument, or reasoning. The only way one could take something as evident in this sense is by being able to treat other people as having the same responses—by empathy with them, in the weak sense of following their thought. Brentano's philosophical claim is that without some stopping point at what is self-evident, justifications fall into infinite regress. This view is radically opposed to much of conventional philosophy. The usual solutions to the regress problem rely on problematic claims about the supposed hidden transcendental structure behind reasoning. In contrast, empathy is a genuine natural phenomenon and a better explanation for the actual phenomenon of making sense of the reasoning of others. What is evident to all who are capable of understanding is an empirically defined subset of this class.

"Empathy" is a contested and ambiguous term, associated with the individual experience of feeling something about another person. If we understand empathy in semantically standard English as "a person's controlled conscious reaction to the emotional experience of another person" (Gladkova 2010: 280), it is something that requires conscious effort—control. The subjective character of this experience, its character as a form of "feeling," and the immunity of private feelings to outside checks makes it a poor candidate as a source of knowledge. Nor is empathy in this strong sense, or its related senses, a particularly stable object of analysis. Empathy is claimed to vary culturally (Aaker and Williams 1998; Shimuzi 2000). "Empathy" and empathy-related terms, such as "sympathy," are semantically different in different languages (Gladkova 2010). The term itself, and its German source term, *Einfühling*, are relatively recent creations.

The discussion of empathy has changed radically in recent years as a result of the discovery of mirror neurons and subsequent discoveries of their extensive and special roles in various forms of human interaction. If we try to understand empathy in relation to mirror neurons, things get even more complicated and contentious. On the one hand, there is a range of phenomena associated with the mirror neuron system that fit with empathy, including a wide range of measurable neural "mirror" responses to the pain of others, to the movements of others, and to such things as the focus of attention of another on an object. On the other hand, the relation between mirror neurons and conscious thought is in general not understood, and the relation between mirror neurons and empathy in the sense of simulation is itself contentious. As Shaun Gallagher explains in his contribution to this issue, it seems clear that mirror neurons play a supporting role in simulation, which plays a supporting role in conscious empathic thinking, but also that mirror neuron system activation, simulation, and empathy are three different processes, and that mirror neurons alone are insufficient to account for empathy in the most fully elaborated sense of the term.

In this chapter I will be concerned with the very low-level form of "empathy," the weak sense, which does appear to be closely associated with mirror neurons and does not involve a high level (or perhaps any level) of consciousness, but which is nevertheless significant in relation to some important, indeed fundamental, philosophical issues. My concern will not be with the mirror neuron evidence itself, nor with either simulation or higher-level controlled or conscious empathy, but rather with the class of primal understandings of others that occur at a most basic, largely unarticulable, and preconscious level.

PRIMAL UNDERSTANDING

The philosophical literature often appeals to a primal kind of understanding of others or of ideas, an understanding at a level so basic that it barely seems like understanding at all, and certainly not like "interpretation." In a much-quoted comment on Wittgenstein's concept of rule-following, Rush Rhees said, "We see that we understand one another, without noticing whether our reactions tally or not. Because we agree in our reactions, it is possible for me to tell you something, and it is possible for you to teach me something" (conversation quoted by Winch [1958] 1990: 85). The point of these qualifications about "noticing whether our reactions tally" is to avoid the thought that agreeing in our reactions is determined by an inference from the behavior of the other person. The agreement in reactions is either there or it is not: A reaction is direct, not something inferred from something else using some inductive procedure or theory, even an implicit theory. The "agreement" itself may not even need to be recognized. To "see" that we understand each other may simply amount to never having occasion for questioning that we do.

Terms like "agree" in the quotation from Rhees are metaphorical or analogical—agree is a concept imported from law, used here to do double duty as an analogical description of an act and its normative sequelae, the thought being that agreements once made are to be kept, so that to agree is to accept a rule. With such terms there is always a question of what is doing the work of explanation and description and what is mere baggage. "Agreement," as Rhees uses it, like empathy in the strong sense, is one of those middle terms that needs to be separated from its baggage of metaphor and then reconstructed. In this case, reconstruction would include distinguishing it from empathy in the strong sense and asking what else might the underlying class of phenomena to which agreement belongs include. As it happens, Wittgenstein, whom Rhees was explicating, makes a parallel distinction in his discussion of rules, in connection with the term "interpretation," where he stresses that to follow a rule is not to interpret a rule (Wittgenstein [1953] 2009: 86, §198).[1]

"Following" is a term that points to something that is part of interpretation, but is primary, whereas "interpretation," which usually is understood to involve some sort of additional thought, is after the fact. It is thus a term that captures the distinction, without adding some of the baggage associated with these other terms. It points to a class of related terms, which share the characteristic of being primal and tacit, with conscious or explicit analogues. Some of these have been discussed in the neuroscience literature, such as the phenomenon of joint attention. This is a very rudimentary form of following the thought of another. It does not require "consciousness," as empathy in the strong sense does, but might be done consciously and intentionally, at which point it becomes a form of empathic thinking.[2] Another closely related case would be ostensive definition. "Definition" is normally explicit, a relation of words with words. Ostensive definition, pointing at something to explain what it means, requires following the intention of another to use pointing to define something and also following the direction of the thought toward the object.

EVIDENZ AND EMPATHY

Some early twentieth century writers, notably Weber, put the understanding of the actions of other people and the understanding of abstract ideas under the same heading, and used the same epistemic language to characterize the goal of understanding in both cases. In the methodological introduction to the text that was published as *Economy and Society* (Weber [1922] 1978), he indicated that both the understanding of ideal objects, which for him included abstractions, abstract values, and the like, as well as the understanding of intentional, or, as he called it, meaningful action, sought the same epistemic end, which he called *Evidenz*.

Weber gives the example of a man chopping wood. We have, he said, direct observational understanding of the subjective meaning of the act—simultaneously for the man and for us, the observer. We do not, as Weber describes this, infer the subjective meaning of the act by deriving it from its elements—the axe, the moving arm, the wood chips flying, and so on. Nor do we infer the content of something invisible, an intention, from these visible elements. If asked for a justification we could invent some such reasoning,[3] but it would not be what we had actually done. Weber does not say that these identifications cannot be in error or, indeed, make any other epistemic claim about them. He simply says, "The highest degree of rational understanding is attained in cases involving the meanings of logically or mathematically related propositions; their meaning may be immediately and unambiguously intelligible"; the situation with empathy, which here he associates with emotion, is parallel: "Empathic or appreciative accuracy is attained when, through sympathetic participation, we can adequately grasp the emotional context in which the action took place" (Weber [1922] 1978: 5).[4]

Evidenz thus means "immediate and unambiguous intelligibility." The term "*Evidenz*" has a complex history, which is primarily associated with the notion of self-evidence. In Weber's own time it was associated with Brentano, who traced it from Descartes through many other figures, including John Stuart Mill and some of his contemporaries, such as Christoph von Sigwart. For Brentano as well as Weber, the term refers to a kind of understanding—Brentano used the Kantian term "judgment"—that is noninferential and ungroundable. Bretano, however, added something striking to the notion of self-evidence that altered it from the Cartesian notion. For Brentano, the two core elements of the idea of *Evidenz* are these: That which is evident must also be evident to others and to be evident is also to be something which cannot be further analyzed, justified, or given criteria for.

The same idea appears in many other guises in the analytic tradition. Wittgenstein's distinction between saying and showing, for example, fits the notion of *Evidenz*: What is shown has the dual features that it cannot be analyzed further and must be "shown" for everyone. *Evidenz* is philosophically problematic because of this feature of unanalyzability: That which is evident can never be further established, but neither can it be gotten rid of and replaced.[5] Brentano was concerned with the philosophical work that the concept could do, and specifically with one task—providing a solution, in the form of a radical alternative, to the Kantian and neo-Kantian problem of a priori truth. His student Oskar Kraus explained the argument:

> Brentano has shown, repeatedly and in detail, that it is "an absurd undertaking to try to use reasoning to guarantee the *evidence* of what is self-evident." He has been reproached for "never having considered the problem of the logical presuppositions of his so-called a priori evident judgments." If he is guilty of this charge, at least he may be said to have asked why anyone should suppose that there is such a problem. Presumably these mysterious "logical presuppositions" are themselves

> known. What is the nature of this knowledge, then? Does *this* knowledge also have "logical presuppositions," or is it ultimate—that is to say, directly evident and justified in itself? Surely one is not blind to the fact that either (i) we should give up all talk about knowledge, or (ii) we may reason in a vicious circle, or (iii) we must admit that there is ultimate knowledge—i.e., that there are judgments which are self-evident and justified in themselves. If there is anyone who doesn't see this, then, as Aristotle put it, we can only leave him behind. (Kraus [1930] 1966: xv–xvii; emphasis in the original)

Brentano's radical idea, in short, is that the standard philosophical strategy of inquiring into the "presuppositions" of what is evident results not in some deeper form of a priori knowledge, but in a vicious circle, because our quest for ultimate knowledge can only end in something we take to be evident. Better to acknowledge the ultimacy of that which is already evident. Previous accounts of self-evidence, Descartes's error, Brentano argued, attempted to give criteria for calling something evident. This had fatal consequences: It produced a regress in which it was necessary, but at the same time impossible, to produce an adequate justification for the criteria for "evidence." The trick is to get an explication of self-evidence or being evident that does not itself require justification.

Brentano's account of *Evidenz* evolved and changed significantly from his most elaborate discussions in *The Origin of Our Knowledge of Right and Wrong* (Brentano [1889] 2009); his final comments, which include his definition, take the form of a set of fragments. For Brentano, unlike Weber, there were no degrees of evidence—something was evident or not. *Evidenz* in this sense was restricted to logical and mathematical truths, about which one had "insight"—even knowledge of one's own existence was only "evident to me," and not evident in the general sense—evident to all (Brentano [1915] 1966c: 131–32). Brentano noted, "One usually says 'This is evident' and not 'This is evident to me.' Probably because of the faith that what is evident to me is evident to all" (Brentano [1915] 1966b: 126). The "all" he defines more precisely in terms of "the person who judges about a thing in the way in which anyone whose judgments were evident would judge about the same thing," meaning that anyone who was capable of making judgments with *Evidenz* on this thing would make the same judgment (Brentano [1915] 1966a: 122).[6]

Because of Brentano's vacillations on the question of what judgments or insights could have *Evidenz*, some comment is appropriate. The point of Brentano's discussion of *Evidenz* is to get rid of the notion of presupposed a priori truth or framework. It would be contrary to this program to make a priori or criteria-based claims about what class of judgments could have *Evidenz*: It is a kind of empirical question as to whether all who understood would judge something to be evident. It would be possible to exclude classes, such as those for which illusion is possible, but that is itself a kind of empirical claim. There can be no problem of relativism for this account: If anyone else would fail to make the same judgment of evidence the fact being judged would by definition not be evident. But fallibilism with respect to what we judge others would take to be evident is appropriate.

The insistence that to have *Evidenz* was to be evident to all was critical to the argument: It overcame the objection, still formulated by the logical positivist Moritz Schlick, that *Evidenz* was just a subjective feeling (Schlick [1910] 1979: 60–61, 98). Another is the suggestion that evident to all is a criterion for evidence. If so, it has the same problems that Descartes's and Husserl's accounts had, namely that it invites a regress: How would one know that the criterion had been met? It would seem that we would need empathic access to the minds of others to know what is evident to them, and this would require its own criteria and these could not, as Brentano frames the problem, be applied to *Evidenz*.

This is not a problem for Weber's use of the term, but it is for Brentano's. Brentano rejected the idea of degrees of *Evidenz* because he was concerned to preserve the idea that *Evidenz* implied truth. But what we get is something more like this: It is impossible to reject that which is evident, because there is no alternative; anyone who was capable would judge the same way. But if we drop the problematic concern with truth and add back Weber's use of *Evidenz* and degrees of *Evidenz* as they apply to the subjective meaning of action, we can use his basic idea of "evident to all" in a different way: as an account of the kind of understanding we have of such things as subjective meaning, or of the kind of tallying of reactions in the quotation from Rhees. The understanding we have, or fail to have, is an understanding of how others understand the same thing. To have *Evidenz*, an understanding must also be evident to others, and to all the others who are capable of understanding. This is not a criterion, but a definition of *Evidenz* in terms of empathy. We can expect to achieve *Evidenz* in this sense most readily with the low-level sort of empathy that corresponds to the tallying of reactions and ostensive definition, and to the kinds of following of the reasoning of others that are given in primitive form in the phenomenon of joint attention.

PSYCHOLOGISM AND REGRESS

Self-evidence has had a bad press in twentieth century philosophy as a result of Gottlob Frege's and Edmund Husserl's critiques of psychologism. Frege's argument, which is now an elementary piece of conventional philosophy, is that there is a difference between truth, such as mathematical and logical truth, and taking to be true—which is precisely what *Evidenz* is concerned with. The error of psychologism is one of confusing "true" with "taken to be true." Being true is independent of being taken to be true. Thus, as Frege puts it,

> If being true is thus independent of being acknowledged by somebody or other, then the laws of truth are not psychological laws: they are boundary stones set in an eternal foundation, which our thought can overflow but never displace. (Frege [1893] 1964: 13)

This difference, in present terms, is related to the difference between what people do and what they ought to do—to normativity. Arithmetic, for him, is a normative science. What people believe about natural numbers (although what Brentano speaks about is not what people in fact think, but what "anyone whose judgments were evident would" think) has nothing to do with the truths about them. Even a community of arithmetic users could be wrong about doing sums, or do them incorrectly: Nothing depends on what is in their heads or what they do. *Evidenz*, in contrast, does depend on what people think (or at least what people whose judgments were evident would think): It is therefore a psychological fact, not a fact about mathematical truth.

But this line of argument ends badly. Frege himself has no solution to the regress problem. As he concedes,

> the basic laws of logic cannot be justified. Logical justification comes to an end when we reach these laws. However, to argue that our nature or constitution forces us to abide by the laws of logic is no longer a logical justification; it is to incorrectly shift from logical to psychological or biological considerations. (Kusch 2007: n.p.; cf. Frege [1893] 1964: 13–15; Kusch 1995: 30–41)

So in a sense, Brentano's point stands—there is no getting rid of *Evidenz* or something like it, because even on Frege's account we must take these laws to be evident. Moreover, contrary to his expressed aim of avoiding a shift from logical to psychological considerations, even Frege must resort to psychological language in his discussion of concepts. People must somehow relate to these concepts in order to understand and use them. So he uses a term which appears repeatedly in the analytic tradition, "grasping" (Frege [1893] 1964: 23). This term is a surrogate for psychological terminology, but it is loaded: It makes sense only if there is something to be grasped. But it is difficult to see what grasping consists in other than the achievement of *Evidenz* described by Weber and Brentano. If the only difference is that grasping implies that there is something being grasped, the usage is misleading: it pre-decides the issue of the nature of concepts and conceptual experience in favor of the idea that concepts are external and object-like.

If we return to the point where this particular intellectual shortcut has not gained currency, it becomes apparent that grasping, psychological normalcy, and *Evidenz* are closely related ideas. This closeness is exhibited in the classic discussion of regress problems, Lewis Carroll's "What the Tortoise said to Achilles." Achilles offers a Euclidean proof. The Tortoise, however, rejects the evident character of the final step and insists on asking what would happen "if I failed to see its truth," asking merely that it be written down so that it can be justified by another step, D. After noting that only obtuseness would prevent anyone from doing so, Achilles does so and says,

> "Now that you accept A and B and C and D, of course you accept Z."
> "Do I?" said the Tortoise innocently. "Let's make that quite clear. I accept A and B and C and D. Suppose I still refused to accept Z?"
> "Then Logic would take you by the throat, and force you to do it!" Achilles triumphantly replied. "Logic would tell you, you can't help yourself. Now that you've accepted A and B and C and D, you must accept Z! So you've no choice, you see."
> "Whatever Logic is good enough to tell me is worth writing down," said the Tortoise. "So enter it in your note-book, please. We will call it (E). If A and B and C and D are true, Z must be true. Until I've granted that, of course I needn't grant Z. So it's quite a necessary step, you see?"
> "I see," said Achilles; and there was a touch of sadness in his tone.

And with this we are off to an infinite regress. This little story is usually taken to show the need for rules of inference in logic, but Carroll's language of seeing is more to the point. What is needed is something that can be shown, even, in this case, to the obtuse. But explicating showing in terms of presuppositions, in this case a presupposed rule of inference, leads merely to a regress.

We do not live in a world where people fall into regresses because they continually demand further justifications of the reasons given by others. Why? The standard answer is that there is a pre-given normative structure that people in general, or users of a common language, or some other group share, which is the basis for their rationality and for the commonality or sharing of their rationality. The reasoning here is rarely articulated, but goes something like this:

1. There are no infinite regresses of this kind in actual reasoning.
2. For there to be a regress of the Tortoise type the Tortoise would have to deny rational common ground—to fail to acknowledge the reasons of Achilles, indefinitely.
3. To end a regress is to arrive at and acknowledge a reason that is shared.
4. Reasons are normative.
5. Reasons come in connected structures of reason.
6. To acknowledge a reason is thus to arrive at a common normative structure.
7. The regress stops when we reach this common normative structure of reasons, concepts, categories, synthetic a priori truths, or the like.
8. There is, because there must be, a common normative structure of this sort.

What is in common in these views, and common to dozens of thinkers who could be added, is the idea that there is some kind of more or less autonomous shared structure external to the person which must be grasped or internalized as a precondition of mutual understanding.

The early Wittgenstein, in the *Tractatus*, claimed that "the tacit conventions on which the understanding of everyday language depends are enormously complicated" (Wittgenstein [1921] 1961: 37, §4.002). The structural relation is clear in this case: There is everyday language, and there is the structure on which it rests. It is ambiguous in this passage whether these "conventions" are local or whether the structures in question are universal. John McDowell in *Mind and World* criticizes "this idea: that when we work at making someone else [who is 'initially opaque' to us] intelligible," we are relying on a "system of concepts within which the other person thinks," meaning a local system of concepts (McDowell 1994: 34–35). Instead, he thinks, we rely on a deeper set of concepts we already share with the other person, "a standpoint from which we can join her in directing a shared attention at the world, without needing to break out through a boundary that encloses the system of concepts" (McDowell 1994: 35–36). Robert Brandom, who focuses on linguistic normativity and on understanding language as a structure of inferential moves, thinks that the inferential structures are local, community relative, or as he calls them, "social," and take the form of a system of practices (Brandom 1994).

The Tortoise, for McDowell and Brandom, is engaged in denying the things that would end the regress. The problem is not obtuseness, but a normative failure—a failure to acknowledge things that he must acknowledge if he is, for McDowell, a rational being, bound by the norms of reason, or for Brandom, a normatively bound member of a community. The term "community" is important here: To the extent that they deal with "local" normativity, these accounts rely on the notion that there is a collectivity of some sort behind every normative regress stopper, in the form of a consensus about correctness or proprieties, for example. Even the universal, Kantian structure of normative reason seems to depend on a collectivized notion of the common possession of this structure by the community of rational beings.

STRUCTURE AND EMPATHY

The standard answer to the regress problem with which I began this chapter appeals to an autonomous structure of reasons, meanings, score-keeping systems, premises, or concepts that serve as regress-stoppers because they are the things that Achilles and the Tortoise share. Sentences, judgments, and the like are true, intelligible, or valid by virtue of the existence of a structure that underlies and warrants them: They depend on something hidden. We communicate by virtue of our shared possession of the tacit structure that makes meanings and the like the same for each of us. In the language of the neo-Kantians of Brentano's time, a language that is very much still with us, this shared hidden structure was made of "presuppositions," which could be revealed by transcendental reasoning. The other view is that "nothing is hidden." This was also Brentano's view: that *Evidenz* did not depend on any offstage or prior structure. Things with *Evidenz* are regress-stoppers directly, because they are universally accepted as evident, and I can know that they are, or have faith that they would be, on the basis of my empathic powers.

We can contrast what we might call "empathist" to "structuralist" accounts as follows. The empathist thinks nothing is hidden in the sense that empathy works on externals. For the "structuralist," agreement always is a result of some hidden fact, which can perhaps be made explicit, such as Brandom's score-keeping systems and proprieties. The structuralist account depends on transcendental arguments, arguments that the structure in question is the unique condition for the possibility of that which is being explained. The empathist account depends on something more akin to inference for the best explanation, consilience with other kinds of facts, such as the fact that we can empathize, and a preference for explanations that do not invoke problematic abstract entities. Because the structuralist's arguments are transcendental arguments, based on the necessity of accepting the structuralist conditions for the possibility of a given outcome, such as communication, the existence of a genuine alternative explanation is a problem. The alternative account is not merely a rival; it is a refutation, because it shows that the structuralist conditions are not "necessary."

Structuralist accounts do not lend themselves to the consideration of alternative explanations. As we have seen in the very brief list of examples I gave earlier, there is no agreement on what the hidden structure is, what it is supposed to explain, or what it is supposed to do, other than to serve as a regress-stopper. So the project of giving an alternative account of what it is that the structuralist purports to explain is stymied at the start. This is no accident. Structuralist arguments are typically transcendental arguments or arguments that have properties in common with transcendental arguments, and the structure of transcendental arguments is typically circular, with the circularity concealed. They depend on characterizing the subject matter to be explained in such a way that alternative explanations are ruled out not by some empirical feature of the things to be explained but by the definitions of the terms used in the preferred descriptions of the theorist. The descriptions are not the kind of descriptions familiar from science, which themselves evolve in the course of the development of experiment and theory, but capture supposedly essential features of the subject matter, whether it is thought, language, concepts, or whatever, which a theory is then supposed to account for. Not surprisingly, the only theory that can account for a particular set of features described in a particular way is one which respects the ontology of the description itself. If the description is implicitly "normative," for example, the theory will have to be as well, in order to account for it. The typical conclusion, that language, thought, concepts, and so on are "normative," merely reaffirms the commitments implicit in the description. Accepting the principle that only something normative can account for something normative precludes any alternative explanation.

If we take these kinds of explanations as a group, however, the strengths of this kind of reasoning become a weakness. The arguments work too well, in the sense that they generate a myriad of hidden structures. This simply reflects the exceedingly various potential regresses to be found in ordinary reasoning: over meanings, over the justification of logical claims, over normative claims of various kinds, over things like legality, over claims about the empirical world, and so forth and so on. Each of these seems to require a different kind of structural explanation, with a different source of normativity. The alternative to appealing to structures in this ad hoc way is to give some sort of account of the relations between these structures. Brandom suggests that all normativity is reducible to "the social practice idiom" (Brandom 1979: 190n7); McDowell takes a more traditionally Kantian approach and argues for universal reason. Another approach holds that local norms are nested within more universal norms. But the fact that normativists have sought to eliminate this problem by claiming that all of them have the same source is indicative of the suspicion that there is a problem here.

Given this list of issues, and the specific character of the arguments advanced for structuralist normativist accounts, what would an alternative empathist account need to establish in order to provide enough of an alternative to improve on normativist structuralist accounts based on transcendental arguments, and thus eliminate the claim to necessity on which transcendental arguments depend? Because of the peculiarity of normativist descriptions of phenomena, the fact that they are descriptions already loaded with normative content so that only normative explanations can count as explanations, we need to step back and consider the phenomenon itself rather than the phenomenon as precharacterized by the normativist.

In short, we need to make the question more like a question about rival scientific theories. If the empathist can establish that an account, any reasonable account, can be given of the main issues listed above, and the account can be linked reasonably closely to a body of scientific fact—something that is excluded by definition in standard normativist accounts, such as Brandom's, which insist on the principle that only the normative can explain the normative—the empathist wins, at least in the temporary, prospective, fallibilist way that scientific accounts "win." The point applies equally to the argument that naturalistic accounts are excluded by definition—the existence of such accounts shows the definitions to be circular. The descriptions themselves become an issue: Hanging on to a favored description when there is no empirical difference in the face of a better alternative account is special pleading. The same result is reached if the account given by the empathist fits with a broader range of fact than that covered by the structuralist account. As we will see, however, we can go beyond this: to use the empathist argument to account for some oddities in the alternative theories, oddities which, once explained, also discredit these alternatives.

IS EMPATHY TOO WEAK A REED?

Is empathy up to this challenge? The usual issues with empathy have to do with the epistemic flaws of empathy—the ease with which we err in our empathic projections onto others. But these issues are issues primarily with empathy in the strong sense, the higher forms of empathy. They take a different shape in the case of following the thought of another person, and also in relation to *Evidenz*. If we ask the question of whether our teacher means what we mean when we write "2 + 2 = 4" on the blackboard, and then ask if what is evident to us is also evident to the teacher, we do not need deep insight into the mind of the teacher. Moreover, we have a great deal of supplementary support for our empathic sense that what is evident to her is the same as what is evident to us, and that indeed she sees it as evident. We have taken the tests, been corrected, and have observed other students being corrected. We have gone through exercises with apples and oranges that help convince us that the expression is evident, and so forth. Whereas none of these things is a criterion for evidence, and none on its own would warrant our acceptance of the expression as evident, or justify our faith that anyone else would see it as evident, there is nevertheless little room for error with respect to this empathic projection. We can safely dismiss any actual case of a person failing to see that this is evident as a case of error, misunderstanding, insanity, or something similar.

This account, then, explains what the rivals explain, and explains deviations in the same way. Indeed, it is striking that Frege indulges in psychological language, as when he says that if there were people who denied the laws of logic, we would say that "we have here a hitherto unknown type of madness" (Frege [1893] 1964: 14); that Saul Kripke comments that "they might lead me to go insane, even to behave according to a quus-like rule" (Kripke 1982: 27). What is different between the empathist and the structuralist is that the empathist does not need to rely on notions like community or other collective facts in addition to psychological facts.

The same goes for grasping a concept or a rule. The normative structuralists also have to deal with the fact that some people fail to grasp. And in accounting for this they must appeal to some set of psychological facts. The empathist must as well. But the core of the empathist's account is the thought that learning something human or intellectual will have an empathic element. It is a demystification of something that remains mysterious in structural accounts. For the empathist, learning basic arithmetic is a matter not of absorbing, through some unknown mechanism of transmittal, a system of tacit premises or presuppositions that would enable the student to take 2 + 2 = 4 as evident, but of understanding the teacher and other students and coming to see 2 + 2 = 4 in a way that would empathically universalize—such that anyone else who could take it as evident would take it as evident. This is an awkward formulation, but the thought is simple. One aspect of learning is figuring out what the teacher wants, which is a problem of empathy. The empathist's point is that this, together with the other kinds of input the student gets, both empathic (for example, through seeing other students learn) and empirical (by counting apples and oranges, for example), is sufficient to account for the evident character of the equation.

How does this relate to the problem of the collective character of structure? For the empathist, nothing need be hidden. The empathic projections in question in this and other cases work on the surface—on what the teacher says and does, for example. What is added to the surface is added by empathic projection. Nothing more is necessary. The sense of *Evidenz*—the faith in the universalizability of the evident—may, in specific cases, as we will see shortly in connection with such things as cultural differences or past historical agents, require supplementation. But in the ordinary case there is nothing other than our empathy by virtue of which this projection is possible. This is simply to say that empathy is a plausible candidate for the task of providing what needs to be added to feedback to account for the patterns of actual conduct that the structure hypothesis purports to account for, namely regress stopping.

The next question is whether empathy is enough of an answer, or the right kind of answer. Structure accounts claim to produce objectivity: The structure is, by definition, the same for everyone. Empathy is not objective, but intrinsically subjective. The traditional problems with empathy involve reliability: We often err in our empathic projections, although primarily with empathy in the strong sense. So empathy alone is not an objective regress-stopper. But this is only part of the story. As we have noted, much of the time our empathic errors are corrected by feedback: If we think we understand the arithmetic teacher, but do not, we are liable to be unable to account for what needs to be accounted for. The question is whether empathy, or low-level empathy plus feedback, is enough, or to put it differently, whether there is anything more to be had. In the case of "+ 2" it is doubtful that anything more is needed. To the extent that there are actual deviants who are unable to match their use of "+ 2" to that of their teachers and fellow students it is likely that there is a more serious and pervasive problem of understanding other people or performing mathematical tasks. Intersubjectivity of the sort produced by mutual comprehension based on empathy plus feedback produces as much "objectivity" in this case as there is to be had, a point to which we will return. And universal intersubjective agreement—literal rather than analogical agreement behind the surface agreement—is as much as there is to objectivity. But more than one intelligible inference may fit the facts, and the facts may underdetermine our judgments and allow for more than one intelligible alternative in a given situation.

If we are considering these accounts as rival theories, as we would rival scientific theories, limiting the issues to the role of empathic universalization in these philosophically central cases is misleading. Empathic universalization is not restricted to the evident, the obvious, or the truths of logic, and the implications of the notion go beyond these issues. Empathy may, in fact, account for a great deal of actual conduct, social interaction, and so forth. This was a point made by Weber and later by Alfred Schutz. As with *Evidenz* itself, empathy is impossible to eliminate as a part of social interaction and the explanation of social interaction. This becomes clear when we consider failures of empathy, cases where our capacity to understand is challenged, or in which we cannot initially understand, empathically or rationally, what the behavior in question means. If we are to explain a Hindu ritual of purity, for example, which initially seems strange, even unintelligible to us, such as the treatment of untouchables, we attempt to give an account of it which in some sense normalizes it, and normalizing it amounts to making it intelligible. But making it intelligible in this context amounts to bringing to bear facts which allow us to describe it in a way that allows us to empathize. The idea of defilement by touch is already intelligible to us as a part of our own thinking. We know, and find intelligible, the kind of thinking that goes into the notion of contagion by touch already—from such diverse sources as the laying on of hands of the apostolic succession to the child's game of tag. So our problem of making the Hindu practice intelligible in the end relies on us filling in the rest of the context in such a way that we can match it up with something intelligible to us.

Intelligibility here bottoms out not in a theory of rationality, but in an actual point of empathic contact. Contagion thinking seems to be universal, and thus universally intelligible. But contagion inferences are not "necessary": We can follow them without accepting them. The inferential part of this thinking is ungroundable, final, and so forth. Perhaps it is rooted in the primal mirrorable experience of the nonmechanical effects of touch, which provides a template for the notion that touching produces nonmechanical transformation. But there is no reason for us to think that this kind of inference will always be correct as a matter of empirical fact. And indeed more generally, empirical fact falls into a different category from following the thought of another, shared attention, and so forth. The traditional Cartesian issues of illusion, for example, cannot be resolved by appeals to evidence, for by definition another person, with knowledge of the illusory effect, would not judge the illusory effect as evident. This is why Brentano distinguished "evident to me" from *Evidenz* as such, which he associated with "insight." As with Weber's discussion of indirect understanding of action, based on inferences, we need to confirm contagion inferences, if they are inferences about actual causal relations, for example about disease. Whether they predict or not is a question separate from the question of whether we can follow the thinking. Following is empathic, final in the sense that there is no further explanation of it. Contagion reasoning itself is a matter of *Evidenz*, in the sense that there is no additional justification of it to be had. But of course it is not evident in the sense that it is necessary or necessarily "true."

WHEN EMPATHY GOES WRONG

The obvious objection to appeals to empathy of any kind is this: Empathy is not a reliable guide to anything. The reasoning is this: Our empathic attributions often go wrong. Empathy produces results with *Evidenz* only in simple cases, such as Weber's example of a man chopping wood (Weber [1968] 1978: 8). And even these empathic imputations, to the extent that they rest on empirical facts, are fallible. So the assumption underlying empathic universalization, on which this whole account is based, namely that empathy is an autonomous source of knowledge, is simply false. In what I have said here I have tried to separate empathy and empathic universalization from truth and objectivity by arguing that whereas empathic universalization leading to intersubjective agreement is enough for truth and objectivity, empathic universalization is a broader phenomenon, and it applies to anything that another person can "follow" in the thinking of another, or, in this sense, understand. This formulation has the effect of inverting the relationship between *Evidenz* and truth that informed the earlier discussion: The evident is not a problematic subtype of truth, as it is in the earlier picture. It is a feature of mutual reasoning, which may or may not lead to truth (whatever that might mean in the contexts of logic and mathematics that concerned Brentano), that better matches the idea of intelligibility. The true is a subtype of the intelligible, and the intelligible is that which can be empathically understood. *Evidenz* is a property of the subtype of the intelligible for which there is no alternative which one could accept. This leads to a different picture of empathic universalization—not as a criterion for the acceptability of "certain" or evident statements, but as a commonplace, and essential part of ordinary human interaction.

The picture we get out of these considerations is this: Potential regresses are everywhere, and they end. But they do not end in analogical facts, such as agreements or assumptions. Nothing is hidden. They end at the point that people—or Tortoises—find that they can follow each other and that the step in their reasoning is evident. *Evidenz*, that is, ending a regress at a point that the parties can each follow, is indispensable. Seeming to be evident and being evident are, in this setting, the same thing. Being evident means being evident to everyone—subject to the usual limitations of "everyone" being sane, capable of recognizing what others would take to be evident, and so forth. But being evident in this sense is not necessarily permanent and thus is not a guarantee of truth in the sense of "there are no alternatives." Alternatives which we did not previously imagine can be invented, and consequently what seems evident can cease to be evident, as Euclidean space ceased to be evident, in the sense that it ceased to be without alternatives. But this does not mean that it ceased to be immediately intelligible, or that we no longer understand Euclidean geometry. Nor would the invention of an alternative form of counting mean that we no longer understood 2 + 2 = 4. The only evidence we have of successful empathy is indirect—through the success of our interactions. But it is not reducible to these interactions, or to any empirical evidence. As Weber says, we "understand what a person is doing . . . on the basis of the facts of the situation, as experience has accustomed us to interpret them" (Weber [1968] 1978: 5). Our experiences, and thus our capacity to empathize, vary individually. And what and how we experience is itself partly the product of this variable capacity to interpret. The fact that we can empathize is not derived from anything and needs no justification. It is a natural fact. To deny it is to deny one of the causal conditions of learning such things as language, communicating, and much more.

Is this picture better than the normative structuralist's picture? It certainly explains more phenomena. But it also sheds light on a peculiarity of the normative structuralist's case. The treatment of Kripke's discussion of rule-following relied heavily on the claim that there was a distinction between community acceptance of what counted as following a rule in the community and the correct application of the community's rule. There is a parallel issue in Husserl. In what is usually taken as his attack on Brentano, he discusses insight with evidence and argues that there is a need for a modal category of the concept of insight with evidence, namely a concept of possible insights with evidence, which in turn must be grounded in "rational consciousness in general" (Husserl [1931] 1962: 354). The oddity of both of these cases is that there are no examples of a community which is in complete error about the correct application of its rules or of a possible insight with evidence that is not actualized. The reason, in the latter case, is that once one gave such an example and explained it so someone would accept it as evident, it would already be an actual insight with evidence. The very process of making it evident to others, in short, would make it evident in the sense of actual empathy. Something parallel happens with the case of community acceptance. Imagine that there was a community which had been taught a rule of arithmetic, such as the + 2 rule, incorrectly, and that this had been learned in the ordinary way, that is to say that the thoughts of the teacher had been followed and it was understood empathically what she meant by "+ 2," and that this understanding was generally accepted in the community. In what sense would this be a case of community error? What would the error be? If they understood the teacher, the teacher's usage was intelligible, and they did as the teacher did, they would simply be following a different rule which they call "+ 2." This would be something like the case of non-Euclidean geometry, which makes the axioms of Euclid understandable but no longer evident. Any case of actual error, in contrast, would be a case in which the rule had somehow been misunderstood at the beginning. But if the beginning is with a teacher and the teacher's thought had been correctly followed, there is no error. And there is no way to get error by the entire community if it involves teaching together with empathic following of the thought of those who are teaching. The case for normative structuralism is that there is something left over to be explained. But there is nothing.

11 Collective or Social?

Tacit Knowledge and Its Kin

The terms "social" and "collective" are often used interchangeably, or without distinction, and this lack of discrimination is especially evident in the cognitive science literature. In the literature of social theory and sociology, in contrast, the terms are sharply distinguished, at least in theoretically sensitive contexts. Indeed, the terms represent an important dividing line between traditions. Émile Durkheim made a point of criticizing his rival Gabriel Tarde for replacing

> the expression "collective psychology" by "interpsychology." The first expression appeared to him to be tainted with ontology, because it seems to imply that there is a collective psychology proper. (Durkheim 1906: 133)

The issue marked a major fault line within French sociology. One of the cardinal points made by Tarde was that the mechanisms for explaining social phenomena involved processes between individuals, notably imitation, which incidentally plays a large role in cognitive science discussions of social interaction, rather than anything "collective" (Tarde [1890] 1903). This led to the use of the term "social" as distinct from, and in contrast to "collective." Durkheim of course rejected this bottom-up approach to the explanation of social phenomena. Durkheim's sociologization of Kant involved the idea that there were collective, shared psychological contents, contents irreducible to the processes of individual psychology, and that appeals to these collective contents were necessary to account for social life. His approach was explicitly "collective." This fault line has persisted. In American sociology, movements such as Symbolic Interactionism rejected any such reasoning and attempted to explain such things as "significant symbols," to use the expression of G. H. Mead ([1934] 1972), in terms of social interaction, but also from the bottom up, as products of the interactive process.

Outside of these contexts, however, confusion in the use of these terms reigns. "Collective" is used, especially in the context of cognitive science, for processes that are not collective but social. "Social" is routinely used in a way that does not discriminate between "collective" and "social" in the sense of social interaction. The point may be illustrated with a text by Michael Tomasello. On the one hand, he uses the "collective" language of "shared intentionality":

> Underlying these two singular characteristics of human culture—cumulative artifacts and social institutions—are sets of species-unique skills and motivations for cooperation. . . . [W]e may refer to the underlying psychological processes that make these unique forms of cooperation possible as "shared intentionality." (2009: xiii)

But when he explains the underlying psychological processes, they are social; they involve interaction between individuals, where one individual is engaged with other individuals in ways that transform the other individuals.

> First, humans actively teach one another things, and they do not reserve their lessons for kin. . . . Second, humans also have a tendency to imitate others in the group simply in order to be like them, that is, to conform. (2009: xiv)

Imitation is an imperfect one-on-one process which does not produce collectively standardized results; teaching might be designed to produce standardized results as external behavior, but what people take away from the actual interactive experience of being taught, the internal psychology, is individual. They may be good or bad at arithmetic. They are disciplined to be standard in the answers they give to arithmetic questions. Being disciplined and desiring to conform produce social results. The skills and the desires allow teams to work together. But "shared intentionality" implies something more, a common mental content together with a common motivation.

Some of the confusion about these terms is legitimate. It is not always obvious which term is the correct one. There are widely used but problematic notions, such as "sharing," that make sense primarily as a collective fact, but which might also be understood as part of interaction, for example in relation to joint attention, with "social" but not "collective" implications. Yet it is easy to slide from facts about interaction to collective claims, despite their very different implications. Moreover, there are definitional issues that confuse matters. One may of course redefine the notions of "sharing" and "intention" in a way that eliminates the oddity of saying that multiple people have the same intention. One might redefine "intention" in terms of some common external goal, for example, such as winning a war, and treat as "sharing" anything intentional directed toward that goal. But this merely has the effect of allowing a huge variety of very different intentional and psychological causal structures and backgrounds, involving, for example, different and conflicting beliefs about the world, to count as "the same" intention, and thus something that could be said to be shared. But this is not a "collective" notion of intention in the sense that there is significant shared or collective internal or psychological content. Indeed, we may have very different concepts even of an external goal such as winning a war.

COLLINS AND THE IDEA OF COLLECTIVE TACIT KNOWLEDGE

In this chapter I will try to sort out some of these distinctions in relation to the case of tacit knowledge, which presents them in a particularly clear form. It is one of the virtues of Harry Collins' recent book *Tacit and Explicit Knowledge* (2010) that it sharpens this issue. My basic thesis will be a simple one. Claims about "collective" facts normally depend on transcendental, "conditions for the possibility of" arguments; the actual empirical evidence only supports noncollective "social" claims. This argument has direct bearing on the problem of tacit knowledge. One role of the concept of tacit knowledge has been to account for mutual interaction and understanding. In this role tacit knowledge is assumed to be shared, a common possession of those interacting, for example as speakers of a common language, and it is further assumed that this shared tacit knowledge is a condition for the possibility of the kind of communication through meaningful speech that language permits. Another role, however, has been to account for highly individual skills and competences, such as the skill of using one's own physically distinctive body to perform complex tasks such as riding a bicycle. These roles are very different and not obviously congruent, a point made by Collins.

Collins argues that the "bicycle" model of tacit knowledge, based on the standard example of embodied but inarticulable tacit knowledge of how to ride a bicycle, is unable to account for certain facts that tacit knowledge should account for. A "collective" kind of tacit knowledge would explain what is needed. This is a paradigmatic argument from explanatory necessity, with a transcendental argument as a solution, although Collins puts his claim somewhat differently—as an assertion about what the most parsimonious explanation is. Whether this self-explication is appropriate is a question to be dealt with later. Ontologically, it is anything but parsimonious. Collins joins a long line of historical figures as well as contemporary thinkers who believe that there is some sort of collective mental element that is out there, in some sense, is assimilated or acquired by the participants, and functions as a shared structure which is in turn a condition for certain performances that cannot be explained or accounted for in any other way. What makes these arguments resemble transcendental arguments is that "collective tacit knowledge," "collective intentionality," and so forth are the condition for the possibility of outcomes that Collins and similar users of these arguments believe cannot be explained in any other way. We are supposed to accept its existence and his characterization of it because it meets this explanatory necessity. It is this general kind of conclusion that will concern me here, as it has in many other places. In general, the issue is this: The leap to a "collective" solution is unwarranted and the characterization of things to be explained as themselves "collective" is also unwarranted. But here I propose to discuss the distinction between collective and social in general, explicitly, and with an eye to explaining its sources and the case to be made against appeals to collective facts, as well as its undeniable attractions.

My basic point will be this: "Collective" mental objects, of which tacit knowledge in Collins' account is an instance, are accessible only through transcendental arguments or arguments that share the problems of transcendental arguments. What I will show here is that these arguments are, as a group, defective in important ways that are relevant for any empirical explanatory account of the subject matter of tacit knowledge. Collins himself concedes one of the central issues with these accounts, the problem of how collective tacit knowledge is acquired. In contrast, "social" explanations, that is to say those involving interpersonal interactions and interpersonal processes such as imitation, are not subject to these defects; however, social mechanisms of the kinds that are generally known and accepted as genuine causal and psychological processes never produce, account for, or explain the kinds of facts that collective accounts proceed from. But social explanations have their own issues.

To keep track of the relevant issues, it is useful to think in terms of a scoreboard. The advantages of the "collective" model, in Collins' case, the idea of Collective Tacit Knowledge, are these:

a) Fills an explanatory need in a simple, "parsimonious" way.
b) Enables understanding of other people.
c) Enables claims about the content of what is tacit.

The disadvantages are these:

a) Underdetermination: As with all regress or transcendental arguments, the Achilles' heel of these arguments is the fact that the same overt results can be accounted for in different and inconsistent ways.
b) The problem of location: It is difficult to get a coherent answer to the question of where the collective stuff is located, and consequently how it interacts with ordinary causal and interpersonal processes.
c) Transmission: There is no good way of accounting for how it is that the collective stuff is acquired by individuals, especially for how it is that the "same" stuff becomes part of the individual psychological or cognitive processes that are directly involved in thought and action explanation.

d) Circularity: Much depends, in these arguments, on characterizing the thing to be explained in such a way that only collective explanations qualify as explanations.

"Individual" or "social interaction" accounts have their own issues, but they come down to three major problems:

a) How can individual content and interactive processes operating between individuals aggregate to produce collective outcomes, such as a common language, cooperation, teams, joint collective action, and so forth?
b) How are we to understand meaning, language, the worldviews of others, and practices if we do not treat these as collective facts?
c) How can we understand alien cultures and contexts of knowledge if not by reference to their shared presuppositions, assumptions, tacit knowledge, and meanings?

In short, despite the oddity of their claims, collective accounts seem to be about something and serve some important cognitive purposes. The question is whether these purposes can be served by a better alternative explanation.

The focus of my discussion here will be with the undeniable intellectual attractions of collective notions as means of achieving understanding. To know that the people of the Middle Ages "assumed" something different than we do about God's place in a hierarchical teleological order of the world, for example, illuminates and makes intelligible some of the otherwise puzzling things that they wrote and believed. So to vindicate noncollective social explanations, these achievements also need to be accounted for, and in a way that is consistent with a reasonable understanding of the mechanisms that these noncollective social explanations employ. So in much of this chapter I will be concerned with giving an account of what sort of understanding one gets by attributing presuppositions, collective tacit knowledge, and the like to a group of people, or to the individuals who compose the "group." This is also the focus of much of Collins' book, under the heading of the problem of making tacit knowledge explicit, something he does through the notion of strings. My account, however, will dispense with the whole apparatus of presuppositions, strings, collective tacit knowledge, and the like as misleading and unnecessary.

SOME DEEP HISTORY

The idea of collective mental properties or possessions begins inadvertently, with Kant. Kant contributed the idea of a transcendental argument and the notion that our possibilities of experience were shaped by categories that were the conditions of the pre-organized experience of the sort that we actually conversed and thought about. Such apparent features of the world as space and causality were the products of this mental pre-organization. The underlying organizing principles were tacit, although Kant did not use this language (in fact, there is a problem in translating the term "tacit knowledge" into German in the first place, but the usual translation, *Implizites Wissen*, already transforms it into a quasi-Kantian notion) in the sense that they were normally not articulated, but could be.

Kant had no intention of introducing a "collective" account of these presupposed conditions of thought. And despite the psychological language of the mental and of cognition that he employed, he insisted that he was not offering a psychology at all, but rather an account of the logical conditions of knowing. Nevertheless, someone had to possess these conditions, in some sense, to be a knower. Kant thought that the most basic conditions at least were common to all rational beings and indeed a condition of rationality. The philosophical argument for their presence and necessity worked with two notions. The first was the idea of a regress, in which premises needed to be justified by more basic premises. The second was the idea that this kind of analysis could produce a unique result that excluded the possibility of alternative premises for the same conclusions (Paulson [1934] 1992). If the claim to exclude alternatives worked, it would obviate any need to consider the possibility that, for example, different people had different presuppositions or implicit knowledge yet nevertheless managed to get around in the world, and even communicate; there would be only one possible set of presuppositions for everyone.

The neo-Kantians radicalized this argument by applying it not only to the certain knowledge of the physical world supplied by physics, but to a whole range of domains of thought in which objective knowledge was possible. Hermann Cohen, the key radicalizer, applied the basic idea of a domain of thought organized in a tacit but reconstructable logical hierarchy of concepts to ethics, which he argued had the character of a logically organized domain because jurisprudence, which was organized around the constitutive ethical concept of will, was itself a logically organized domain. The "fact of science," the fact that there was an organized domain, implied that there was a set of presuppositions and a logical hierarchy of concepts that constituted it. The circularity is evident in the characterization of the domain: What else could account for a domain with this kind of conceptual order than an explanation of that order, and what would explain it other than a hierarchical arrangement of the concepts in terms of their logical relations?

Cohen interpreted this kind of analysis epistemologically as distinct from psychologically, like Kant. This turns out to be a crucial and problematic distinction that reappears in Collins, for example when he criticizes Dreyfus for failing to deal with "the nature of knowledge" (2010: 104). Kant had made a great point of claiming that, as Warren Schmaus put it, "he was not offering his theory of categories as an empirical, psychological account of the origin of experience" (2004: 30), but rather of what was presupposed by experience. Thus, as Schmaus paraphrases Kant, "to say, for instance, that the category of quantity is necessary for experience . . . is to say only that one could not experience objects without their having some quantity or another" (2004: 30–31).

But the application of these ideas to historically specific domains, such as the law, and then to the various academic disciplines, including theology, had the effect of localizing them to the individual members of these disciplines who were actually "knowers" thinking in terms of the organized concepts of their discipline. The trick of saying "one could not experience objects without their having some quantity or other" does not work with the objects of specialized disciplines: One can experience the actions of agents of the law without presupposing anything specifically "legal." And one can understand the theological beliefs of others without presupposing the existence of God. So the "conditionality" could not be bound to experience and migrated to the knower. When the idea of a domain constituted by hierarchically organized concepts was extended to the "historical a priori," which is to say to the presuppositions of a past epoch that distinguished it from our own, the localization was made even more apparent. To say that people in the Renaissance experienced *Il Duomo* differently than we do implies that the difference is in them, not in *Il Duomo*. For localized domains, the categories and concepts involved were not conditions of experience as such, but of the highly specific objectivity inducing experiences of people who in some sense possessed the constituting concepts. In the law, for example, this would be people trained in the law, who could agree on objective facts of legal science.

The presuppositions in these cases had to belong to the people who were of the time, or of the discipline. And because the function of the presuppositions was to assure or explain the "objectivity" of results in the domain, they had to be uniform or shared. None of this was argued for: It was a given in the Kantian lineage of the idea of objectivity and constitution. Because these were not thought of as matters of psychology, but as matters of the logic of concepts—Cohen, for example, claimed to be making inferences from the facts of universal jurisprudence, a mythical discipline unconnected to actual lawyers—there was no sense that a psychological account was needed. Eventually, various neo-Kantians saw the need to provide accounts that made sense of the facts of localization. Hans Vaihinger's philosophy of "as if" was one solution: It converted the presuppositions to hypotheticals, which were therefore optional. Another solution was dualism: One could ignore psychology by arguing that the facts in question were facts in the symbolic realm, as Cohen's student and successor Ernst Cassirer argued ([1923–1929] 1955). But these solutions merely evaded the major consequence: By applying the Kantian approach to these domains, by attributing a specific symbolic realm or conceptual order to a particular group of people, the neo-Kantians had inadvertently come to assert social facts about groups of people and historical facts about the people of an epoch.

This pair of ideas—epistemic as distinct from psychological and local or historical—produced a peculiar and confused result. What was the relation between the fact of localization, the fact that only a set of related people were knowers of this kind, and the epistemic content, the presuppositions, themselves? Was it possible to avoid questions like "how did the presuppositions get acquired by these knowers, and why did some people have them and others not have them?" In short, can one historicize, socialize, or sociologize epistemology without at the same time psychologizing it?

For these localized presuppositions there was no avoiding the question of where they came from and what sort of reality they had. This question was, indeed, what Ernst Cassirer's account of the symbolic was designed to answer. His answer was that the symbolic realm was a real constitutive tacit order of collective knowledge, one in which relations held between symbols, which individuals drew from and employed in their own thought and expression. The idea that there are relations of some sort of logical or inferential kind that exist at the level of the symbolic or semantic is a consistent theme in this literature and persists today in the philosophical literature on normativity (Williams 2010) and in the "practice" literature, in which practices as a collective phenomenon are supposed to exhibit "coherence" of a sort that cannot be reduced to the coherence produced by individual cognitive psychological processes.

For Cassirer, this led to the idea of a generic symbolic order open to all, which individuals or particular societies accessed. But the more common and plausible solution to the problem of where the presuppositions came from and had their real existence was to place them into some sort of collective mind. The group mind is a solution to the problem created by localization. But it is a concept with its own history. Ontologizing the problem of collective mental life introduced a novel and problematic entity. Part of the Kantian legacy was to separate mind and brain, which facilitated the idea that groups could have minds without the causal accouterments of brains. But there were still nagging problems about cause. If the presuppositions of the group were not given in experience and thus accessible to individual reflection, they had to be acquired. And if they were presupposed by experience, they had to be acquired some way other than ordinary learning, which operates through experience, with empirical inputs, and produces individual mental results, like habits and beliefs, rather than collective possessions. What is this way? Collins acknowledges that this is a problem, but makes no attempt to solve it.

The larger problem here is about the distinction between "epistemic" and "psychological" inherited from Kant: the status of the presuppositions, concepts, and categories which are the conditions of explicit knowledge. If we grant that they are logically required, does this imply that they are therefore necessarily causally real in some sense? This kind of reasoning seems to generate causal claims from transcendental arguments. And there is a long tradition of transcendental reasoning which implies something like this, but it is vague or evasive about what is implied (Turner 2010a: 14–30). The reasons for vagueness or evasiveness are not difficult to understand. In the next two sections, I will illustrate two of these reasons: the problem of transmission and the problem of underdetermination.

BRINGING THE TRANSCENDENTAL DOWN TO EARTH: TRANSMISSION

Cassirer's solution, to posit a universal symbolic order, fails, as all universalistic solutions do: The things to be accounted for at the local level are far too diverse and various to be fit under any universal scheme, no matter how elaborate. The neo-Kantians knew this, which is why they eventually turned to ideas of "form" as the universals and handled content as subordinate and relativistic. But the basic idea that what we take to be ordinary facts, or common sense, or what is known, is the product of the presuppositions we unconsciously employ to constitute our world, and has persisted as conventional wisdom. The anthropologist Clifford Geertz puts it this way, speaking about sex: "Common sense is not what the mind cleared of cant spontaneously apprehends; it is what the mind filled with presuppositions . . . concludes" (Geertz 1983: 84).

Hans Freyer wrote one of the classic defenses and explications of the idea of the "objective mind" which dealt extensively with the puzzle of how the objective mind interacted with life and with the intellectual history of this puzzle. He notes that

> when Dilthey formulated his theory of the *Verstehen* of the human sciences, he was forced necessarily to raise the question: What actually is that "interior" that inheres in such objects as states, churches, customs, books, and works of art? What is it that we comprehend with understanding in these objects? Answer: the "interior" is nothing psychic; we are not doing psychology, at least as we have formulated it. Rather, this interior is an entity of the mind with a "characteristic" structure and legitimacy. (Freyer [1923] 1998: 11)

Dilthey, in short, wants, like Kant, to talk about the mind and understanding in a nonpsychological way, objectively, in terms of the real meanings of things. But because these things—*Il Duomo*, for example—have local meaning, we need an account that corresponds to the local fact, but is not merely psychological, meaning a matter of the beliefs and feelings of individuals, but rather of the conditions of their experience. Here is how Dilthey solves this conundrum:

> It is the "spirit" of a definite law, a definite religion, or art, that has its existence in the external apparatus of the objectivation. Examples will follow in which this fact of objective mind is provisionally demarcated from the sphere of actual-psychic things. The world of objective mind, as is repeatedly found, has its natural organization; it consists of relatively independent cultural systems, even if they are bound to a nexus of activity. The formal structure of cultural systems and the historical diversity of their contents can be comprehended through specific concepts ("second order concepts of the human sciences"). (Freyer [1923] 1998: 11)

A culture is an objective reality, relatively independent of "actual-psychic things," such as the contents of individual minds. It is, to put it in terms of collective tacit knowledge, itself a kind of knowledge or condition of knowledge, in the sense that the Kantian categories are, but unlike these categories localized to a "nexus of activity," a real social world of some sort.

Freyer was a kind of sociologist as well as a philosopher. This way of formulating the issue reflected the intellectual situation of his time. After the rise of *Lebensphilosophie*, the questions that dogged the neo-Kantians about the relation of these intellectual forms to life were typically framed in terms of the fixity of the contents of the objective mind and the vitality and changeable character of the "life" they were supposed to be a condition of. The problem was this: There were individual psychological facts, and there was activity, all of which had properties unlike the relatively autonomous and fixed, but meaning-conferring properties of culture. This posed the problem of the relation of the two orders of fact. The relation could not be unidirectional: "Life" had to somehow produce cultural forms, just as the forms produced experience. Freyer puts the problem thus:

> The forms of objective mind bear in themselves, as it were, by virtue of their psychic origin, the indelible yearning to be bound again to life. They are not dependent upon the particular action of realization; they transcend it and remain meaningful forms, even if a particular action passes them by. Nevertheless, they are in need of actual life because it is the source out of which they arose. It is of no use to separate these two qualities; both of these qualities must be considered together in the concept of objective mind. The forms of objective mind, no matter how high they are lifted out of the stream of activity, are still merely the concluding pieces in a circular course that runs from soul to soul, from life to life. They represent a higher level of what we, at a lower level, called tools: objectified fragments of living processes—tools of life. The triumph of subjective mind is that the objective structures with their own validity and their own permanency, which subjective

> mind has produced out of itself, never become entirely free from it. They must always be reclaimed by subjective mind in order to be fully actual. (Freyer [1923] 1998: 82)

The last phrase points to the problem of transmission. To actually have any effect on people, the objective mind must be incorporated into the subjective mind. Merely having it "out there" in the form of objective spirit is not enough. Even if it is not a psychological fact, or not reducible to psychological facts about individuals, it has to also become a psychological fact to have any effect on the individual. To make this account work, there must be a way to get these objective forms into the heads of people. It is not enough to say "but the forms are a condition of experience itself." By localizing, we psychologize the problem of how objective spirit is acquired, or known, even as a condition of experience. Collins has this problem as well. Knowledge is individual: How does the social "superorganism" (2010: 134) and its contents relate to the contents of individual minds?

UNDERDETERMINATION AND AUDIENCES

One of the issues that Freyer's somewhat mystical appeal to objective spirit conceals is the question of the actual content of this spirit. It is possible, and we will see this is also Collins' thought, to claim that the shared conditions of experience are not fully articulable. But this does not preclude attempts to articulate these conditions, to, in the language of tacit knowledge, make the tacit explicit. The record of these attempts, however, reveals another problem. Kantians, freed from ordinary empirical considerations by the epistemology-psychology distinction, could attribute presuppositions to a logical space that was not identifiable with any particular actual knowers, and thus avoid "psychology" and the identification of this logical space with an unspecified "we." They could then come up with impressive results by identifying the presuppositions of particular phenomena. Consider a famous discussion of "reactive attitudes" by P. F. Strawson, explicated recently by Stephen Darwall:

> Strawson dubbed the distinctive attitudes involved in holding people responsible "reactive attitudes," with prominent examples being indignation, resentment, guilt, blame, and so on. And Strawson pointed out what commentators have since stressed, namely, that reactive attitudes implicitly address demands. They invariably involve "an expectation of, and demand for" certain conduct from one another ([1962] 1968: 85). Reactive attitudes invariably concern what someone can be held to, so they invariably presuppose the authority to hold someone responsible and make demands of him. Moral reactive attitudes therefore

> presuppose the authority to demand and hold one another responsible for compliance with moral obligations (which just are the standards to which we can warrantedly hold each other as members of the moral community). But they also presuppose that those we hold accountable have that standing also. They address another, Strawson says, in a way that "continu(es) to view him as a member of the moral community; only as one who has offended against its demands" ([1962] 1968: 93). (Darwall 2006: 17)

Darwall comments: "It follows that reactive attitudes are second-personal in our sense, and that ethical notions that are distinctively relevant to these attitudes—the culpable, moral responsibility, and, I argue, moral obligation—all have an irreducibly second-personal aspect that ties them conceptually to second-personal reasons" (2006: 17). "Second-personal" is Darwall's language for "we" reasons, reasons that are collective, shared, and so on within the "we" in question.

What is of interest in this quotation is, first, how readily Strawson generates a vast set of "presuppositions" out of the mere fact that people feel resentment, indignation, and so on. How does he do this? Phrases like "implicitly address" are an indication of his procedure: He is attempting to make sense of a physical reaction in terms of what would make it a justifiable act. And to justify it would require a long list of beliefs about the act and its objects of the sort he gives. This is apparently a case of making explicit something that is implicit. But there is an ambiguity here—is this a claim that the people involved actually have in their heads something corresponding to these "presuppositions"? If not, what is the point of calling them either "pre" or "suppositions"? But this is not Strawson's meaning: He is not making some sort of empirical claim about how people who are indignant actually think. Indeed, the whole point of reactive attitudes is that they are "reactive," meaning a more or less instantaneous response of the kind familiar to cognitive science. They are not the product of elaborate reasoning, implicit or otherwise. But Strawson does mean something stronger than "might imply, under the right circumstances" or "would be required for a correct theoretical justification." The presuppositions he provides are intended as an explanation rather than an *ex post facto* justification. And Darwall, by referring to a real "we," also connects them to actual persons.

Even in the limited sense "would be required for a correct theoretical justification," however, the explanation is very odd. There is an immediate question about who the audience for this justification is. The reactive attitudes—let us just take indignation as an example—are reactions that are taken to be human universals. But the concepts that are supposedly "presupposed" are native to a highly specific intellectual culture: ours. The idea of "moral community," and the attendant idea that such a community is a source of moral authority, is a modern idea with a distinctive set of intellectual antecedents. One could be indignant about the violation of a tabu or the profanation of a sacred object without either of these involving ideas about, for example, moral community: The sacred is a relation with God; tabu is a relation with the world. Neither is merely "for us." The philology of the term "indignation" takes us back to the notion of dignity, which is part of the "honor" family of concepts, and normally is part of a web of beliefs about social roles and statuses. Yet Strawson never mentions status, honor, or dignity and appeals only to abstract notions of moral obligation and community.

So what does it mean to generate lists of presuppositions as Strawson does? Clearly these are not psychological claims. But "reactive" identifies a psychological phenomenon. It is puzzling why reactions would have "presuppositions" in the first place. If we interpret the problem Strawson wants to solve as an explanatory one, of explaining why people react to what they react to, perhaps it would makes sense to say that the account Strawson gives is, for a certain audience, one possible account of the "meaning" of indignation that would make sense to that audience. But one might give an equally good explanation, or for that matter an equally good justification, in other terms, for example, in terms of the root concept of dignity itself. There is, in short, a problem of underdetermination: Whatever regress the "presuppositions" are supposed to end can also be ended in other "presuppositions." Perhaps the regress can end in no presuppositions at all, if we choose to make the reaction of indignation in question some sort of primitive inference whose force we directly understand. Moreover, the explanation seems necessarily to be an explanation for a particular audience, one that understands the presuppositions. For other audiences, one would give another explanation. For a South Sea Islander, one might explain the same phenomenon in terms of tabu. None of this would fit very well with the idea that these presuppositions are part of some sort of objective cultural fact that could be made explicit. But they might fit with the idea that there was something hidden or tacit that couldn't be made explicit, but could be restated in an explicit functional substitute for the audiences for which the substitute was functional.

SEPARATING THE LOGICAL AND THE PSYCHOLOGICAL

The fact that "presuppositions" are underdetermined, audience relative, and ontologically problematic suggests, but does not directly imply, that perhaps there is no stable object corresponding to it. This is a troubling conclusion. We think that there ought to be some sort of close relationship between the logical and the psychological or the social: Freyer, and even Darwall with his "we," seems to be talking about something that is in people's heads and accessible, to some extent, to them. The fact that we can sometimes self-explicate our presuppositions, or make our tacit knowledge explicit through explaining ourselves more fully, or do this for others by identifying their presuppositions, seems to indicate that we are saying something about what is already there in the mind. But the logical and the psychological work in quite different ways. So this sense may simply be an illusion.

Consider the following comment by Hans Kelsen about the interpretation of the League of Nations covenant, paragraph 1 of article 4. It reads in part, "The Council shall consist of Representatives of the Principal Allied and Associated Powers." As he points out, it would have made the US and Japan permanent members of the council, despite the fact that the US never ratified the treaty and Japan withdrew. As Kelsen says,

> a literal interpretation of paragraph 1 certainly does not correspond to the intentions of the authors of the statute. They assumed as a fact that all the "Principal Powers" would ratify the Treaty of Versailles at least and thereby become members of the League. They did not think at all of the case where one of these states, after having ratified the Treaty, would withdraw from the League. They therefore refrained from stipulation that only members of the League could be represented on the Council. (1939: 48)

The two middle sentences of this passage are related as follows: There is a claim about an "assumption" and another claim about something "they did not think at all." The initial claim about what they assumed is not in conflict with the second claim about the psychological fact of not having noticed the possibility that countries would fail to ratify or leave the League. The second claim is, rather, a clarification or psychological explanation of the first. In this case the fact is not, however, an occurrent fact (i.e., something that the person is currently conscious of or is otherwise manifest), but an omission or the absence of a psychological fact. Yet both the psychological claim and the "assumption" claim are true and they are consistent with one another. Indeed, as Kelsen's passage reads, the assumption claim is in some sense supported and explained by the psychological one.

So what sort of fact is the fact about the assumption? One way of approaching this question is to ask for whom it is a fact. If it is not a fact in a psychological sense of introspectability—one cannot introspect an omission—it was therefore not an introspectable fact for the signatories. Is it a fact for the interpreter, who is providing an explanation of the failure to make the logically possible inference that countries might withdraw from the treaty? Is the explanation the kind of explanation that makes the inference intelligible—intelligible to the interpreter and the audience of the interpreter?

The issues here become a little clearer if we consider some different ways of formulating Kelsen's comment and the relation between the "did not think" and the "assumption" parts of the sentence. If we treat the assumption part as an "as if" statement, namely that the writers of the document proceeded "as if" nations would not withdraw from the covenant, we capture the meaning without adding any term, such as "assuming," that suggests something psychological or suggests that the "assumption" is a transcendental condition. The sentence becomes one in which the "as if" clause allows us to give an intelligible interpretation, although not necessarily a correct one. The notion of "as if" is explicitly an appeal to a fiction in Vaihinger's sense ([1911] 1966). But it is a fiction that allows us to make sense of something.

It is a fiction that, for a particular audience, makes sense of the conduct of the authors of the document. First, it is an audience that already understands the meaning of the terms of the fiction. But second, the need for this particular kind of sense making is restricted to people who have noticed the problem of withdrawal from the covenant, and only for those people. The people who wrote the treaty did not need to think about, or use, the "assumption" because they all failed to notice the issue. They also did not understand each other in the fictive or hypothetical "as if" sense; they were living in a world in which this possibility had not come to notice.

The failure to notice was a "failure" only from a different perspective. From theirs, there was only agreement and mutual understanding, and nothing to explain. They all noticed, and attended to, the same things. If we had the power to appear from the future and proposed a clause which resolved the problem, they might say, "we did not notice that," or they might say, "you are assuming that nations will withdraw from the covenant." But we wouldn't have "assumed" anything either. We would simply have had a different experience—in this case the historical experience of withdrawals from the league. If we had not had that experience, we might also fail to notice this possibility. Indeed, as there was no legal procedure in the covenant for withdrawal, there is a sense in which the possibility of withdrawal was itself invented by those who wished to withdraw, and by their insistence on treating the covenant as merely a treaty which could be repudiated in the normal manner of formal repudiations of treaties, something that was not intended or even imagined by the original authors of the covenant.

This gets us to an odd result: Claims about "assumptions" say no more than "as if" claims. The point of appealing to claims, in this practical context of interpretation, is to make sense of some belief or action that we do not understand. The aid to understanding that claims about assumptions provide is relative to the beliefs, noticings, and so forth of the persons interpreting the claims. The correctness of claims about assumptions as well as the content of the "as if" claims are relative to the specific misunderstanding; without a misunderstanding there is nothing for the claim to be about.

This does not mean, however, that someone—the authors of the covenant, for example, would not assent to the attribution of the assumption—as a clarification of what they meant, or even produce the "assumption" if they were faced with a question that implied withdrawal was possible. The question itself, in this case, would have brought the possibility to notice, or at least brought to notice the fact that the questioner had imagined this possibility. So to answer "yes, that is what was assumed" tells us nothing about a state of mind in the past. It is merely a retrospective interpretation provided in response to a new question which implied a possibility that had not been considered.

This, indeed, is a model for what happens when the tacit is made explicit: The person making the tacit explicit tells the hearer what he thinks would enable the hearer to make sense of the relevant inferences.

WHAT HAPPENS WHEN THE TACIT IS MADE EXPLICIT?

One of Collins' major themes is the question of what happens when the tacit is made explicit. His answer goes in the opposite direction from the one I have indicated in relation to the Kelsen example. For Collins, there is some stable content that the speaker makes explicit by lengthening the "string" he uses to explain what was tacit. And this does fit with one of the puzzling features of claims about tacit knowledge: the sense one has, from the use of fixed terms such as "skill," "concept," and the like, that one is talking about something with an intrinsic character, and a character that one can give an account of in terms not far removed from the terms used in the analogical notion of "knowledge" itself, so that one can speak of tacitly possessed concepts, ideas, assumptions, and the like. This sense fits with the idea that there should be some reasonably determinate psychological content that corresponds to the tacit knowledge in question. The fact that persons with tacit knowledge can sometimes, but not always, explain themselves explicitly, which we are inclined to think of as making the tacit knowledge explicit, underwrites these notions.

The problem of making the tacit explicit has been thought of in a variety of ways. One is that the tacit can always be made explicit. Jürgen Habermas, for example, speaks of "individual elements" being "made thematic" as though this was an activity analogous to psychoanalytic revelation ([1981] 1984–1987: 82). It is a recurring theme of some of Polanyi's admirers in science that there is nothing mysterious about tacit knowledge and that all Polanyi meant by tacit knowledge was knowledge that scientists had that no one had bothered to write down. Another is that embodied knowledge is impossible to "write down," perhaps because of its complexity, but also because we have no access to this knowledge. We cannot explain how to ride a bicycle so that someone could actually go and do it based on our instructions, but this is not because novice bicyclists would have to train their bodies by trial and error. This suggests that the reason this knowledge is inaccessible and impossible to make explicit is that it is another kind of knowledge, nonconceptual knowledge.

Collins (2010: 15–32) tries to solve the problem as follows. Communication is done through strings of elements that are themselves inert and require interpretation to have meaning. Sometimes short strings do the job of communication. Other times longer strings are needed. In the case of cultural differences, for example, it may take a considerable amount of additional material—a longer string, in his terms—to convey what is needed. In some cases, no amount of lengthening the string will communicate the knowledge in question; it has to be conveyed by social contact. This, for him, is a model for understanding the problem of making tacit knowledge explicit; some can't be, some can by adding to the length of the explanation, and the normal, indeed exclusive, means of conveying tacit knowledge is direct personal contact.

This amounts to a kind of composite of the idea that tacit knowledge can be thematized and the admission that some of it cannot, and on the surface that seems like a reasonable solution to the problem of what tacit knowledge is. However, a little reflection shows that "lengthening the string" is a misleading image. To explain in words something that one knows but does not normally articulate requires a target—some audience or person whom we can already imagine not knowing something that we are able to explain. It is trivially true that, if we are repairing a failed communication, in explaining to someone who does not know something that is needed in order to understand a communication, we must say more than we said when the communication failed.

But if we are attempting to communicate and fail, we may also simply state something differently and get our point across or, alternatively, find another way to get the result we wanted from the communication. Indeed, it is routinely the case that we can substitute one way of expressing one thing for another. We can call this functional substitutability. In the case of making tacit knowledge "explicit" we are performing this kind of substitution. But the kind of substitution that is functional in a given situation may not be in another. It depends on the audience or individual recipient of the substitute, and on what "functions" the substitute needs to perform.

This is a point that is obscured by many of the standard examples, but becomes obvious when we are dealing with the problem of other cultures. To take a simple example, it is customary for the Chinese to respond to statements that are unwelcome or to which they object with silence—silence conveys the message that the statement is objectionable. But would the person who was raised with this custom be able to find the appropriate functional substitute for it, when faced with a foreigner who was oblivious to the message being sent by silence? Would the Chinese who were not aware of the specificity of this custom, and for that matter the fact that it was a custom and not the normal human response to unpleasant speech, even understand that the person who was behaving badly by continuing to speak in an unwelcome way was in need of an explanation of the silence?

This case is a simple example of tacit knowledge being made explicit. It is found in business travel books on how to behave in China. The behavior of the Chinese is interpreted as a rule which can be formulated as an explicit functional substitute—"silence means that your hearer is waiting for you to say something different and more welcome." But this is a rule for someone in a culture in which there is an expectation that people signal and then explain their displeasure with an utterance. If the textbook were for travelers from a culture in which failure to respond produced an extreme loss of prestige for the person failing to respond, the advice would differ—perhaps the correct functional substitute would be "the failure of the Chinese to respond is an insult, which actually produces a kind of prestige for the silent person, and you are expected to show deference by acting differently."

They are functional substitutes only for people whose expectations are formed by those societies. "We" are unaccustomed to thinking in terms of prestige and deference, and would need to have the specific concepts of "prestige" and "deference" translated, explained, and illustrated with examples before we would find the second rule usable. Neither rule is in the head of the Chinese ready to be made explicit—indeed, treating these as "rules" at all is merely to employ a convenient analogy. They are rules for travelers to use to interpret behavior and act in ways that are functional substitutes for the way they would act within their own society. But they are substitutes only. Truly fluent interaction, of the kind that is possible in the situations in which one is most familiar, would involve the full use of our capacity to attribute intentions and beliefs to others, our capacity to repair and revise attributions, and our capacity to make ourselves understood by others who have misinterpreted us through providing repairs to their inferences.

This way of formulating the problem of what it is that we do when we articulate tacit knowledge has the effect of shifting the problem from the act of stating the tacit to the social interaction between the person doing the stating and the person for whom the stating is being done. In discussing the Kelsen quote, I have already stressed the sharp differences between the psychological facts and the use of the notion of "assumption." Assertions about "assumptions," this discussion suggested, are better understood as attempts to provide functional substitutes for a particular audience, often an audience different from the audience in the original setting, in the case of the signatories of the League of Nations, the original audience being the diplomats of the day and the other audience being the later observers who experienced the withdrawal of states and wondered why this wasn't provided for in the treaty itself. But the use of the term "audience" raises a different problem. As I have noted, we are routinely called upon to explain ourselves to people who don't understand us, and we do so by empathically imagining what it is that they have wrongly inferred or wrongly believe or "assume" that we can correct by providing information that will repair the relevant inference.

This interactive process does not appeal, in any essential way, to the notion of rules, or to anything "collective." "Functional substitutes" are invented on the fly as a normal part of interaction, and the ability to do this, which depends perhaps on our capacity to empathically think through or simulate the thinking of the other, applies to a huge variety of tasks, including the understanding of historical figures. When Kelsen explains the thinking of the original negotiators of the League of Nations treaty provisions, similarly, the explanation is one that could just as well be applied to a single individual: Woodrow Wilson, for example.

David Lewis has commented on this kind of invention on the fly in the language of presupposition, in a way that undermines the stability of the notion of presupposition. As Lewis says, "At any stage in a well-run conversation, a certain amount is presupposed. The parties to the conversation take it for granted; or at least they purport to, whether sincerely or just 'for the sake of the argument'. Presuppositions can be created or destroyed in the course of a conversation" (1979: 339). This is because we invent the presuppositions needed for the conversation as we go.

> Say something that requires a missing presupposition, and straightway that presupposition springs into existence, making what you said acceptable after all. (Or at least, that is what happens if your conversational partners tacitly acquiesce—if no one says "But France has *three* kings!" or "Whadda ya mean, '*even* George'?"). That is why it is peculiar to say, out of the blue, "All Fred's children are asleep, and Fred has children." The first part requires and thereby creates a presupposition that Fred has children; so the second part adds nothing to what is already presupposed when it is said; so the second part has no conversational point. It would not have been peculiar to say instead "Fred has children, and all Fred's children are asleep." (Lewis 1979: 339)

These invented "presuppositions" are neither "pre" nor "supposed": They were not there until they were needed to repair the inference, and there was no act of intellectual acquiescence to them; they were produced by the hearer.

If we look past the problematic language of "presupposition" to the interactive processes themselves, we get an image of social life and mutual understanding like this: We interact with one another in terms of gestures and statements of various kinds, which we interpret in ways that make sense to us. When they do not, we quickly generate alternative ways to make sense of what we are told. We can do this effortlessly and unconsciously. But on occasion we also do it consciously and explicitly, for example in trying to understand people who are very different from us and live in very different societies or hold very different beliefs. These attempts at explanation, like the rule about the meaning of silence for the Chinese, are audience relative and underdetermined, just as our unconscious supplying or inventing of presuppositions is for Lewis. The fact that we interact with people who are similar to us in many respects means that our usual inferences about the actions of others, their intentions, the relations between their words and deeds, and the inferential relations between the different kinds of things they say become habitualized and automatic. Moreover, our interactions with others increases the extent to which our habitualized responses serve the purposes of understanding the people around us. To the extent that there is tacit knowledge, it is contained in these habitualized responses.

There is nothing "collective" or even "social" about this: The habits are ours as individuals. The social element is found in the capacity to guess what other people need to know in order to understand us when an interaction goes wrong, our capacity to invent and attribute inferences to others—to repair what has gone wrong when our habitualized responses fail, or those of the person we are interacting with fail. This capacity to read their minds and determine what they need to be told explicitly to repair the interaction may be rooted in such parts of the neuro-cognitive system as mirror neurons and simulation. But in any case these capacities are social rather than collective in their reach. The "we" that might be asserted about people like us is only a descriptive we: It does not designate a collective fact. The diplomats who signed the treaty establishing the League of Nations, like Woodrow Wilson himself, failed individually to anticipate withdrawals from the treaty. Saying "we" failed is simply to record this fact. Similarly for the notion of audience I have employed here. It is merely a collection of individuals, not a body with some sort of shared collective mental content.

THE SCORECARD

The "scorecard" with which I began was a list of issues with collective accounts and with their rival noncollective social accounts. How do these issues look after these considerations? It no longer looks as though collective tacit knowledge fills an explanatory need in a simple, "parsimonious" way. It is not clear that there is a need that the concept fills: We can account for understanding in an ontologically more parsimonious way by reference to social rather than collective processes. The understanding of other people enabled by the idea of collective tacit knowledge and the content it supposedly gives us access to turn out to be more readily accounted for by our capacity to invent inference repairs. It is of course possible to describe the things to be explained in ways that force us to appeal to collective facts. But it is always possible to describe these differently without loss of empirical content.

The idea of collective tacit knowledge, like all similar ideas, faced some basic issues related to the idea that these were stable objects of some kind. One was underdetermination: As we saw in relation to Strawson, there is no stable thing corresponding to the presuppositions of something like a reaction of indignation. There are, rather, multiple possible explications, some of which will be intelligible to certain audiences, none of which is uniquely determinate. One might insist that this inaccessibility through regress arguments is precisely the point: The shared tacit stuff is mentally inaccessible, tacit in the deepest sense, but still shared. But to say this creates another problem: If the stuff is inaccessible, how did it get into the heads of the people who supposedly possess it in the first place? This is the downloading problem, and it is insoluble: Even if there was a stable determinate object that was shared, it would be impossible to explain how this stable object was related to the fact of activity and the constant flux created by normal social interaction. The fact that the location of this supposed object and the problem of its interaction with the causal world has been a problem ever since Kant, and indeed the sheer diversity of conceptions about what is supposedly out there or in the mind and where it is located, suggests that there is no stable determinate object of this kind.

Can "individual" or "social interaction" accounts avoid these problems yet account for what needs accounting for: a common language, cooperation, teams, joint collective action, practices, and so forth? All of these involve mixtures of explicit beliefs, habits, mutual understandings, and sometimes common material objects. They all work through interaction, interaction that pushes inferences into the habitual and therefore tacit. The mystery elements in these phenomena are the aspects that are inaccessible to consciousness or accessible only through the attribution of presuppositions. If we understand presuppositions in the sense of David Lewis, there is no mystery. The constant invention of these things is a normal part of social interaction. There is nothing that needs to be located outside the mind, transmitted, downloaded, or to exist in some mysterious causal relation to ordinary cognitive processes. The creation of these repairs is an ordinary cognitive process. Cultures and the like are not things with essences or jointly motivating spirits. They are not causes at all. These terms are simply aggregate descriptions and typifications of what people do and believe, and they do so habitually and therefore tacitly in ways that are different from what we do.

Collins is a major representative of what could be understood as a naturalistic approach to the study of science. The most famous text on naturalistic epistemology, Quine's, took the view that epistemology would eventually collapse into or be replaced by scientific knowledge of the process of knowing (Quine 1969). Kant's distinction between psychology and the epistemic was a target of this claim, just as Kant's analytic synthetic distinction was the target of "Two Dogmas of Empiricism" (Quine 1951). It is not a small irony that Collins proves to be the heir not of naturalism, but of Kant and these two problematic distinctions, as they were carried through in the equally problematic tradition of the collective mind.

Notes

NOTES TO THE INTRODUCTION

1. Bourdieu actually claims, "The unconscious is never anything other than the forgetting of history which history itself produces by incorporating the objective structures it produces in the second nature of *habitus*" (1977: 78–79). This is a nice solution: It puts the origins of the tacit in the explicit. But Bourdieu cannot explain how "forgetting" produces what it is supposed to explain, namely the dispositions that *habitus* is supposed to consist of. That "history" is given the job of "producing" this is a nice metaphorical touch, but it illustrates the problem it attempts to solve: metaphors standing in for explanations which can be explained only by more metaphors. Nor does it solve the problem of sameness. We forget and remember differently from one another, unless there are rituals that enforce memories.
2. For a discussion of a recent version of Wittgenstein that does just this see Turner (2010b).

NOTES TO CHAPTER 1

1. One may also question whether Bradie adequately formulates the issue, for the "problem" of refuting Goldbach's conjecture in this fashion, i.e., by finding a number, is apparently insoluble. A short retort by Polanyi might be to deny that insoluble problems are problems, or simply to restrict the paradox to soluble problems, or to deny that the problem of refuting a conjecture is properly speaking a "problem," although indeed it may involve searching.

NOTES TO CHAPTER 4

1. One reviewer of *The Social Theory of Practices* took the view that the problem of norm- identifying that figured in the book—the fact that people need to have cognitive or subcognitive access to the rules they were supposed to be following—could be resolved by supposing that people were endowed with little search engines (presumably symbolic processing or rule based) for identifying the rules. The idea was later suggested by Kelly and Stich (2007). The problem with this solution is that the results would be, from what we know about social life, greatly underdetermined, or to put it differently, the search engines for the tacit social rules in situation *X* would produce lots of matches, and would produce different ones depending on how the search was framed. So the result would be the same: The practices that they identified would be their individual solution to the problem of coping, not a matter of identifying and internalizing the true collective practice.

NOTES TO CHAPTER 5

1. Perhaps Joseph Rouse (2002), to the extent that it is an account of practices, could be construed as such an attempt.
2. For an example of Polanyi's deflationary approach to consensus and ratification, see *Meaning* (Polanyi and Prosch 1975: 145).
3. The argument, very briefly, was that the causal character of learning precluded the possibility of "sharing" in the sense required by practice theory (Turner 1994).
4. One difficulty with this theoretical object, which Kelsen acknowledged at the end of his career, is that they cannot be both true and normative themselves, because this would beg the question and refer it back to a regress—the question of what grounds their normativity. Kelsen was thus led to regard the *Grundnorm* as a fiction in the strict sense of being false and impossible.

NOTES TO CHAPTER 6

1. Tarde proceeded from the relentless application, and conceptual expansion, of the concept of imitation; Ellwood's approach was an application of the functional psychology of Dewey and Mead of the 1890s to social topics (cf. Ellwood n.d.). Ellwood is of more than historical interest, but he is also arguably the historical source of the symbolic interactionist critique of the concept of society advanced by Blumer, who was Ellwood's student. Lizardo complains about the pragmatism of *The Social Theory of Practices*, a topic I won't pursue. For a discussion that suggests it ought to be more pragmatist, see Kilpinen (2009).
2. And they are very few. Most of the references are to the book as a whole. But there are some direct references. After saying that I claim that "the transmission of practical skills from one agent to another cannot occur by way of imitation," he cites page 45. There is nothing of the sort on this page. Moreover, the book repeatedly discusses emulation, which would be an example of this kind of transmission.
3. Mysteriously, however, he uses this same cognitivist language, especially "functional presuppositions," himself. This is an important point in the larger history of practice theory, particularly in relation to the term "concept." Oakeshott, as I have noted elsewhere, sought to replace this Kantian language with different terms, precisely to avoid the implications of their use (Turner 2003a [chap. 7 in this volume], 2005b).
4. As Nehaniv and Dautenhahn point out, exact copying, even with similar embodiment, is almost never possible: One never has exactly the same agents with exactly the same kinds of bodies in exactly the same settings when the behavior of one agent is said to match that of another, as they must differ at least in their situatedness in time and/or space, not to mention numerous other details (2002).

NOTES TO CHAPTER 7

1. Compare Barry Smith (1997).
2. For example, Arthur Reber (1989), a psychologist who has shown experimentally the presence of "tacit" learning as a result of subconscious patterned inputs, has been taken to have confirmed some key ideas of Polanyi (cf. Bechtel and Abrahamsen 1991: 229, 236), and he is also a figure in the background to the understanding of connectionism approaches to the mastery of symbolic systems (Bechtel and Abrahamsen 1991).

3. One might add to this list Ryle's (1945–1946) distinction between knowing how and knowing that, which appears in an article in the *Proceedings of the Aristotelian Society*, with more extensive discussions in *The Concept of Mind* (Ryle 1949: 25–61). For Oakeshott's comments on this, see *The Voice of Liberal Learning* (Oakeshott 1989: 50–56), and it has figured in later discussions of skills, which some later writers, notably John Searle (1995) and Hubert Dreyfus ([1998] 2002), have linked to cognitive science.
4. I have discussed the merits or otherwise of the various concepts of practice and tradition among these thinkers elsewhere. With respect to social theory and the historical context of the 1940s, see Turner (1999). For a discussion of the comparative superiority of Oakeshott's account, see Turner (2003b). For treatments of Polanyi, see Turner (1998a&b, 2002).
5. The issue is usually formulated in terms of language and grammatical structure, and the arguments involve the question of whether grammatical rules can be accounted for without appealing to some sort of "rules in the mind" that are analogous to and logically of the same type as the grammatical rules of language, although more sophisticated and able to account for exceptions. But similar problems arise because people can learn to follow rules. As Bechtel and Abrahamsen suggest, "The pre-connectionist assumption has been that in order for people to function as conscious rule-interpreters it is necessary that they function internally as rule-processing systems" (1991: 249). The more radical alternatives to this "rules behind the rules" approach discussed by various connectionists, as Bechtel and Abrahamsen characterize them,

    > begin with the idea that the novice human acquires the ability to interact with the external symbols by lower level processes (such as connectionist pattern recognition) that do not involve a direct internalization of these symbols. That is the infant *learns how* to use external symbols (1991: 249).

    "On this view symbols are primarily human artifacts such as linguistic and mathematical expressions, but they may eventually be internalized in the same format as non-symbolic expressions" (1991: 253).
6. See also, throughout this book, his comments on "judgment" (Oakeshott [1933] 1978).
7. For a clear formulation of the issues in these terms, see Hookway (2000).
8. An example of this is his discussion of freedom in connection with Henry Simons (Oakeshott 1962c: 38–39).
9. In a sense, this is an example of a more general problem with cartels and holisms, such as one described by Paul Roth (1987) as the paradox of language learning. If only sentences taken as an interrelated group make sense—Quine's view—we are faced with the puzzle of how infants, who should find any single sentence to be meaningless, could learn to speak, as they must, by learning individual sentences (1987: 21).
10. This is nicely formulated in Ramberg (2000).

NOTES TO CHAPTER 8

1. For useful discussions see R. Lamb (2009a&b).
2. Skinner has a generic theory, quoted earlier, about the motives of ideological innovators, namely to impose a vision. This doesn't fit well with his critique of Leo Strauss's *Persecution and the Art of Writing* (1952), which is attacked for offering a generic motive, namely the need to write in such a way as to avoid persecution in the face of the religiously intolerant regimes of premodern Europe and elsewhere (Skinner 2002, Vol. 1: 71), although Strauss is far more cautious, *pace* Skinner, and his suggestion itself far more plausible. The

more important issue is this: Does Skinner's account of "manipulation" and "imposing a vision" fit cases like *Uncle Tom's Cabin*. Certainly there was a "vision" of the humanity of slaves, but wasn't there also a real intellectual and moral problem about slavery to which this romanticized vision of slaves was an intelligible response? A similar issue arises with Ian Hacking's version of the child abuse story, and for the same reason: Charges of manipulation make sense only when salient facts are omitted (Turner 1998c).

NOTES TO CHAPTER 9

1. For a discussion of priming cases see Wegner (2002: 58, 128–29).
2. Wegner gives a much more aggressive account, based on an extensive overview of psychological research, of the limits and illusions of consciousness, which not only applies to the case of will, but to such things as the sense of collective belonging. Needless to add, many of his most pointed observations, especially on the phenomenon of individuals' tendency to invent sense making (and intentionalizing) reasons for behavior that is in fact determined by other things, apply *mutatis mutandis* to the phenomenon of making tacit knowledge explicit (2002: 171–86).
3. I provide a discussion of the thin sense in "The Strength of Weak Empathy" (2012b [chap. 10 in this volume]).

NOTES TO CHAPTER 10

1. "Rule," as used in much of the discussion of Wittgenstein, is, like "agreement," an analogical term, in which something explicit, a rule in the normal sense, is analogized to something that is tacit. I leave aside the issue of Wittgenstein's own usage, other than to note that he limited it to the purpose of therapy and disavowed the idea that his account was a theory.
2. The "bodily" analogue to this kind of understanding is well attested to in the mirror neuron literature, for example, in relation to professional dancers: They are adept at recognizing the dance moves of other dancers, better able to identify the moves of dancers of the same sex, and become more adept at identifying these moves as they become more expert dancers. But one may ask whether this is the same cognitive process and ask, as Gallagher does with respect to the strong sense of empathy, whether mirror neurons, or other known or hypothesized cognitive processes, actually explain the phenomenon in question.
3. As Wegner points out, we routinely invent "intentions" as justifications for our actions even when the real cause of the action is otherwise—for example, in cases of brain damage where the left side of the brain is interpreting actions produced by the right side of the brain (Wegner 2002: 172).
4. Elsewhere he uses empathy to cover the task of the historian of law in understanding the legal thinking of past judges (Weber [1911] 2000: 53).
5. A useful discussion is found at http://de.wikipedia.org/wiki/*Evidenz* (accessed May 2, 2013).
6. Brentano does treat perception as "evident to me" as distinct from *Evidenz* in the full sense, but he need not have done so. For example, he could have argued that if the same empirical facts were evident to all who understood, they would at least have the status of appearances that any theoretical account should have, and thus are genuine facts.

Bibliography

Aaker, Jennifer, and Williams, Patti. (1998) "Empathy versus pride: The influence of emotional appeals across cultures," *Journal of Consumer Research* 25: 241–61.

Aristotle. ([350 B.C.E.] 1915) *Nichomachean Ethics*, Bk 2, trans. W. D. Ross. Oxford: Clarendon Press.

Barsalou, L. W. (1993) "Flexibility, structure, and linguistic vagary in concepts: Manifestations of a compositional system of perceptual symbols," in A. C. Collins, S. E. Gathercole, and M. A. Conway (eds.), *Theories of Memory*. London: Lawrence Erlbaum Associates, 29–101.

Barsalou, L. W. (1999) "Perceptual symbol systems," *Behavioral and Brain Sciences* 22(4): 577–660.

Barsalou, L. W., Simmons, W. K., Barbey, A., and Wilson, C. D. (2003) "Grounding conceptual knowledge in modality-specific systems," *Trends in Cognitive Sciences* 7: 84–91.

Barsalou, L. W., Solomon, K. O., and Wu, L. L. (1999) "Perceptual simulation in conceptual tasks," in M. K. Hirage, C. Sinha, and S. Wilcox (eds.), *Cultural, Typological, and Psychological in Cognitive Linguistics, The Proceedings of the 4th Conference of the International Cognitive Linguistics Association*. Amsterdam: John Benjamins, 209–28.

Bates, Elizabeth, and Elman, J. (1993) "Connectionism and the study of change," in Mark Johnson (ed.), *Brain Development and Cognition: A Reader*. Oxford: Blackwell, 623–42.

Bechtel, William, and Abrahamsen, Adele. (1991) *Connectionism and the Mind: An Introduction to Parallel Processing in Networks*. Malden, MA: Blackwell.

Becker, Carl. ([1932] 1959) *The Heavenly City of the Eighteenth-Century Philosophers*. New Haven, CT: Yale University Press.

Beiser, Frederick C. (2009) "Normativity in neo-Kantianism: Its rise and fall," *International Journal of Philosophical Studies* 17(1): 9–27.

Blake, Randolph, and Shiffrar, Maggie. (2007) "Perception of human motion," *Annual Review of Psychology* 58: 47–73.

Boghossian, Paul. (1989) "The rule-following considerations," *Mind* 98: 507–49.

Bourdieu, Pierre. (1977) *Outline of a Theory of Practice*, trans. Richard Nice. Cambridge: Cambridge University Press.

Bradie, Michael. (1974) "Polanyi on the *Meno* paradox," *Philosophy of Science* 41(2): 203.

Brandom, Robert. (1979) "Freedom and constraint by norms," *American Philosophical Quarterly* 16: 187–96.

Brandom, Robert. (1994) *Making It Explicit: Reasoning, Representing and Discursive Commitment*. Cambridge, MA: Harvard University Press.

Brandom, Robert. (1998) "Action, norms, and practical reasoning," *Philosophical Perspectives* 12: 127–39.

Brandom, Robert. (1999) "Interview," *Epistemologia* 22: 143–50.

Brentano, Franz. ([1889] 2009) *The Origin of Our Knowledge of Right and Wrong*, ed. Oskar Kraus, English edition ed. Roderick M. Chisholm, trans. Roderick Chisholm and Elizabeth H. Schneewind. New York: Routledge.

Brentano, Franz. ([1915] 1966a) "On the thesis: '*Veritas Est Adequatio Rei et Intellectus*,'" in Oskar Kraus (ed.), *The True and the Evident*, trans. Roderick M. Chisholm, Ilse Politzer, and Kurt R. Fischer. London: Routledge & Kegan Paul, 120–22.

Brentano, Franz. ([1915] 1966b) "The evident," in Oskar Kraus (ed.), *The True and the Evident*, trans. Roderick M. Chisholm, Ilse Politzer, and Kurt R. Fischer. London: Routledge & Kegan Paul, 126–29.

Brentano, Franz. ([1915] 1966c) "On the evident," in Oskar Kraus (ed.), *The True and the Evident*, trans. Roderick M. Chisholm, Ilse Politzer, and Kurt R. Fischer. London: Routledge & Kegan Paul, 130–32.

Bruner, J. (1990) *Acts of Meaning*. Cambridge, MA: Harvard University Press.

Bruza, P., Kitto, K., Nelson, D., & McEvoy, C. (2009) "Extracting spooky-activation-at-a-distance from considerations of entanglement," in P. D. Bruza, D. Sofge, W. Lawless, C. J. Van Rijsbergen, M. Klusch (eds.), *Lecture Notes in Artificial Intelligence*, Vol. 5494 (*Proceedings of the Third Quantum Interaction Symposium*, Saarbruecken, March 25–27, 2009). Berlin & Heidelberg: Springer-Verlag, 71–83.

Calvo-Merino, Beatriz, Grèzes, Julie, Glaser, Daniel E., Passingham, Richard E., and Haggard, Patrick. (2006) "Seeing or doing? Influence of visual and motor familiarity in action observation," *Current Biology* 16: 1905–10.

Carnap, Rudolf. (1992) "Empiricism, semantics, and ontology," in Richard Rorty (ed.), *The Linguistic Turn: Essays in Philosophical Method*. Chicago: The University of Chicago Press, 72–84.

Cassirer, Ernst. ([1923–1929] 1955) *The Philosophy of Symbolic Forms*, trans. J. M. Krois. New Haven, CT: Yale University Press.

Cavell, Stanley. (1969) *Must We Mean What We Say? A Book of Essays*. New York: Charles Scribner's Sons.

Cicourel, Aaron. (1986) "Social measurement as the creation of expert systems," in Donald W. Fiske and Richard Shweder (eds.), *Metatheory in Social Science: Pluralisms and Subjectivities*. Chicago: The University of Chicago Press, 246–70.

Collins, H. M. (1974) "The TEA set: Tacit knowledge and scientific networks," *Science Studies* 4: 165–86.

Collins, H. M. (1985) *Changing Order: Replication and Induction in Scientific Practice*. Chicago: The University of Chicago Press.

Collins, H. M. (1990) *Artificial Experts: Social Knowledge and Intelligent Machines*. Cambridge, MA: MIT Press.

Collins, H. M. (2001) "Tacit knowledge, trust and the Q of sapphire," *Social Studies of Science* 31: 71–85.

Collins, H. M. (2010) *Tacit and Explicit Knowledge*. Chicago: The University of Chicago Press.

Collins, H. M., Green, R. H., and Draper, R. C. (1986) "Where's the expertise?: Expert systems as a medium of knowledge transfer," in Martin Merry (ed.), *Expert Systems 85*. Cambridge: Cambridge University Press, 323–34.

Collins, Patricia Hill. (1997) "Comment on Hekman's 'Truth and method: feminist standpoint theory revisited': Where's the power," *Signs* (22)2: 375–81.

Cowling, Maurice. (1980) *Religion and Public Doctrine in Modern England*. Cambridge: Cambridge University Press.

Crook, Paul. (1994) *Darwinism, War and History: The Debate over the Biology of War from the 'Origin of Species' to the First World War.* Cambridge: Cambridge University Press.

Cross, Emily S., Hamilton, Antonia f. de C., and Grafton, Scott. (2006) "Building a motor simulation *de novo*: Observation of dance by dancers," *NeuroImage* 31: 1257–67.

Cuzzins, Adrian. (1990) "Content, conceptual content, and non-conceptual content," in York Gunther (ed.), *Essays on Non·Conceptual Content.* Cambridge, MA: MIT Press, 133–63.

Darwall, Stephen. (2006) *The Second-Person Standpoint: Morality, Respect, and Accountability.* Cambridge, MA: Harvard University Press.

Dautenhahn, Kerstin, and Nehaniv, Christopher. (2002) "The agent-based perspective on imitation," *Imitation in Animals and Artifacts.* Cambridge, MA: The MIT Press, 1–40.

Davidson, Donald. ([1972] 2005) "The third man," *Truth, Language, and History.* Cambridge: Oxford University Press, 159–66.

Davidson, Donald. ([1973] 1984) "On the very idea of a conceptual scheme," *Inquiries into Truth and Interpretation.* Oxford: Clarendon Press, 183–98.

Davidson, Donald. (1985) "A new basis for decision theory," *Theory and Decision* 18: 87–98.

Davidson, Donald. ([1986] 2005) "A nice derangement of epitaphs," in Ernest LePore (ed.), *Truth and Interpretation: Perspectives on the Philosophy of Donald Davidson.* Cambridge: Basil Blackwell, 89–108.

Davidson, Donald. ([1990] 2004) "Representation and interpretation," *Problems of Rationality.* Oxford: Clarendon Press, 87–100.

Davidson, Donald. ([1994] 2005) "The social aspect of language," *Truth, Language, and History.* Cambridge: Oxford University Press, 109–26.

Davidson, Donald. (1999) "Reply to Pascal Engel," in Lewis Hahn (ed.), *The Philosophy of Donald Davidson.* Chicago: Open Court, 460–62.

Dilthey, Wilhelm. ([1959] 1988) Preface. *Introduction to the Human Sciences: An Attempt to Lay a Foundation for the Study of Society and History,* eds. Rudolf A. Makkreel and Frithjof Rodi. Princeton, NJ: Princeton University Press, 47–53.Dreyfus, Hubert L. ([1998] 2002) "Intelligence without representation—Merleau-Ponty's critique of mental representation: The relevance of phenomenology to scientific explanation," *Phenomenology and the Cognitive Sciences* 1: 367–83. http://www.class.uh.edu/cogsci/dreyfus.html (accessed April 30, 2013)

Durkheim, Émile. ([1895] 1982) *The Rules of Sociological Method and Selected Texts on Sociology and Its Method*, ed. Steve Lukes. New York: The Free Press.

Durkheim, Émile. (1900) "Review of Charles A. Ellwood, 'Prolegomena to social psychology,'" *Année Sociologique* (1st series) 3(1): 183–84.

Durkheim, Émile. (1906) "Review of Gabriel Tarde, 'L'Interpsychologie'" (*Bulletin de L'Institut Général Psychologique*, June 1903, 1–32), *Année Sociologique* 9: 133–35.

Durkheim, Émile. ([1912] 1995) *The Elementary Forms of Religious Life*, trans. K. E. Fields. New York: The Free Press.

Ellwood, Charles. (1899) "Prolegomena to social psychology I: The need of the study of social psychology," *American Journal of Sociology* 4(5): 656–65.

Ellwood, Charles. (1901) "The theory of imitation in social psychology," *The American Journal of Sociology* 6(6), 721–41.

Ellwood, Charles. (n.d.) "Sociological life history of Charles Ellwood," L. L. Bernard Papers, University of Chicago Library Special Collections.

Elster, Jon. (1983) *Sour Grapes: Studies in the Subversion of Rationality*. Cambridge: Cambridge University Press.

Engel, Pascal. (1999) "The norms of the mental," in Lewis Hahn (ed.), *The Philosophy of Donald Davidson*. Peru, IL: Open Court Publishing, 447–59.

Ericsson, K. Anders. (2006) "The influence of experience and deliberate practice on the development of superior expert performance," in K. Anders Ericsson, Neil Charness, Paul Feltovich, and Robert R. Hoffman (eds.), *The Cambridge Handbook of Expertise and Performance*. Cambridge: Cambridge University Press, 683–703.

Feyerabend, Paul. (1962) "Explanation, reduction, and empiricism," in Herbert Feigl and Grover Maxwell (eds.), *Minnesota Studies in the Philosophy of Science*, Vol. 3. Minneapolis: University of Minnesota Press, 28–97.

Fleck, Ludwik. (1979) *Genesis and Development of a Scientific Fact*, ed. Thaddeus T. Trenn and Robert K. Merton, trans. Fred Bradley and Thaddeus J. Trenn. Chicago: The University of Chicago Press.

Freeman, David. (1985) "Statistics and the scientific method," in William M. Mason and Stephen Flenberg (eds.), *Cohort Analysis in Social Research: Beyond the Identification Problem*. New York: Springer-Verlag, 343–66.

Frege, Gottlob. ([1893] 1964) *The Basic Laws of Arithmetic: Exposition of the System*, trans. and ed. Montgomery Furth. Berkeley: University of California Press.

Freyer, Hans. ([1923] 1998) *Theory of Objective Mind: An Introduction to the Philosophy of Culture*, trans. Steven Grosby. Athens: Ohio University Press.

Friedman, Michael. (1996) "Exorcising the philosophical tradition: Comments on John McDowell's *Mind and World*," *Philosophical Review* 105: 427–67.

Friedman, Michael. (2001) *The Dynamics of Reason*. Stanford, CA: CSLI Publications.

Gadamer, Hans Georg. (1975) *Truth and Method*, trans. and ed. Garrett Barden and John Cumming. New York: Seabury.

Gallese, Vittorio. (2000) "The inner sense of action: Agency and motor representations," *Journal of Consciousness Studies* 7: 23–40.

Gallese, Vittorio. (2003) "The roots of empathy: the shared manifold hypothesis and the neural basis of intersubjectivity," *Psychopathology* 36: 171–180.

Gallese, Vittorio. (2003) "The manifold nature of interpersonal relations: The quest for a common mechanism," *Philosophical Transactions: Biological Sciences* 358(1431): 517–28.Gallese, Vittorio, and Goldman, Alvin. (1998) "Mirror neurons and the simulation theory of mind-reading," *Trends in Cognitive Sciences* 2(12): 493–501.

Gallese, Vittorio, and Lakoff, George. (2005) "The brain's concepts: The role of the sensory-motor system in conceptual knowledge," *Cognitive Neuropsychology* 22(3): 455–79.

Gallese, Vittorio, and Metzinger, T. (2003) "Motor ontology: The representational reality of goals, actions and selves," *Philosophical Psychology* 16: 365–88.

Garfinkel, Harold. (1967) *Studies in Ethnomethodology*. Englewood Cliffs, NJ: Prentice Hall.

Gavison, Ruth (ed.). (1987) *Issues in Contemporary Legal Philosophy: The Influence of H. L. A. Hart*. Oxford: Clarendon Press.

Geertz, Clifford. (1983) "Common sense as a cultural system," *Local Knowledge: Further Essays in Interpretive Anthropology*. New York: Basic Books, 73–120.

Gilbert, Margaret. (1990) "Walking together: A paradigmatic social phenomenon," *Midwest Studies in Philosophy* 6: 1–14. (Reprinted in Gilbert 1996, 177–94).

Gilbert, Margaret. (1996) *Living Together: Rationality, Society, and Obligation*. Lanham, MD: Rowman and Littlefield.

Gladkova, Anna. (2010) "Sympathy, compassion, and empathy in English and Russian: A linguistic and cultural analysis," *Culture Psychology* 16(2): 267–85.
Glymour, Clark. (1983) "Social science and social physics," *Behavioral Science* 28(2): 126–34.
Goldman, A. (2005) "Mirror systems, social understanding, and social cognition" (plus 10–12 responses to commentaries), in G. Origgi and D. Sperber (mods.), *What Do Mirror Neurons Mean? Theoretical Implications of the Discovery of Mirror Neurons* (a virtual workshop sponsored by the European Science Foundation), 82–87. http://www.interdisciplines.org/medias/confs/archives/archive_8.pdf (accessed May 1, 2013)
Griffiths, T. L., Steyvers, M., and Tenenbaum, J. B. (2007) "Topics in semantic representation," *Psychological Review*, 114, 211–44.
Gross, Neil. (1998) "Review," *Theory and Society* 27(1): 117–27.
Habermas, Jürgen. ([1981] 1984–1987) *The Theory of Communicative Action*, trans. T. McCarthy. Boston: Beacon Press.
Hacker, P. M. S. (1996) "On Davidson's idea of a conceptual scheme," *Philosophical Quarterly* 46: 289–307.
Hacking, Ian. (1982) "Language, truth, and reason," in Martin Hollis and Steven Lukes (eds.), *Rationality and Relativism*. Cambridge, MA: MIT Press.
Hacking, Ian. (1983) *Representing and Intervening: Introductory Topics in the Philosophy of Natural Science*. Cambridge: Cambridge University Press.
Hampshire, Stuart. (1959) *Thought and Action*. London: Chatto and Windus.
Hart, H. L. A. (1982) *Essays on Bentham*. Oxford: Oxford University Press.
Haugeland, John. (1998) *Having Thought: Essays in the Metaphysics of Mind*. Cambridge, MA: Harvard University Press.
Hayek, Friedrich. (1973) *Law, Legislation and Liberty*, Vol. 1: *Rules and Order*. Chicago: The University of Chicago Press.
Hodges, Nicola J., Starkes, Janet L., and MacMahon, Clare. (2006) "Expert performance in sport: A cognitive perspective," in K. Anders Ericsson, Neil Charness, Paul Feltovich, and Robert R. Hoffman (eds.), *The Cambridge Handbook of Expertise and Performance*. Cambridge: Cambridge University Press, 471–88.
Hollis, Martin. ([1970] 1977) "The limits of irrationality," in Bryan Wilson (ed.), *Rationality*. Oxford: Blackwell, 214–20.
Hookway, Christopher. (2000) "Epistemic norms and theoretical deliberation," in Jonathan Dancy (ed.), *Normativity*. Oxford: Blackwell, 60–78.
Hume, David. ([1748] 1995) *An Inquiry Concerning Human Understanding*. Upper Saddle River, NJ: Prentice Hall.
Hunt, Earl. (2006) "Expertise, talent, and social encouragement," in K. Anders Ericsson, Neil Charness, Paul Feltovich, and Robert R. Hoffman (eds.), *The Cambridge Handbook of Expertise and Performance*. Cambridge: Cambridge University Press, 31–38.
Hurley, Susan L. (1992) "Intelligibility, imperialism, and conceptual scheme," *Midwest Studies in Philosophy* 17(1): 89–108.
Hurley, Susan. (2008) "The shared circuits model. How control, mirroring, and simulation can enable imitation and mind reading," *Behavioral and Brain Sciences* 31(1): 1–22. http://www.ppls.ed.ac.uk/ppig/documents/Hurley-05252004_preprint.pdf (accessed April 29, 2013)
Hurley, Susan, and Chater, Nick. (2005) *Perspectives on Imitation: From Neuroscience to Social Science* (2 vols). Cambridge, MA: The MIT Press.
Husserl, Edmund. ([1931] 1962) *Ideas: General Introduction to Pure Phenomenology*, trans. W. R. Boyce Gibson. London: Collier Books.
Iacoboni, M. (2009) *Mirroring People: The Science of Empathy and How We Connect with Others*. New York: Farrar, Strauss and Giroux.

Jhering, Rudolph von. ([1877] 1968) *Der Zweck im Recht*, Vol. 1 (English version): *Law as a Means to an End*, trans. Isaac Husik (Modern Legal Philosophy Series 5). New York: A. M. Kelley.

Kelly, D., and Stich, S. (2007) "Two theories about the cognitive architecture underlying morality," in P. Carruthers, S. Laurence, and S. Stich (eds.), *The Innate Mind*, Vol. III: *Foundations and the Future*. Oxford: Oxford University Press, 348–66.

Kelsen, Hans. (1939) *Legal Technique in International Law: A Textual Critique of the League Covenant*. Geneva: Geneva Research Centre.

Keysers, C., Kohler, E., Umiltà, M. A., Nanetti, L., Fogassi, L., and Gallese, V. (2003) "Audiovisual motor neurons and action recognition," *Experimental Brain Research* 153: 628–36.

Kilpinen, Erkki. (2009) "The habitual conception of action and social theory," *Semiotica* 173(1/4): 99–128.

Koselleck, Reinhart. (2002) *The Practice of Conceptual History: Timing History, Spacing Concepts*, trans. Todd Presner. Stanford, CA: Stanford University Press.

Koselleck, Reinhart. (2004) *Futures Past: On the Semantics of Historical Time*, trans. Keith Tribe. New York: Columbia University Press.

Kraus, Oskar. ([1930] 1966) "Introduction," in Oskar Kraus (ed.), *The True and the Evident*, , trans. Roderick M. Chisholm, Ilse Politzer, and Kurt R. Fischer. London: Routledge & Kegan Paul, xi–xxix.

Kripke, Saul. (1982) *Wittgenstein on Rules and Private Language: An Elementary Exposition*. Oxford: Blackwell.

Kuhn, Thomas. ([1962] 1996) *The Structure of Scientific Revolutions*. Chicago: The University of Chicago Press.

Kuhn, Thomas. (1977) *The Essential Tension: Selected Studies in Scientific Tradition and Change*. Chicago: The University of Chicago Press.

Kusch, Martin. (1995) *Psychologism: A Case Study in the Sociology of Philosophical Knowledge*. London and New York: Routledge.

Kusch, Martin. (2007) "Psychologism," in Edward N. Zalta (ed.), *Stanford Encyclopedia of Philosophy*. http://plato.stanford.edu/entries/psychologism (accessed May 2, 2013)

Lakoff, George. (1999) "Philosophy in the flesh: A talk with George Lakoff." http://www.edge.org/3rd_culture/lakoff/lakoff_p2.html (accessed April 29, 2013)

Lamb, Charles. (1888) "A dissertation on roast pig," *Essays of Elia*. London: J. M. Dent.

Lamb, Robert. (2009a) "Recent developments in the thought of Quentin Skinner and the ambitions of contextualism," *Journal of the Philosophy of History* 3(3): 246–65.

Lamb, Robert. (2009b) "Quentin Skinner's revised historical contextualism: A critique," *History of the Human Sciences* 22(3): 51–73.

Landauer, T. K., Laham, D., Rehder, B. & Schreiner, M. E. (1997) "How well can passage meaning be derived without using word order? A comparison of latent semantic analysis and humans," in M. G. Shafto and P. Langley (eds.), *Proceedings of the Nineteenth Annual Conference of the Cognitive Science Society*. Mahwah, NJ: Lawrence Erlbaum Associates, 412–17.

Langley, Pat, Simon, H. A., Bradshaw, Gary L., and Zytkow, Jan. (1987) *Scientific Discovery: Computational Explorations of the Creative Processes*. Cambridge, MA: MIT Press.

Laymon, Ronald. (1988) "The Michelson-Morley experiment and the appraisal of theories," in Arthur Donovan, Larry Laudan, Rachel Laudan (eds.), *Scrutinizing Science: Empirical Studies of Scientific Change*. Dordrecht: Kluwer Academic Publishers, 245–66.

Lewis, David. (1979) "Scorekeeping in a language game," *Journal of Philosophical Logic* 8: 339–59.

Lizardo, Omar. (2007) "'Mirror neurons', collective objects and the problem of transmission: reconsidering Stephen Turner's critique of practice theory," *Journal for the Theory of Social Behaviour* 37: 319–50.

Loula, Fani, Prasad, Sapna, Harber, Kent, and Shiffrar, Maggie. (2005) "Recognizing people from their movement," *Journal of Experimental Psychology* 31(1): 210–20.

Lovejoy, A. O. (1961) *The Reason, the Understanding, and Time*. Baltimore: Johns Hopkins Press.

Machery, E. (2009) *Doing without Concepts*. Oxford: Oxford University Press.

MacIntyre, A. (1966) *Short History of Ethics*. London: Routledge & Kegan Paul.

MacIntyre, Alasdair. ([1970] 1977a) "Is understanding religion compatible with believing?" in Bryan Wilson (ed.), *Rationality*. Oxford: Blackwell, 62–77.

MacIntyre, Alasdair. ([1970] 1977b) "The idea of a social science," in Bryan Wilson (ed.), *Rationality*. Oxford: Blackwell, 112–130.

MacIntyre, A. ([1981] 2007) *After Virtue: A Study in Moral Theory* (3rd ed.). Notre Dame, IN: University of Notre Dame Press.

Masterman, Margaret. (1970) "The nature of a paradigm," in I. Lakatos and M. Musgrave (eds.), *Criticism and Growth of Knowledge*. Cambridge: Cambridge University Press, 59–79.

Mauss, Marcel. ([1935] 1979) "Body techniques," *Sociology and Psychology: Essays by Marcel Mauss*. London: Routledge & Kegan Paul, 97–135.

McCormmach, Russell. (1983) *Night Thoughts of a Classical Physicist*. New York: Avon.

McCumber, John. (1990) "Hegel on habit," *The Owl of Minerva* 21(2): 155–65.

McDowell, John. (1994) *Mind and World*. Cambridge, MA: Harvard University Press.

McDowell, John. (1998) *Mind, Value, and Reality*. Cambridge, MA: Harvard University Press.

Mead, George Herbert. ([1934] 1972) "The vocal gesture and the significant symbol," *Mind Self and Society from the Standpoint of a Social Behaviorist*. Chicago: The University of Chicago Press, 61–67. http://www.brocku.ca/MeadProject/Mead/pubs2/mindself/Mead_1934_toc.html (accessed May 2, 2013)

Mead, Margaret. (1928) *Coming of Age in Samoa: A Psychological Study of Primitive Youth for Western Civilization*. New York: Blue Ribbon Books.

Meehl, Paul E. (1986) "What social scientists don't understand," in Donald W. Fiske and Richard A. Shweder (eds.), *Metatheory in Social Science: Pluralisms and Subjectivities*. Chicago: The University of Chicago Press, 315–38.

Meltzoff, Andrew N. (2005) "Imitation and other minds: The 'like me' hypothesis," in Susan Hurley and Nick Chater (eds.), *Perspectives on Imitation: From Neuroscience to Social Science*, Vol. 2. Cambridge, MA: MIT Press, 55–77.

Meltzoff, Andrew N., and Moore, M. Keith. (1977) "Imitation of facial and manual gestures by human neonates," *Science* 198(4312): 75–78.

Meltzoff, Andrew N., and Moore, M. Keith. (1989) "Imitation in newborn infants: Exploring the range of gestures imitated and the underlying mechanisms," *Developmental Psychology* 25(6): 954–62.

Meltzoff, Andrew N., and Moore, M. Keith. (1997) "Explaining facial imitation: A theoretical model," *Early Development and Parenting* 6: 179–192.

Nagel, Thomas. (1986) "Thought and reality," *The View from Nowhere*. New York: Oxford University Press, 90–109.

Nandan, Yash (ed.). (1980) *Émile Durkheim: Contributions to* L'Année Sociologique. New York: The Free Press.

Nehaniv, Christopher, and Dautenhahn, Kerstin. (2002) "The correspondence problem," *Imitation in Animals and Artifacts*. Cambridge, MA: The MIT Press, 41–62.
Oakeshott, Michael. ([1933] 1978) *Experience and Its Modes*. Cambridge: Cambridge University Press.
Oakeshott, Michael. (1962a) "Political education," *Rationalism in Politics and Other Essays*. London: Methuen, 111–36.
Oakeshott, Michael. (1962b) "Rationalism in Politics," *Rationalism in Politics and Other Essays*. London: Methuen, 1–36.
Oakeshott, Michael. (1962c) "The political economy of freedom," *Rationalism in Politics and Other Essays*. London: Methuen, 37–58.
Oakeshott, Michael. (1975) *On Human Conduct*. Oxford: Clarendon.
Oakeshott, Michael. (1989) *The Voice of Liberal Learning: Michael Oakeshott on Education*, ed. Timothy Fuller. New Haven, CT: Yale University Press.
O'Connor, Flannery. ([1979] 1988) *The Habit of Being: Letters of Flannery O'Connor*, ed. Sally Fitzgerald. New York: Ferrar, Straus, and GirouxPaulson, Stanley. ([1934] 1992) "The neo-Kantian dimension of Kelsen's Pure Theory of Law," *Oxford Journal of Legal Studies*, 12(3): 311–32. First appeared in Hans Kelsen ([1934] 2002) *Introduction to the Problems of Legal Theory* (*Reine Rechtslehre*, 1st ed.), trans. B. Paulson and S. Paulson. Oxford: Clarendon Press. http://www.jstor.org/stable/764769 (accessed May 7, 2013)
Pickering, Andrew. (1995) *The Mangle of Practice*. Chicago: The University of Chicago Press.
Pickering, Andrew. (1997) "Time and a theory of the visible," *Human Studies* 20(3): 325–33.
Pickstone, John. (2001) *Ways of Knowing: A New History of Science, Technology and Medicine*. Chicago: The University of Chicago Press.
Plato. ([380 BCE] 1999) *Meno*, trans. Benjamin Jowett. http://classics.mit.edu/Plato/meno.html (accessed July 8, 2013)
Polanyi, Michael. ([1946] 1964) *Science, Faith and Society*. Chicago: The University of Chicago Press.
Polanyi, Michael ([1958] 1998) *Personal Knowledge: Towards a Post-Critical Philosophy*. Chicago: The University of Chicago Press.
Polanyi, Michael (1966a) *The Tacit Dimension*. London: Routledge.
Polanyi, Michael. (1966b) "The logic of tacit interference," *Philosophy* 41(1): 1–18.
Polanyi, Michael. (1967) *The Tacit Dimension*. New York: Anchor Books.
Polanyi, Michael, and Prosch, Harry. (1975) *Meaning*. Chicago: The University of Chicago Press.
Postema, Gerald J. (1987) "The normativity of law," in Ruth Gavison (ed.), *Issues in Contemporary Legal Philosophy: The Influence of H. L. A. Hart*. Oxford: Clarendon Press, 81–104.
Prinz, J. J. (2002) *Furnishing the Mind: Concepts and Their Perceptual Basis*. Cambridge, MA: MIT Press.
Quine, W. V. O. (1951) "Two dogmas of empiricism," *Philosophical Review* 60: 20–43.
Quine, W. V. O. (1960) *Word and Object*. Cambridge, MA: MIT Press.
Quine, W. V. O. (1969) "Epistemology naturalized," *Ontological Relativity and Other Essays*. New York: Columbia University Press, 69–90.
Quine, W. V. O. (1980) "Sellars on behaviorism, language, and meaning," *Philosophical Quarterly* 61(1–2): 26–30.
Ramberg, Bjørn. (2000) "Post-ontological philosophy of mind: Rorty versus Davidson," in Robert Brandom (ed.), *Rorty and His Critics*. Malden, MA: Blackwell, 352–69.

Reber, A. (1989) "Implicit learning and tacit knowledge," *Journal of Experimental Psychology: General* 118: 219–35.
Rorty, Richard (ed.). (1992) *The Linguistic Turn: Essays in Philosophical Method*. Chicago: The University of Chicago Press.
Roth, Paul. (1987) *Meaning and Method in the Social Sciences: A Case for Methodological Pluralism*. Ithaca, NY: Cornell University Press.
Rouse, Joseph. (2002) *How Scientific Practices Matter: Reclaiming Philosophical Naturalism*. Chicago: The University of Chicago Press.
Rouse, Joseph. (2007) "Social practices and normativity," Philosophy of the Social Sciences 37(1), 46–56.
Rubinstein, David. (2004) "Language games and natural reactions," *Journal for the Social Theory of Behavior* 34(1): 55–71.
Ryle, Gilbert. (1945–1946) "Knowing how and knowing that: The Presidential Address," *Proceedings of the Aristotelian Society* (New Series) 46: 1–16.
Ryle, Gilbert. (1949) *The Concept of Mind*. London: Hutchinson.
Sachs, Joe. (2005) "Aristotle: Ethics," *Internet Encyclopedia of Philosophy*. http://www.iep.utm.edu/aris-eth (accessed April 1, 2013)
Schatzki, Theodore. (1996) *Social Practices: A Wittgensteinian Approach to Human Activity and the Social*. Cambridge: Cambridge University Press.
Schatzki, Theodore. (2002) *The Site of the Social: A Philosophical Account of the Constitution of Social Life and Change*. University Park: Pennsylvania State University Press.
Schlick, Moritz. ([1910] 1979) "The nature of truth in modern logic," *Philosophical Papers*, Vol. 1 (1909–1922), trans. Peter Heath, H. L. Mulder, and B. F. B. Van de Velde-Schlick. Dordrecht: Reidel, 41–103.
Schmaus, Warren. (2004) *Rethinking Durkheim and His Tradition*. Cambridge: Cambridge University Press.
Schmitt, Carl. ([1932] 1996) *The Concept of the Political*, trans. George Schwab. Chicago: University of Chicago Press.
Schneider, Walter, and Shiffren, Richard M. (1977) "Controlled and automatic processing: Detection, search, and attention," Psychological Review 84(1), 1–66.
Searle, John. (1980) "Minds, brains and programs," *Behavioral and Brain Sciences*, 3: 417–57. http://journals.cambridge.org/action/displayAbstract?fromPage=online&aid=6573580 (accessed April 23, 2013)
Searle, John. (1995) *The Construction of Social Reality*. New York: The Free Press.
Searle, John. (2010) *Making the Social World: The Structure of Human Civilization*. Oxford: Oxford University Press.
Sellars, Wilfrid. (1963) "Imperatives, intentions, and the logic of 'ought,'" in Hector-Neri Castaneda and George Nakhnikian (eds.), *Morality and the Language of Content*. Detroit, MI: Wayne State University Press, 159–218.
Sellars, Wilfrid. (1980) "Behaviorism, language, and meaning," *Philosophical Quarterly* 61(1–2): 3–25.
Shimizu, Hidetada. (2000) "Japanese cultural psychology and empathic understanding: Implications for academic and cultural psychology," *Ethos* 28(2): 224–47.
Simon, Herbert. (1971a) *Models of Discovery*. Dordrecht: Reidel.
Simon, Herbert. (1971b) "The logic of heuristic decision-making," *Models of Discovery*. Dordrecht: Reidel.
Simon, Herbert A. (1976) "Bradie on Polanyi on the *Meno* Paradox," *Philosophy of Science* 43(1): 147–50.
Skinner, Quentin. (1969) "Meaning and understanding in the history of ideas," *History and Theory* 8(1): 3–53.
Skinner, Quentin. (1970) "Conventions and the understanding of speech acts," *Philosophical Quarterly* 20: 118–38.

Skinner, Quentin. (2001) "The sovereign state: A genealogy," in Hent Kalmo (ed.), *Sovereignty in Fragments: The Past, Present and Future of a Contested Concept*. Cambridge: Cambridge University Press, 26–46.

Skinner, Quentin. (2002) *Visions of Politics*. Cambridge: Cambridge University Press.

Smith, Barry. (1997) "The connectionist mind: A study of Hayekian psychology," in S. F. Frowen (ed.), *Hayek: Economist and Social Philosopher: A Critical Retrospect*. London: Macmillan, 9–29.

Smith, Dorothy. (1997) "Comment on Hekman's 'Truth and method: Feminist standpoint theory revisited,'" *Signs* 22(2), 392–98.

Stalnaker, Robert. ([1998] 2003) "What might non-conceptual content be?" in York Gunther (ed.), *Essays on Non-Conceptual Content*. Cambridge, MA: MIT Press, 95–106.

Stanley, Jason, and Williamson, Timothy. (2001) "Knowing how," *Journal of Philosophy* 98(8): 411–44.

Stein, L. A. (1995) "Imagination and situated cognition" in K. M. Ford, C. Glymour, and P. Hayes (eds.), *Android Epistemology*. Cambridge, MA: MIT Press, 167–182.

Stich, Stephen. (1992) "What is a theory of mental representation?" *Mind* 101(402): 243–61.

Strauss, Leo. (1952) *Persecution and the Art of Writing*. Glencoe, IL: The Free Press.

Strawson, P. F. ([1962] 1968) "Freedom and resentment," in P. F. Strawson (ed.), *Studies in the Philosophy of Thought and Action*. London: Oxford University Press, 71–96.

Suppe, Frederick (ed.). (1974) *The Structure of Scientific Theories*. Urbana: University of Illinois Press.

Tarcov, Nathan. (1982) "Quentin Skinner's method and Machiavelli's Prince," *Ethics* 92: 692–709.

Tarde, Gabriele. ([1890] 1903) *The Laws of Imitation*, trans. Elsie Clews Parsons. New York: Henry Holt & Co.

Taylor, Charles. (1989) *Sources of the Self: The Making of Modern Identity*. Cambridge, MA: Harvard University Press.

Thornton, Tim. (2004) *John McDowell*. Chesham, Bucks: Acumen Publishing.

Tomasello, Michael. (2009) *Why We Cooperate*. Cambridge, MA: The MIT Press.

Tomasello, Michael, and Carpenter, Melinda. (2005) "Intention reading and imitative learning," in Susan Hurley and Nick Chater (eds.), *Perspectives on Imitation: From Neuroscience to Social Science*, Vol. 1. Cambridge, MA: MIT Press, 134–48.

Turner, Mark. (1991) Reading Minds: The Study of English in the Age of Cognitive Science. Princeton, NJ: Princeton University Press.

Turner, Stephen. (1979) "Translating ritual beliefs," *Philosophy of the Social Sciences* 9: 401–23.

Turner, Stephen. (1980) *Sociological Explanation as Translation* (Rose Monograph Series of the American Sociological Association). Cambridge: Cambridge University Press.

Turner, Stephen. (1983) "'Contextualism' and the interpretation of the classical sociological texts," *Knowledge and Society* 4: 273–91.

Turner, Stephen. (1986) *The Search for a Methodology of Social Science: Durkheim, Weber, and the Nineteenth Century Problem of Cause, Probability, and Action*. Dordrecht: Reidel.

Turner, Stephen. (1994) *The Social Theory of Practices: Tradition, Tacit Knowledge, and Presuppositions*. Oxford: Polity Press; Chicago: The University of Chicago Press.

Turner, Stephen. (1998a) "Making normative soup from non-normative bones," in Alan Sica (ed.), *What Is Social Theory? The Philosophical Debates*. Oxford: Blackwell, 118–44. Reprinted in *Brains/Practices/Relativism: Social Theory after Cognitive Science*. (2002) Chicago: The University of Chicago Press, 120–41.

Turner, Stephen P. (1998b) "Polanyian in spirit: A reply to Gulick," *Tradition and Discovery: The Polanyi Society Periodical* 25: 12–20.

Turner, Stephen. (1998c) "The limits of social constructionism," in I. Velody and R. Williams (eds.), *The Politics of Constructionism*. London: Sage, 109–20.

Turner, Stephen. (1999) "The significance of Shils," *Sociological Theory* 17: 125–45.

Turner, Stephen. (2000) "Imitation or the internalization of norms: Is 20th century social theory based on the wrong choice?" in Hans Herbert Kögler and Karsten R. Stueber (eds.), *Empathy and Agency: The Problem of Understanding in the Human Sciences*. Boulder, CO: Westview Press, 103–18. Reprinted in *Brains/Practices/Relativism: Social Theory after Cognitive Science*. (2002) Chicago: University of Chicago Press, 58–73.

Turner, Stephen P. (2002) *Brains/Practices/Relativism: Social Theory after Cognitive Science*. Chicago: The University of Chicago Press.

Turner, Stephen. (2003a) "Tradition and cognitive science: Oakeshott's undoing of the Kantian mind," *Philosophy of the Social Sciences* 33(1): 53–76. [chap. 7 in this volume]

Turner, Stephen. (2003b) "MacIntyre in the province of the philosophy of the social sciences," in Mark C. Murphy (ed.), *Alasdair MacIntyre*. New York: Cambridge University Press, 70–93.

Turner, Stephen. (2005a) "Normative all the way down (Review essay of Joseph Rouse, *How Scientific Practices Matter: Reclaiming Philosophical Naturalism*)," *Studies in History and Philosophy of Science* 36: 419–29.

Turner, Stephen. (2005b) "The English Heidegger (Review essay of Terry Nardin, *The Philosophy of Michael Oakeshott*)," *Philosophy of the Social Sciences* 35(3): 353–68.

Turner, Stephen. (2007a) "Cognitive science, social theory, and ethics," *Soundings* 90(135–60).

Turner, Stephen. (2007b) "Social theory as a cognitive neuroscience," *European Journal of Social Theory* 10(3): 359–377.

Turner, Stephen. (2007c) "Practice relativism," *Crítica, Revista Hispanoamericana de Filosofía* 39(115): 3–27. [chap. 5 in this volume]

Turner, Stephen. (2007d) Explaining normativity," *Philosophy of the Social Sciences* 37(1): 57–73.

Turner, Stephen. (2007e) "Practice then and now," *Human Affairs* 17(2): 110–25. [chap. 4 in this volume]

Turner, Stephen. (2010a) *Explaining the Normative*. Oxford: Polity Press.

Turner, Stephen. (2010b) "Webs of belief, practices, and concepts," *Archives européennes de sociologie* 51: 397–421.

Turner, Stephen. (2012a) "Making the tacit explicit," *Journal for the Theory of Social Behavior* 42(4): 386–402. [chap. 9 in this volume]

Turner, Stephen. (2012b) "The strength of weak empathy," *Science in Context* 25(3): 383–99. [chap. 10 in this volume]

Vaihinger, H. ([1911] 1966) *The Philosophy of 'As If': A System of the Theoretical, Practical and Religious Fictions of Mankind* (2nd ed.), trans. C. K. Ogden. New York: Barnes and Noble.

Wacquant, Loïc. (1996) "Toward a reflexive sociology: A workshop with Pierre Bourdieu," in Stephen Turner (ed.), *Social Theory and Sociology: The Classics and Beyond*. Oxford: Blackwell, 213–34.

Warwick, Andrew. (2003) *Masters of Theory: Cambridge and the Rise of Mathematical Physics*. Chicago: The University of Chicago Press.
Weber, Max. ([1911] 2000) "On legal theory and sociology," in Arthur J. Jacobson and Bernhard Schlink (eds.), *Weimar: A Jurisprudence of Crisis*. Berkeley: University of California Press, 50–54.
Weber, Max. ([1915] 1946) "Religious rejections of the world and their directions," in H. Gerth and C. W. Mills (eds.), *From Max Weber: Essays in Sociology*. New York: Oxford University Press, 323–58.
Weber, Max. ([1922] 1988) *Gesammelte Aufsätze zur Wissenschaftslehre*. Tübingen: J. C. B. Mohr (Paul Siebeck).
Weber, Max. ([1968] 1978) *Economy and Society: An Outline of Interpretive Sociology* (3 vols), ed. Guenther Roth and Claus Wittich. Berkeley: University of California Press.
Weber, Max. (2003) *The History of Commercial Partnerships in the Middle Ages*, trans. Lutz Kaelber. Lanham, MD: Rowman & Littlefield.
Wegner, Daniel. (2002) *The Illusion of Conscious Will*. Cambridge, MA: The MIT Press.
Weizenbaum, Joseph. (1976) *Computer Power and Human Reason: From Judgment to Calculation*. New York: W. H. Freeman.
Wikipedia. "Charles Taylor." http://en.wikipedia.org/wiki/Charles_Taylor_%28philosopher%29 (accessed April 4, 2013)
Williams, Michael. (2010) "Pragmatism, minimalism, expressivism," *International Journal of Philosophical Studies* 18(3): 317–30. http://dx.doi.org/10.1080/09672559.2010.492116 (accessed May 7, 2013)
Wilson, Bryan (ed.). ([1970] 1977) *Rationality*. Oxford: Blackwell.
Winch, Peter. ([1958] 1990) *The Idea of a Social Science and Its Relation to Philosophy*. New York: Humanities Press.
Winch, Peter. ([1970] 1977) "Understanding a primitive society," in Bryan Wilson (ed.), *Rationality*. Oxford: Blackwell, 78–111.
Wittgenstein, Ludwig. ([1921] 1961) *Tractatus Logico-Philosophicus*, trans. D. F. Pears and B. F. McGuiness. London: Routledge & Kegan Paul.
Wittgenstein, Ludwig. ([1938] 1967) "Lectures on aesthetics," in Cyril Barrett (ed.), *Lectures and Conversations on Aesthetics, Psychology and Religious Belief*. Berkeley: University of California Press.
Wittgenstein, Ludwig. ([1953] 2009) *Philosophical Investigations* (4th ed.), trans. and ed. P. M. S. Hacker and Joachim Schulte. Oxford: Wiley-Blackwell.
Wittgenstein, Ludwig. (1969) *On Certainty*, ed. Gertrude E. M. Anscombe and Georg Henrik von Wright, trans. Denis Paul and Gertrude E. M. Anscombe. Oxford: Blackwell.
Wu, L. L. (1995) "Perceptual representation in conceptual combination," Ph.D. diss., University of Chicago.

Index

D

E

F

G

H

S

T